I0817478
NAVY
2206
HSL-34
S

Kaman H-2 SEASPRITE

Kaman H-2 SEASPRITE

US NAVY SHIPBORNE HELICOPTER

NAVY
HSL-84
3543
NW
S
CHWR
E
04

Schiffer
Military History
4880 Lower Valley Road
Atglen, PA 19310

OTHER SCHIFFER BOOKS BY THE AUTHOR

Green Hornets: The History of the US Air Force 20th Special Operations Squadron,
978-0-7643-2779-7

Lockheed P-2V Neptune: An Illustrated History,
978-0-7643-0151-3

The US Air Force Air Rescue Service: An Illustrated History,
978-0-7643-6480-8

Library of Congress Control Number: 2024941478

Designed by Jack Chappell
Cover design by Brenda MacCallum
Type set in Bahnschrift/Diamante/Times/Univers

ISBN: 978-0-7643-6933-9
Printed in India

10 9 8 7 6 5 4 3 2 1

Published by Schiffer Publishing, Ltd.
4880 Lower Valley Road
Atglen, PA 19310
Phone: (610) 593-1777; Fax: (610) 593-2002
Email: Info@schifferbooks.com
Web: www.schifferbooks.com

FSC
www.fsc.org
MIX
Paper | Supporting responsible forestry
FSC® C016779

ACKNOWLEDGMENTS

The creation of this book would not have been possible without the kind and generous assistance and support of many individuals. Many are veterans who came aboard my project as core resources to preserve their history and the record of the Seasprite helicopter. Adding to their ranks are systems engineers, technicians, writers, photographers, and historians who shared my intent to document this long-overdue history. Many friends upon whom I relied in other writing projects stood by, ready to share their expertise and material. They include fellow writer and researcher Lennart Lundh, David A. Hansen, lifelong aviation photographer Stephen H. Miller, Gary Verver, Erik Roelofs, and fellow helicopter aficionados Don Brabec, Ray Wilhite, John Hairell, and Johan Ragay. Special thanks go to writer, senior editor of *Seapower Magazine*, and former NFO Rick Burgess, lt. cmdr., US Navy (ret.); my Polish comrade and writer/historian Milosz Rusiecki; Vietnam Seasprite combat veterans Ronald D. Milam, Michael J. Rigby, David J. McCracken, and Scott Milner; Rod Stoker on behalf of his father LaRon Stoker; Robert Clark; Walker A. Jones; Peter P. Papadakos, executive director, Gyrodyne Helicopter Historical Foundation; Mark Aldrich, *Tailhook Magazine*; Gordon I. Peterson; Gordon Permann; Kaman engineer Richard L. Goudreau and son Kevin; and Kelly McLarney. My sincere thanks to Richard Collier; Mark Donovan, USS *King* Association; Bonnie Towne, researcher, National Naval Aviation Museum; Orbie Robertson; Beth L. Crumley; Timothy Jara; writer/historian Bruce Browne; Robert Kuhlmann; Jack Long; Brian Miller; Santiago Rivas; Michael Mau; Jeff Evans; Jodi V. Wilcox, reference librarian, Aviation Technical Library, Ft. Rucker, Alabama; David W. Moulton Sr., capt., US Navy (ret.); Mike Pocalyko; Rich Jaeger; Michael Brattland; Bruce Butler; Bob Daniel; Judy Snyder; Howard Tillison; Charles R. Leo; Jeff Massey; Robert Daniel; Earle Rogers; Joe Copalman; Benjamin Kristy, collections chief, National Museum of the Marine Corps; Pam Bone, Pax River Naval Air Museum; Joe Skrzypek, Naval Helicopter Association Historical Society; Michael Coumatos; Doug Slowiak; Jim Burridge; Don Cogger; Larry Trick; Alex Drake; R. A. Scholefield; Terry Fogarty, Kaman Air Vehicles; Mike Wilson; Andrew Bonallack; Bill Personius; Eric Oxendorf; Elijah Palmer; Barry Fryer; writer Marc Liebman; Robert Beach, Hampton Roads Scale Modelers; Rick Morgan; David Holmes; Bob Jones; Brian Stecher; Curtis Price; Martin S. Kaufman; Martyn Swann; and David D. Diamond, cmdr. USN (Ret.). And I'm grateful for the interactive participation by members of social media groups that preserve the history of US Navy units in which they served. They answered my questions and provided insight that could come only from Seasprite veterans.

EDGMENTS

I am indebted to the following organizations: Naval Helicopter Association, Naval Helicopter Association Historical Society, the Tailhook Association, National Museum of the Marine Corps, Patuxent River Naval Air Museum, New Zealand Defence Force–Defence Public Affairs, American Aviation Historical Society, National Naval Aviation Museum, Gyrodyne Helicopter Historical Foundation, USS *King* Association, Vietnam Helicopter Pilots Association, and Emil Buehler Naval Aviation Library. It is my fervent hope that this book pays fitting tribute to those who climbed aboard Seasprite helicopters to perform their duties, and to the maintainers who made those missions possible. The lives they saved stand as testimony to their skill and dedication. To them this book is dedicated.

INTRODUCTION

Although seldom in the limelight as often as more-publicized helicopters, Kaman's H-2 Seasprite helicopter forged its history through the process of evolution to meet US Navy fleet requirements. US Navy staff during the mid-1950s formulated plans for a high-performance, all-weather helicopter. Although regarded as a utility-rescue helicopter, the aircraft was envisioned capable of a variety of other roles. Through numerous accomplishments, in the hands of skilled, dedicated aircrews, it outgrew its "utility" designation, earning its place in aviation history.

The Seasprite, Kaman's model K-20, was a radical departure from the company's twin-intermeshing-rotor concept characteristic of Kaman's family of helicopters: mainly the US Air Force H-43 Huskie, born of the US Navy and Marine HOK, HTK, and HUK. Aviation pioneer Charles H. Kaman, early in his career, opposed the single-rotor/antitorque tail rotor concept, relying instead on the intermeshing-rotor concept, which promised significant power saving and greater efficiency. To meet the stringent Navy requirement, however, Kaman submitted both its traditional intermeshing-rotor design and a single-rotor configuration. The latter achieved higher speeds, was cheaper to build, and minimized deck space, since the intermeshing arrangement required very long rotor blades. Charlie Kaman's judgment proved sound, in 1957 earning the Kaman Aircraft Corporation the contract to give life to the Seasprite.

At the heart of the Seasprite was the gas turbine engine. Foresight, pioneering, and seven years of intensive research on and development of gas turbines for helicopters undertaken by Charles H. Kaman and engineering vice president John O. Emmerson placed the Kaman Aircraft Corporation in a dominant position in the helicopter industry. Both were convinced that gas turbines—which were lighter and simpler than piston engines—were the answer to powering helicopters, versus the high-power engines designed for jet aircraft during the early 1950s. Kaman and Emmerson turned to Boeing engineers who were working on a small gas turbine to power land and water vehicles. Boeing then proposed to the Navy that their 190-horsepower 502 engine be installed in Kaman's model K-225 helicopter. Navy aeronautical engineers, who welcomed the advent of turbine power, agreed. In 1951, Kaman's K-225 made history as the world's first gas-turbine-powered helicopter. Joint evaluation under sponsorship of Boeing, Lycoming, Kaman, the US Navy, and the US Army paved the way for further development of gas turbines designed specifically to power helicopters. From their efforts came Kaman's HOK-1, HTK, and HUK-1 helicopters, experimentally powered by Lycoming T-53 gas turbine engines, the HOK-1 being the forerunner of Kaman's turbine-powered H-43B "Huskie" helicopter. Close on its heels was the Navy's HU2K-1 Seasprite, powered by a T-58 engine, and both types went into production.

ODUCTION

Kaman's development of helicopters with intermeshing rotors during the late 1940s resulted in the company's production of the HOK-1, which satisfied the Marine Corps search for a rescue and utility helicopter. The Navy ordered a utility version labeled the HUK-1. *Courtesy of US Navy via Jim Ehl*

A US Air Force derivative of the Marine HOK concurrently was developed to fulfill the crash-rescue mission. Success with a turbine-powered version, the H-43B, convinced Kaman engineers that they had the answer to the Navy's search for a utility rescue helicopter, although with the switch made to the single-rotor concept. Like the Seasprite, the H-43's role would extend well beyond the crash-rescue function. This H-43B "Huskie" is seen at Myrtle Beach AFB in April 1966. *Courtesy of Richard Sullivan*

Seasprite prototypes were identified by a blunt nose and extended tailwheel. Its retracting landing gear, which has been an oddity throughout helicopter history, enhanced the YHU2K-1 prototype's "clean" profile. The second prototype, BuNo 147203, recorded the Seasprite's first flight on July 2, 1959. *Courtesy of US Navy*

Improvements for reliability, maintainability, and safety were continually applied to the Seasprite's airframe through modification. Remarkably long lived, Seasprites were cycled through multiple upgrading, test, and conversion programs, resulting in nearly a dozen designations. The adage "Operational usage spawns additional usage" typified the Seasprite. Missions and requirements unheard of in original plans spurred numerous changes. So prevalent were modification programs that by the early 1970s, no Seasprite remained active in its original form. The Seasprite has been improved so often and for so long that some machines have been upgraded more than once, prompting Charlie Kaman to quip, "We have manufactured 250 H-2 helicopters, but we modernized 268 of them."

Vital to the fleet was the plane guard role, in which 1940s-vintage Piasecki HUP helicopters flew protectively near carriers should mishaps occur during flight operations. Appropriately named the "Retriever," the tandem-rotor HUP was powered by a heavy Wright 550 hp, modified radial tank engine, often found to be underpowered and unreliable. The ultimate solution for the plane guard mission was the emerging lighter and more powerful turbine engine. The first Seasprites, assigned to two helicopter utility (HU) squadrons, relinquished the HUPs of plane guard duty in the Atlantic and Pacific Fleets. Other duties included search and rescue (SAR) and general transportation.

Designed as a replacement for the twelve-year-old UH-25 HUP, the UH-2A joined HU-2 in December 1962, giving the squadron all-weather rescue capability. HU-2 provided helicopter rescue and utility service aboard aircraft carriers and other ships of the Atlantic Fleet. This UH-2A, BuNo 149773, wears the original SAR scheme of Engine Gray and Fluorescent Red-Orange. *Courtesy of US Navy*

Kaman UH-2A/Bs, such as this Seasprite BuNo 149755 of HU-2 aboard USS *Franklin D. Roosevelt* (CVA-42) in December 1963, were regular fixtures on aircraft carriers. Squadron standard operating procedure stated that a UH-2A/B should not have a full fuel load if a rolling takeoff could not be made, or if there was a need to hover within the first hour of flight. Lightening the aircraft to maintain a hover required use of the fuel dump. *Courtesy of US Navy*

Some of the world's smallest airports were aboard ships, regularly testing crew skills and providing for anxious moments, especially in stormy seas. Communication between pilots and crewmen in the cabin was vital to ensure that the tailwheel was on deck and the tail rotor pylon was clear of obstacles. This HH-2D, BuNo 150186 of HSL-30, lands aboard a Portuguese destroyer escort (DE-1039). *Courtesy of US Navy*

Despite the benefits of the turbine power plant, engine failures were high. Studies indicated that more than 30 percent of Seasprite losses, mainly at sea, could have been averted with twin-engine power. Kaman returned to the drawing board, and less than three years after the H-2 was introduced to the fleet, it underwent its first major change—"twinning." Within five years, all the fleet's H-2s were cycled back to Kaman for installation of a second engine identical to the original. Besides ensuring a broader safety margin, the twin installation paid dividends in all-around performance.

The twin-engine Seasprite would become a major player in a new dimension of naval warfare. Having studied the use of helicopters since the end of World War II, Navy officials—finally convinced of the helicopter's ability to counter the growing Soviet submarine threat with dipping sonar and air-dropped torpedoes—established a helicopter antisubmarine squadron in early October 1951. Akin to the antisubmarine warfare (ASW) mission, and far ahead of their time, unmanned attack aircraft were making their debut, although with marginal results. Charlie Kaman, with a keen interest in ASW, reasoned that a rotary-wing drone with sonar and torpedoes could serve as the eyes and ears of a ship far beyond its horizon. Kaman's persistent ASW drone research convinced the Navy to stage an industry-wide competition for a Drone Anti-Submarine Helicopter (DASH).

The Navy DASH program continued, mainly in secrecy, until the 1990s, although with limited success. The relentless quest for the ultimate antisubmarine system culminated in the Light Airborne Multi-Purpose System (LAMPS), which identified a helicopter capable not only of ASW beyond the ship's horizon, but of antiship missile defense (ASMD) and antiship surveillance and targeting (ASST), while retaining the search-and-rescue and utility function. The twin-engine Seasprite, relatively new to the Navy, ranked high on the list as the foreseeable LAMPS helicopter.

The model HH-2D SAR Seasprite evolved into the interim LAMPS platform, becoming the torpedo-armed SH-2D. This led to an improved version, designated SH-2F, which became the mainstay of the LAMPS program. During the initial period of LAMPS deployment, the Seasprite was evaluated as a platform for air-to-air and air-to-surface missiles. Additional squadrons were formed, and Seasprites regularly operated from cramped helicopter pads of guided missile cruisers, frigates, destroyers, and support ships called "small boys," which often could not accommodate the Navy's larger Sikorsky Sea King helicopters.

When air operations began in Southeast Asia, UH-2s flew plane guard from carriers, while others aboard small boys flew combat search-and-rescue (CSAR) missions. On a regular basis, skilled and courageous Seasprite crews met the demands of rescuing downed airmen from the Gulf of Tonkin and from heavily defended enemy lairs inland. Combat experience, along with lessons learned from the US Army's evaluation of the Seasprite as a gunship, led to development of an armed and armored Seasprite variant. In later years, improved versions of the H-2 flew the unfriendly skies of the Middle East.

Seasprites assigned to US Coast Guard ships were painted overall International Orange. A UH-2B lands aboard the USCG Wind-class icebreaker *Staten Island* (WAGB-278) during the 1960s. *Courtesy of US Coast Guard*

No image better illustrates the danger of the Seasprite's workplace on the high seas. Days such as this tested the mettle both of Seasprite crews and deck personnel. Seasprite pilot Scott Milner stated, "How we managed to complete seven-to-ten-month deployments without a mishap is a real testament to the skills of our enlisted members." *Courtesy of US Navy*

The Seasprite's versatility was reflected in the long list of duties it was called upon to perform. Ship resupply—termed vertical replenishment, or VertRep—along with courier duty, was commonplace. They flew the extremes of combat and VIP duty. Navy H-2s supported Arctic and Antarctic operations and oceanographic charting. They flew gunfire support and reconnaissance missions. They were tested as airborne firefighters, and in the hands both of dedicated US Navy and Marine Corps aircrew, Seasprites served Navy and Marine Corps air stations in the crash-rescue role.

In the 1980s, Kaman would reopen the Seasprite line to fulfill US Navy requirements. Following retirement from the US Navy at the beginning of the twenty-first century, highly developed SH-2G Seasprites became available for foreign military sales, thereby extending the life of already long-lived Seasprites.

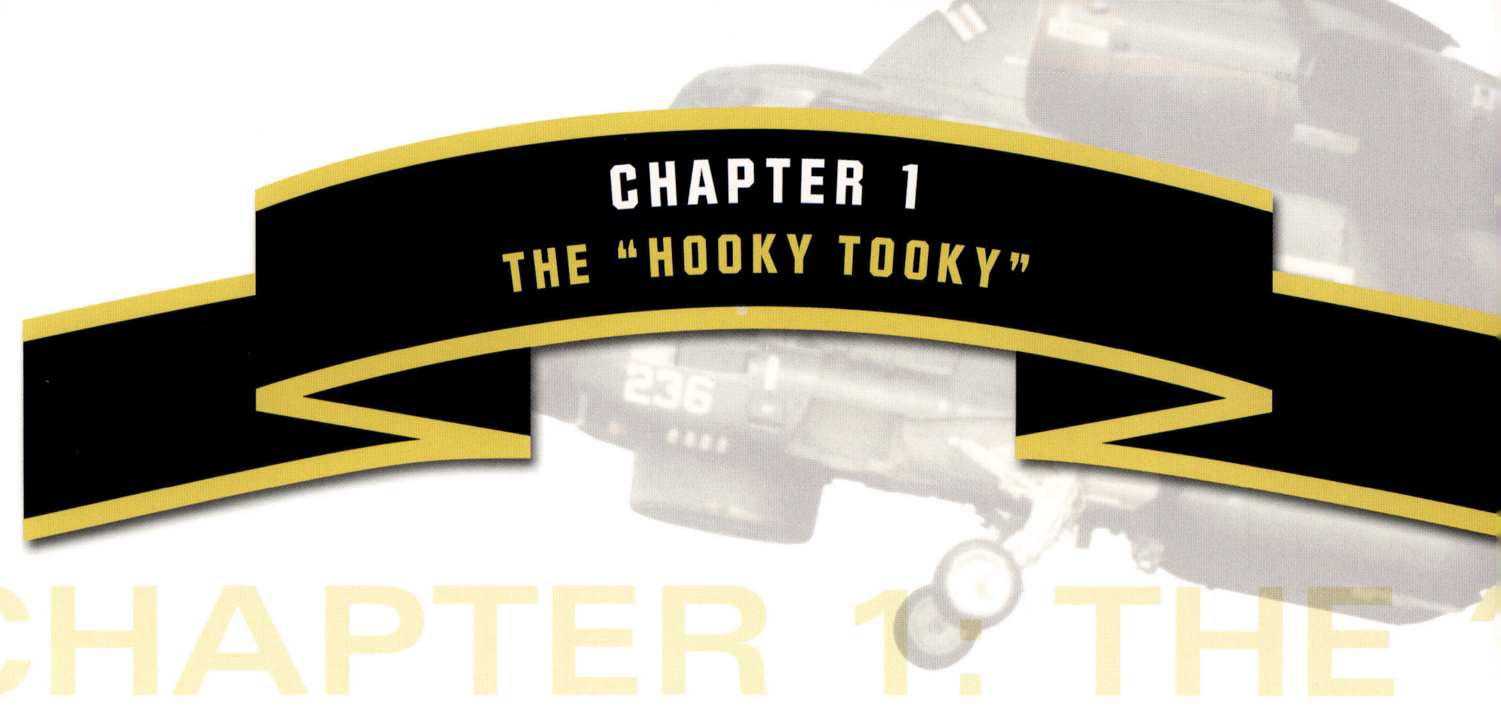

CHAPTER 1
THE "HOOKY TOOKY"

The stringent requirements for a new helicopter announced by Navy planners in 1956 led to a US Navy–sponsored design competition. Demanding specifications called for a high-speed, long-range, all-weather helicopter that would be the least expensive and use minimal deck space. Regarded primarily as a search-and-rescue aircraft, it was to be capable of utility and liaison duty with the fleet.

After the Navy selected Kaman's single-rotor design over entries by established helicopter companies Bell, Sikorsky, and Vertol, the design was given the designation HU2K-1, which in Navy parlance became the "Hukey" and "Hooky Tooky." On November 29, 1957, Kaman received a contract for four YHU2K-1 prototypes and twelve production machines. Kaman's model K-20 embodied numerous features to create an extremely versatile helicopter, the extent of which would be realized in coming years. It was not lost on Kaman engineers and Navy planners that the HU2K-1 harbored not only the capability for ASW operations, but the payload capacity to carry attack weapons and detection gear with significant search endurance. Although it was not deemed an amphibious helicopter, major consideration was given to operations over open seas and the likelihood of emergency water landings, resulting in aluminum construction with a flotation hull. Fuel capacity totaled 276 gallons, which was stored in two tanks beneath the cabin floor; an auxiliary, jettisonable 60-gallon capacity fuel tank was mounted externally on each side of the fuselage. To control rolling on water, emergency inflatable rubber sponsons were contained within both sides of the forward fuselage. A partial bulkhead prevented water entering the cabin from also entering the aft fuselage.

Design criteria also called for the ability to carry twelve persons in the cabin, or two stretchers and four sitting casualties. A retractable 600-pound-capacity, hydraulic rescue hoist was stowed internally above the starboard cabin doorway. Cargo could be loaded through cabin doors on each side of the fuselage. Both pilot doors and cabin doors could be jettisoned, although that feature sometimes provided anxious moments for the crew. Crewmen tell of the Seasprite's bad habit of shedding cabin doors in flight. Thankfully, safety lanyards prevented doors from flying up into the main rotor. Cargo could also be carried externally on a cargo hook of 4,000-pound capacity. The engine and transmission systems were located on top of the aircraft, enabling structural loads to be transmitted to the fuselage frame. To power the four prototypes, Kaman installed a General Electric T58-GE-6 turboshaft engine rated at 875 shaft horsepower (shp). Production HU2K-1s used the more powerful T58-GE-8 engine, rated at 1,250 shp, permitting a maximum gross weight of 10,000 pounds. At a normal gross weight of 8,637 pounds, the HU2K-1 cruised at 152 mph, with a top speed of 162 mph. Maximum range was 670 miles, and service ceiling was 17,400 feet. The HU2K-1 used a fiberglass, 44-foot-diameter, four-blade main rotor

The fixed landing gear of this initial mockup in October 1957 was quickly replaced at the behest of Navy engineers, who noted its interference with operation of a proposed rescue hoist over the cabin doorway. Cleveland pneumatic gear was replaced by more-rugged Dowty gear for rough shipboard duty. Unusual was a four-blade tail rotor, which would not reappear until later models. *Courtesy of Kaman*

Since one of the many stringent Navy requirements for the Seasprite was minimal size to operate aboard ships, Kaman incorporated features that reduced the helicopter's overall length to 37 feet, 10 inches. This was accomplished by folding back the main rotor blades and folding forward the aftmost tail rotor blade and tail rotor pylon tip, plus fully opening the nose doors. The main rotor blades could be folded back in less than a minute without having to support the blade's weight or turn a blade broadside to the wind. The flat surface of the engine cover was reshaped to a dome-like fairing. A dummy weapon attached to this mockup's landing gear was an early suggestion of use beyond rescue and utility. *Courtesy of Kaman*

This mockup shows the switch made to forward-retracting main landing gear and a three-blade tail rotor. Dark-painted components of the tail pylon mark the location of tail rotor driveshaft gearboxes. The wide-chord tail pylon would be narrowed, and the portside engine air intake would be eliminated. *Courtesy of US Navy*

incorporating an in-flight blade-tracking system. Kaman's characteristic servo-flaps, which ensured rotor stability, smoothness, and ease of handling, were carried over from company synchropters. Veteran Seasprite pilot Robert Beach notes the following:

> One point I loved about the Seasprite—you could still fly it without hydraulics. We used to practice flying with the "boost" off, which took some muscle but was perfectly controllable. This was due to the "flaperon" rotor control system, where the small surfaces on the blades were what was deflected[,] which then created axial torque on the blades, causing them to move. Very ingenious[,] and as far as I know, only Kaman used it. It was nice for us since all other helos in the inventory at the time (other than perhaps the Bell TH-57) would be uncontrollable with a full hydraulic failure.

Kaman personnel pose on August 14, 1959, with the second-built YHU2K-1 prototype, BuNo 147203, following ground and hover tests. Known names of those men at the rear are, *left to right*, Kendall, Horn, William Murray, Andrew Foster, F. L. Smith, R. A. Hintermister, Anthony Rita, Campbell, and Standin. In the front row are, *left to right*, Donton, Jack Goodwin, O'Donnell, and Micton. *Courtesy of Kaman*

Night operations demanded that vibration was kept to an absolute minimum to avoid pilot fatigue caused by instrument blur. To ensure the absolute minimum, a vibration absorber in the nose, or in the left forward cabin, became standard on all aircraft. Especially beneficial for shipboard duty were rotor stops that allowed turn-up and shutdown in winds up to 70 mph. Main rotor blades were interchangeable and could be folded back in the horizontal plane. Mounted on a narrow vertical fin, or pylon, was the antitorque, three-bladed tail rotor, which could be folded.

The Seasprite initially was designed with fixed, Cleveland pneumatic landing gear. In anticipation of design growth and obvious interference with rescue hoist operation, Navy engineers insisted on retracting the main landing gear, which also contributed to higher speed. The switch was later made to stiffened Dowty landing gear, which was unique in that effective damping was accomplished by means of a liquid spring shock absorber, the piston of which used compression of oil.

With test instrumentation on its nose, and displaying the Navy scheme for helicopters, the second prototype is seen in November 1959 without engine, transmission, and tail rotor driveshaft covers. A blunt nose and small tailwheel on an elongated strut identified the prototype. *Author's collection*

Landing gear had a tread of 10 feet, 10 inches and fully retracted in two seconds. The levered suspension struts, which used Dowty-designed liquid oleo springs, "broke" in the center, allowing the wheels to swing forward. Kaman developed laterally stiff, low-aspect tires with special chord design to aid damping. *Courtesy of Howard Levy*

Only the four YHU2K-1 prototypes featured a portside engine air intake. Rotor blade folding reduced the Seasprite's overall length, including rotors, from 53 feet to 39 feet. Geometric symbols were applied to the blades for tests of the automatic blade-tracking system. *Courtesy of Howard Levy*

All-weather and night capability was derived from Kaman-designed automatic stabilization equipment (ASE), which provided precise control for pitch, roll, heading, and altitude set by the pilot, thereby relieving him of making continual control corrections. An Instrument Flight Rules (IFR) suite comprised a radar altimeter, automatic navigation system with Doppler radar, navigation computer, tactical air navigation (TACAN), and automatic direction finder (ADF). Vital components were made easily accessible, including navigation and communication equipment housed in the nose behind clamshell doors.

After the second YHU2K-1 prototype, Bureau Number (BuNo) 147203, made a successful maiden flight on July 2, 1959, contracts followed, with production totaling eighty-eight HU2K-1s, the first of which was delivered on December 18, 1962; deliveries were completed in 1965. When production began, the HU2K-1 was officially named "Seasprite."

With the Fleet Indoctrination Program (FIP) scheduled to begin in fall 1960, ample preparation was made to transition the HU2K-1 into the Navy. In mid-May 1960, nearly eighty Navy and civilian personnel attended a two-week maintenance and engineering inspection (MEI) of the HU2K-1 at Kaman Aircraft. The majority of Navy personnel were from Helicopter Utility Squadrons 1 and 2 (HU-1 and HU-2), which were slated to receive the first HU2K-1s. The FIP was accomplished with five HU2K-1s: BuNos 149014–149018. As part of the FIP, in fall 1961, Detachment 1070 of the Naval Air Mobile

Details of the second-built prototype's tail section include the hinged tail rotor pylon tip and horizontal stabilizer, also called the tailplane. The tailplane, which was later fit with braces, provided stability during high speeds and was interconnected with the cyclic stick. The tailplane spanned 10 feet, and tail rotor diameter was 8 feet. *Courtesy of Howard Levy*

Training Group was formed at Naval Air Station (NAS) Memphis. A training detachment was also established at Naval Auxiliary Air Station (NAAS) Imperial Beach (renamed NAS Imperial Beach in January 1968), California. Eventually seventy detachments that included Seasprites were formed at NAS and Marine Corps air stations (MCAS). Training for Navy maintenance personnel was conducted using three full-scale training panels designed and built by Kaman. In his 1960 report on flying the HU2K-1, project test pilot Jack C. Goodwin had high praise for the aircraft:

> Speedy, sprightly, and nice to fly—that's the Seasprite. This helicopter, with its high speed and long[-]range capabilities is also the most comfortable and "pilot kindly" rotary wing aircraft I have ever flown. . . . The obvious effort has been made to engineer an aircraft which will be efficient for people to use, as well as affording space in which to locate electronic, avionic[,] and mechanical components. . . . Control placement within the cockpit and the height and style of control design features also meet this test of pilot needs. . . . The Kaman servo flap control system is as nearly free of vibration as any I have ever flown. . . . The HU2K-1 Seasprite is a pilot's aircraft. . . . It has incorporated in it many changes which helicopter pilots have been seeking for a long time, and it promises to more than satisfy the mission requirements specified by the Navy.

Of note is Canada's contrast to Goodwin's report. Watching closely the development of the Seasprite, the Royal Canadian Navy in 1960 selected the HU2K-1 as the prime candidate for its compact, all-weather, all-purpose helicopter. After the Canadian government approved an initial order for twelve Seasprites, Kaman raised the price significantly, and officials had yet to see the helicopter's performance results from US Navy sea trials. These results did not meet the Royal Canadian Navy's requirements, which led instead to procurement in 1961 of Sikorsky's Sea King helicopter.

During production, in October 1962 the HU2K-1 became the UH-2A under the US military's revised designation system. Production slowed when Navy engineers waffled over design specifics resulting from the expense and shortage of government-supplied IFR equipment. This resulted in the production of two versions having different

Kaman's signature servo-flap, which served as a miniature airfoil attached to the trailing edge of each main rotor blade. Pilot control of the device was transmitted to the entire blade to change flight attitude. The flap stabilized the blade system and eliminated aerodynamic feedback so that the pilot felt no stick and cockpit vibration typical of helicopters. *Courtesy of John Hairell*

From top to bottom, the YHU2K-1's rotor head, transmission mounts, and swash plate with connecting rods. *Courtesy of Howard Levy*

The Seasprite's cockpit was a practical arrangement of flight instruments flanking engine instruments, below which was the 10-inch-diameter dead-reckoning indicator. A wheel-shaped landing-gear lever next to the pilot's collective lever enabled the pilot to lower landing gear and collective pitch simultaneously in event of an autorotation landing. *Courtesy of Howard Levy*

The third-built prototype, BuNo 147204, was used extensively for testing the emergency flotation gear and rescue equipment. During testing of the cheek floats, empty auxiliary fuel tanks were attached to long outriggers as a precautionary measure to maintain flotation. The emergency flotation gear was deemed inadequate for keeping the aircraft upright in the water, resulting in a directive that it be used only in emergencies and for rescue. The purpose of the device mounted below the engine air intake is unknown. *Courtesy of Kaman*

During testing of flotation gear on Lake Congamond, a crane was used to place BuNo 147204 in and out of the water. Lake Congamond is within the Connecticut River drainage basin, near Kaman's plant at Bradley Field, Windsor Locks, Connecticut. *Author's collection*

During tests of the emergency flotation gear, a temporary flotation bag was affixed to the aft fuselage to keep the prototype afloat when the forward bag was deflated. *Courtesy of US Navy*

During a Navy-sponsored open-sea rescue symposium in 1963, YUH-2A BuNo 147204 demonstrates a maneuverable rescue ramp, which facilitated rescue of a survivor. The ramp was lowered by hoist from the cabin doorway and supported by the fish pole boom. The loud hailer system visible on the aircraft's nose was also tested. *Courtesy of US Navy*

The prototypes evaluated a number of rescue systems. With the fish pole boom lowered, BuNo 147204's crew puts the scoop net and floodlights through their paces during a simulated night rescue. *Courtesy of US Navy*

avionics suites. Following construction of eighty-eight UH-2As built with full IFR capability, beginning in August 1963, 102 would leave the factory with simplified day VFR (Visual Flight Rules) instrument suites. This version was labeled HU2K-1U (later UH-2B) although the two models were alike, with the exception of improved liquid spring landing gear and an improved fuel control in the B model. The UH-2A had factory-installed AN/ARN-21 TACAN navigation, AN/APN-130 Doppler ground speed radar, ADF, ANA/ASA-13 navigational computer with tactical display plotting board, and radar altimeter, while the UH-2B had AN/ARN-52 TACAN and only mounts for the remaining equipment. When problems were resolved, all surviving UH-2Bs were retrofit with the IFR package. Although both versions were then identical, UH-2Bs retained that designation, which led to common use of the term UH-2A/B; UH-2Bs were built in three batches: BuNos 150139–150186, 151300–151335, and 152189–152206. The UH-2B first went to sea aboard guided missile cruiser USS *Albany* (CG-10) beginning on August 8, 1963, and UH-2B production was completed during 1965.

A rear view of the special dolly provides details of the auxiliary fuel tank support. *Courtesy of US Navy*

The specially fabricated landing-gear dolly lowered the Seasprite's stance, which allowed it to be transported in cargo aircraft. *Courtesy of US Navy*

For airlift trials with cargo aircraft, UH-2B BuNo 151333 was fitted with makeshift dollies to ensure its fit into a C-124. With the empennage removed, a specially made dolly supported the tail boom. The Globemaster II used for the tests was a C-124C, s/n 52-1082, of the 1501st Air Transport Wing. *Courtesy of US Navy*

A strong feature of the Seasprite design was a self-contained, plug-in field service hoist for handling of the 350-pound T-58 turbine engine and rotor drive system components. The hoist could be collapsed into a compact unit for transport in the aircraft. *Courtesy of US Navy*

Apparent in this view of UH-2A BuNo 149772 is the slant of the tail rotor driveshaft toward the port side of the aircraft. Seasprites commonly wore the name of the ship to which they were assigned for plane guard duty. No. 772 of HC-2, Det. 66, wears the name of the aircraft carrier USS *America* (CVA/CV-66). Home base for HC-2 was NAS Lakehurst, New Jersey. *Courtesy of Lionel Paul*

Prior to its first squadron assignment, HU-1 aboard USS *Constellation*, BuNo 152202 served as a JUH-1B test platform, which required a nose-mounted test probe. *Courtesy of US Navy*

The UH-2A BuNo 147976 is pulled aboard the carrier USS *Bon Homme Richard* (CV-31), to which it was assigned, following a night crash at sea on January 28, 1963. *Courtesy of US Navy*

During the 1960s, UH-2B BuNo 151314 of HU-4 was the star performer for crew and visitors by hoisting and lowering a person on the helicopter deck of command ship USS *Northampton* (CC-1). The Seasprite shared in the ship's role as ambassador, whose many duties included flagship communication test platform and "Floating White House." In later years, no. 314 served in the VIP role at NAS Naples, Italy. Unusual is the small tail rotor warning on the pylon. *Courtesy of US Navy*

Eight of the UH-2A/B's antennas were located on the aircraft's underside. The large teardrop antenna at center corresponded to the AN/ARN-59 ADF. On this Seasprite, Fluorescent Red-Orange was continued from the nose along the underside. BuNo 149778 crashed in the Pacific off Point Loma, California, on June 13, 1969, killing all five aboard. *Courtesy of US Navy*

Positioning of the T58-GE-8 engine in production UH-2A/Bs had both engine air intake and exhaust on the starboard side of the aircraft only. The tail pylon of production Seasprites was of narrower chord than prototypes, and tailplanes were braced. *Courtesy of US Navy*

CHAPTER 2
THE SEASPRITE JOINS THE FLEET

Deliveries of the Seasprite began on December 18, 1962, when Cmdr. A. C. LeFevre, commanding officer of HU-2, flew BuNo 149016 from Kaman's plant to NAS Lakehurst, New Jersey, home base of HU-2 "Fleet Angels." Two weeks later, Lt. (j.g.) Lawrence W. Beguin of HU-1 flew the first Seasprite to touch down at NAAS Ream Field, California, HU-1's home base; Beguin became the first Navy pilot to log one thousand hours in the UH-2. Dispersion of the Seasprite force followed the standard US Navy pattern of East and West Coast communities for service with their respective fleets. On New Year's Eve 1962, the Seasprite accomplished its first SAR mission when Lt. John Thoma and crewman ADR3 S. R. Kryzs of the Naval Air Test Center (NATC) at NAS Patuxent River, Maryland, voluntarily flew in below-zero weather with 70 mph winds to rescue four people stranded on a boat in a frozen marsh near Wallops Island, Virginia. The first rescue by a Seasprite crew of HU-2 occurred on March 25, 1963, when they responded to a civilian plane crash found by the Civil Air Patrol near Atlantic City, New Jersey. The UH-2A flew in concert with another Kaman, an H-43 of Air Force Detachment 48 at Dover Air Force Base, Delaware. Their combined effort resulted in the rescue of three badly injured survivors.

The first shipboard service of the Seasprite occurred aboard USS *Independence* on June 4, 1963. After six months of UH-2A familiarization at Ream Field, on August 1, 1963, HU-1 assumed its role as "Pacific Fleet Angel" with Detachment "Golf" aboard the carrier USS *Oriskany* (CV-34) in the western Pacific.

Initially, the IFR-equipped UH-2As were assigned to ships for plane guard, SAR, and utility duties, while VFR UH-2Bs had been earmarked primarily for operations at US Navy and Marine Corps air stations. At-sea commitments led to the formation of HU-4, which operated Seasprites from US Coast Guard icebreakers, cruisers, and survey ships, leaving the aircraft carriers to the Fleet Angels of HU-1 and HU-2. Three UH-2As usually constituted a carrier detachment, which adopted the ship's hull number, or a single-letter designation. Small-boy detachments typically used one Seasprite. The plane guard position was flown each time the carriers launched and landed aircraft, a practice continued in modern times. During the launch cycle, the "Angel" was the first aircraft to take off, assuming a racetrack orbit off the starboard side at about 150 to 300 feet, with night patterns flown at 300 to 400 feet. The crew consisted of pilot, copilot, and one or two volunteer crewmen, some of whom were "rescue swimmers," highly trained in water survival and rescue techniques. To the reassurance of aircrew, with Seasprites aboard ship came the long-awaited capability of all-weather, day-night rescue by Navy helicopter. Shortly after HU-2 Seasprites were assigned aboard USS *Independence* (CVA-62) as Detachment 62 in June 1963, an intense training program for pilots and maintenance personnel was held at NAS Patuxent River, New Jersey; squadron size then more than doubled. By the end of March 1964, HU-2's inventory included twenty-five UH-2As and four UH-2Bs.

When not flying plane guard, shipboard Seasprite crews maintained busy schedules flying ship-to-ship transfers of men and equipment, flying cargo and mail delivery, and, on Sundays, becoming the "Holy Helo" when flying a chaplain from one small ship to another. They flew medical evacuation and gunfire-spotting missions. Operating from US Coast Guard icebreakers, orange-painted Seasprites flew ice reconnaissance and resupply missions. Pairs of Seasprites relieved radial engine-powered Sikorsky HUS-1 "Seahorses" (later H-34s) of search-and-rescue duty at numerous naval aviation installations worldwide.

The Seasprite's basic design included a number of features that contributed directly to its main mission of search and rescue: the "loud hailer" enabled crewmen to give instructions to survivors, automatic stabilization equipment repeatedly proved its worth, and a radar altimeter proved vital during hovers, especially at night or overwater, where visual references often did not exist. Unique to the Seasprite was the "fish pole" rescue boom, which allowed the pilot to view the rescue and rotate the pole to place the survivor at the cabin doorway.

THE MARINE SEASPRITE

Diversification of the Seasprite soon was underway. Given the relationship between the Navy and Marine Corps, it is no surprise that Seasprites were in the US Marine Corps inventory, although not in large numbers: a total of eleven UH-2Bs during the six-year period from 1964 through 1970.

The UH-2Bs were rotated through three Marine Corps air stations: MCAS Yuma, Arizona; MCAS Cherry Point, North Carolina; and MCAS Beaufort, South Carolina. Assigned to station operations and engineering squadrons (SO&ES), individual aircraft assignments lasted from three months to four years before transfer to other stations or return to the Navy. Cherry Point typically had four UH-2Bs assigned, Beaufort had two or three, and Yuma had two alternatively assigned from July through December 1964. Using the call sign "Pedro," H-2 crews performed crash-rescue and SAR duty and provided emergency services to civilians. Cherry Point crews had the additional duty of SAR for the Coast Guard's Fifth District, along the coastal region of North Carolina. One of the more unusual tasks for Cherry Point crews involved clearing the runways of deer, which sought their warmth in winter. The SAR unit at Beaufort, besides flying missions both for military and civilian emergencies, provided helicopter rescue training for the water survival school at Parris Island, South Carolina. Tail codes for Marine Corps air stations were 5B for Beaufort, 5C for Cherry Point, and 5Y for Yuma, although they are not known to have been included in UH-2B markings.

The Pedros were fully IFR equipped and flew with a highly motivated and well-trained crew comprising pilot, copilot, crew chief, and observer, also called a junior crew chief. Crewmen were helicopter mechanics, with crew chiefs often flying as copilot once qualified through a training syllabus. A pilot of the ten-man Pedro unit at Cherry Point noted, "Our attitude toward the UH-2B is one of complete confidence and satisfaction. For a SAR mission, we can go farther, faster, and stay on-scene longer than we can in any other utility helicopter."

While retained by Kaman as a research-and-test platform, the third-produced Seasprite, conducting a practice session in January 1963, shows the effectiveness of the searchlight positioned for use with the rescue hoist. Five months later, BuNo 147974 was written off following an accident during the evaluation period. *Courtesy of US Navy*

"Chock and chain" crewmen anticipate the landing of BuNo 149778 of HU-2 "Fleet Angels" aboard USS *Independence* (CVA-62). "Starboard delta" was the holding pattern for the plane guard helicopter on the starboard side of the carrier. It flew at low altitude so as not to interfere with fixed-wing aircraft recovery. When the tower radioed the helicopter "Signal Charlie," the crew knew that aircraft recovery was complete, and they could come back aboard. *Courtesy of US Navy*

Model UH-2B Seasprites commonly served as station aircraft at naval air stations. BuNo 150150, the one hundredth Seasprite built, began service at NAS Lemoore, California. No. 150 crashed off the Florida coast in May 1990, killing all aboard. *Courtesy of Clay Jansson via Stephen Miller*

The standard color scheme for US Navy helicopters operating in the Arctic and Antarctic is overall International Orange. Ice reconnaissance and resupply were regular duties performed by Seasprites of helicopter combat support squadrons assigned to US Coast Guard icebreakers. Early Deep Freeze explorations, which were dependent on good sleds and dog teams, came to rely on helicopters for support. *Courtesy of US Navy*

The UH-2B BuNo 150146 of HC-5 on display at Edwards AFB, California, during Armed Forces Week in 1968. A mannequin dressed as a rescue swimmer and on the rescue hoist was included in the display. *Courtesy of US Navy*

The US Marine Corps fully operated IFR UH-2Bs as SAR "Pedro" units mainly at MCAS Cherry Point, North Carolina, and Beaufort, South Carolina, from 1964 to 1970. Use of the fish pole is seen to good advantage, enabling the pilot to manage the rescue. *Courtesy of US Marine Corps*

In Marine service, UH-2Bs retained the standard US Navy color scheme. The kapok "horse collar" sling was the standard device used to hoist survivors from land, sea, or vessels. On January 30, 1964, BuNo 150167 became the first UH-1B assigned to MCAS Beaufort. *Courtesy of National Museum of the Marine Corps*

Of particular interest is the involvement of Cherry Point's SO&ES with the "Fire Fly" experiment. In late 1967, civilian engineers of the Naval Air Development Center (NADC) enlisted Cherry Point Seasprite crews and UH-2B BuNo 151319 to test the feasibility of extinguishing fuel and oil fires from the air, using aqueous film-forming foam (AFFF), or "light water," to float on top of fuel and oil to smother flames.

The Seasprite was well suited for the Fire Fly installation, since its two external fuel tanks could be replaced with light-water tanks that used the aircraft's fuel pressurization system. The fish pole boom proved ideal for attaching a spray nozzle to its tip yet remained fully functional for rescue. Extending the boom enabled the pilot to hover and attack the fire. With the added benefit of rotor wash, pilots became quite adept with the Fire Fly. Plexiglas windows near the pilot's foot pedals often warped from the flames, which had pilots wearing the trouser portion of crash crewmen's flame-retardant suits.

Despite the Fire Fly's effectiveness, the Marines could not justify committing a Seasprite full-time with the system in place of fuel tanks; at least twenty minutes were required to change from light water to fuel tanks, which meant valuable time lost for a SAR mission. When the Navy began to recall UH-2Bs from service for conversion to antisubmarine platforms, Marine Seasprites were replaced by Sikorsky HH-34Js and, later, Boeing-Vertol HH-46D/Es, which flew the Pedro mission until 2015, when the Marine Corps divested itself of the SAR mission.

In 1965 the Navy had experimented with an aerial firefighting system similar to that tried by the Marines. Using the UH-2B BuNo 150172, the Naval Research Laboratory conducted experiments at NAS Miramar to determine the effectiveness of light water for crash-rescue duty. The Seasprite's 60-gallon auxiliary fuel tank contained the film-forming solution, which was discharged by the pilot under pressure through a spray boom that extended from the aircraft's right side. In a procedure

When Marine Seasprites were recalled by the Navy for conversion to ASW variants, they were replaced by Sikorsky HH-34Js and, later, Boeing Vertol HH-46D/Es. This pair of HH-46Es was the final "Pedro" flight at MCAS Cherry Point, in September 2015. *Courtesy of US Navy*

BuNo 150172 undergoes evaluation as an airborne firefighting platform at NAS Miramar, California, in 1965. *Courtesy of US Navy*

The UH-2C BuNo 150142 at Imperial Beach, California, in 1973. The Seasprite and one crewman were lost on March 11, 1977, when it crashed into the Pacific on approach to USS *Sterett* (DLG-31/CG-31). *Courtesy of Mike Wilson*

similar to that perfected by US Air Force local base rescue crews with Kaman's H-43 Huskie, the UH-2B first hovered near fuel fires to allow two rescue crewmen to slide down a 20-foot rope; the pilot then advanced on the blaze, using the spray to open a wide path through the flames. This allowed the rescue men to rescue a dummy from a simulated crashed aircraft. Tests were also conducted aboard a carrier, where C-45 aircraft were set ablaze on a far corner of the carrier deck. Additional tests were conducted by Kaman at its Bloomfield, Connecticut, facility, with US Navy plans in spring 1968 calling for modification of a limited number of UH-2s to be fit with firefighting equipment for use at land air stations. Those plans, however, did not come to fruition.

UH-2Bs of US Marine Corps Station Operations and Engineering Squadrons

BuNo
150152
150164
150166
150167
150179
150180
150181
151306
151308
151319
152189

En route to Australia, the crew of HC-2 rescues a sailor from USS *America* (CVA-66) in the Bismarck Sea on November 16, 1970. *Courtesy of US Navy*

BuNo 151309 of HSL-30 Support Detachment 31's arrival aboard US Sixth Fleet flagship USS *Springfield* (CLG-7) in 1973 with VAdm. Frederick H. Michaelis, commander of Naval Air Forces Atlantic. On the nose of the VIP Seasprite is the Snoopy character and a pennant with three stars. *Courtesy of US Navy*

In March 1972, the HH-2D BuNo 152192 of HC-4, Det. 31, makes an authorized low pass alongside Soviet navy ASW helicopter cruiser *Leningrad* as it steams past the Sixth Fleet flagship *Springfield* in the western Mediterranean Sea. Visible are five Kamov KA-25 ASW "Hormone" helicopters on her flight deck. Although *Leningrad* wore hull no. 845, hull numbers were changed frequently to make it difficult for Western forces to track Soviet navy strength. *Courtesy of US Navy*

CHAPTER 3
THEY LOOKED GOOD IN OLIVE DRAB

THEY LOOKED GO

Early in the life of the UH-2A/B, the US Army took a profound interest in the Seasprite. Missing from published accounts describing Army evaluation of the UH-2A as a high-speed helicopter and gunship is the Army's search for a utility / tactical transport helicopter. Since Bell's UH-1B "Huey" was relatively new to the Army, and the UH-1D "stretched Huey" tactical transport had yet to begin service, Army officials in 1963 were open to options. Historically, the services had no aversion to examining what other services had and how it was used. Although extensive testing of the Seasprite found it unsuitable in the Army utility/transport environment, it received high marks as a high-speed platform with jet augmentation, and in the gunship role.

In March 1963, the US Army Material Command was directed by the Office of the Chief of Research and Development, to evaluate the UH-2A to determine if the helicopter and the T58-GE-8B engine could perform in the Army environment. The job fell to the Army's Test and Evaluation Command, whose intent was to determine if the Seasprite qualified as a high-speed weapons system. The Army's Aviation Test Board was interested too, particularly with regard to how the UH-2A fared in the desert and at high elevations.

On June 15, 1963, the Aviation Test Board took delivery of UH-2A BuNo 149786, loaned from the Navy. Half the time (150 hours) of a normal service test was allotted, which was divided among temperate, desert (at US Army Yuma Proving Ground, Arizona), and high elevation (at Pikes Peak, Colorado).

The overall physical characteristics of the UH-2A as a utility/tactical transport were found unsatisfactory. Major deficiencies were noted in the engine's short service life (due mainly to sand ingestion), complex rotor head, cabin configuration for troop transport and egress, instrument panel layout, and closeness of the cargo hook to the landing gear, which settled deeply into sand. Mission capability tests, held in conjunction with the US Army Airborne, Electronics and Special Warfare Board at Fort Bragg, North Carolina, determined that the UH-2A offered few advantages over Bell's UH-1B "Huey" in the utility / tactical transport role. Noteworthy was the difficulty of paratroopers exiting the Seasprite's cabin; the death blow came when a hapless paratrooper's parachute snagged on the tailwheel when he jumped.

On the brighter side, the UH-2A did meet or exceed the flight characteristics and performance requirements for a utility / tactical transport helicopter. Army officials were impressed with the Seasprite's field hoist, which was capable of lifting all major components forward of the tail group. At the end of testing on August 31, 1963, the Army concluded that the expense of extensive modifications needed for Army use, coupled with the UH-2A's maintenance requirements, was not fair exchange for a modest increase in performance over the UH-1 Huey. In contrast, follow-on testing by the Army of the UH-2A with jet augmentation and in the gunship role met with vastly different results.

Finished in Gloss Olive Drab, the standard for Army helicopters, Kaman's H-2 "Tomahawk" received high marks as the US Army's potential gunship during the early 1960s. Politics entered the picture, and Bell's famed "Huey" was chosen instead. BuNo 149785 crashed in Italy in 1967 and was written off. *Courtesy of US Army*

GUNSHIP SEASPRITE

The second UH-2A to wear ARMY titles was BuNo 149785, handed over from Kaman to the Army Aviation Test Board in October 1963. Earlier that year, the Army had allocated funds for development of the world's first pure gunship helicopter, simultaneously opening a design competition for a low-cost interim gunship pending an advanced aircraft. Kaman, like other helicopter manufacturers during the 1960s, experimented with aerial weapon systems in anticipation of military needs. As manufacturers worked on their designs, the Army announced its requirement for an Advanced Aerial Fire Support System (AAFSS). Lockheed's AH-56 "Cheyenne" and Sikorsky's S-66 "Blackhawk" were chosen; however, their lengthy test, production, and delivery timetables, plus the worsening situation in Vietnam, forced the Army to hasten its search for an interim gunship. Selection came down to Bell's model 209 (precursor to the AH-1G "HueyCobra"), Sikorsky's S-61 (H-3 "Sea King"), and Kaman's H-2 "Tomahawk." Dubbed the "Tommy" by Kaman engineers, the Tomahawk featured stub wings for mounting rocket launchers that carried 2.75-inch folding-fin aerial rockets (FFAR).

The significant modification to the UH-2A was a completely redesigned nose section, which contained a twin-turret system, each housing two 7.62 mm machine guns. Turrets could be fired in sync or independently for vast coverage of targets. Modifications included a liberal amount of armor protection for the cockpit, engine, transmission, and fuel tanks. Army navigation and communications equipment was installed.

The most dramatic modification to create the Tomahawk was made to 785's nose section, which was transformed into an elaborate machine gun system consisting of four 7.62 mm M60 machine guns having a broad range of depression and traverse. *Courtesy of US Army*

Within the Tomahawk's gun package, ample access was provided for loading and maintenance of the four machine guns. On the ground are frangible fore and aft covers for the rocket launchers. *Courtesy of US Army*

Affixed to both sides of the Tomahawk were stub wings with braces for mounting nineteen-tube LAU-3/A, 2.75-inch, folding-fin aerial rocket launchers. *Courtesy of US Army*

The H-2 Tomahawk unleashes rocket salvoes at Hunter Army Airfield, Ft. Stewart, Georgia, on October 21, 1963. Using the chin-mounted turret, the Tomahawk's copilot/gunner was able to consistently hit a 1-gallon can at up to 400 meters. Rocket firings demonstrated point-target accuracy by hitting a wide variety of ground vehicles. Army weapon tests at speeds up to 167 mph showed little or no effect on stability and control of the Tomahawk. *Courtesy of US Army*

The copilot/gunner's reflex sight for the quad M60 machine gun system. *Courtesy of US Army*

In November and December 1965, the three remaining contenders flew comparative tests at Edwards Air Force Base, California, followed by weapon tests at Fort Sill, Oklahoma. The Cobra and Tomahawk, which matched speeds, emerged as the top contenders, and deliberation ensued. A Kaman official noted,

> The Huey was rough as a cob, while our "Tommy" was smooth as silk. Our gun work was about 200 percent more accurate, but our airframe cost was 80 percent more. And there was much quibbling about maintainability, etc. But beating a dead pigeon will help neither us nor the Army.

With regard to weapons accuracy, a former Kaman employee who was involved with the Seasprite's development stated to this author that weapon accuracy standards were lowered until the Bell HueyCobra's range marks fell within acceptable limits. The handwriting was on the wall when the Kaman contingent was told by Bell representatives at the competition, "You're wasting your time here. We're going to win." Regardless, Aviation Test Board officials judged the Tomahawk an extremely capable machine and sought congressional approval to purchase 220 aircraft. Politics came into play after the November 1963 assassination of President John F. Kennedy, with the Tomahawk acquisition plan tabled under the new president, Lyndon B. Johnson. It was no secret that Johnson, a staunch Texan, showed favor in his alliance with Texas-based Bell Helicopter. The competition's model 209 was shipped to Vietnam, where the 1st Cavalry Division put it through its paces; it received final approval from the division's commander, Gen. John Tolson. Thus, competition rules, which held that none of the competing designs could enter production without approval from commanders in the combat zone, cinched the Cobra as the winner.

BuNo 149785 was turned over to the Navy to join the masses being converted to UH-2Cs. No. 785 met its end on January 4, 1967, while assigned to HC-2, Detachment 38, aboard USS *Shangri-La* (CVA-38).

THE COMPOUND SEASPRITE

In view of high marks given the UH-2A after the flight characteristics and performance phase of Army testing, flight test work for the US Army continued. The UH-2A involved in further testing was BuNo 147978, which went from the production line in February 1961 directly to Kaman under a bailment contract. By mid-1964 this Seasprite had amassed one thousand flight hours, having undergone structural improvement and installation of an airframe vibration absorber, among other refinements. The vibration absorber occupied the nose battery compartment to achieve exceptionally low vibration levels, for which the UH-2 was noted. Most publicized was 978's role in high-speed flight testing while modified with a jet pod, and later the addition of wings.

Early in 1964, Kaman, under contract with US Army Transportation Research Command, mounted a GE YJ85 jet engine on 978's starboard fuselage. Developed during the 1950s, the J85 was one of GE's most successful and widely used turbojets. The test was part of high-speed rotor research conducted for the Army's Aviation Material Laboratory, which sought data for the design of high-performance Army helicopters. Besides "unloading," or relieving stress, of the main rotor, the additional engine's horizontal thrust also helped delay blade stall, dampen pitch and yaw, and reduce control sensitivity.

After the compound UH-2 reached a speed of 216 mph, Kaman and Army engineers were convinced that a jet-augmented Seasprite had the potential to reach speeds of 250 mph, and 275 mph with the addition of a second YJ85 jet engine. Engineers further concluded that the addition

As an NUH-2B, BuNo 147978 spent a major portion of its existence as a research platform for the US Army. With a GE YJ85 engine mounted to its starboard side, the Seasprite provided data for the design of fast, maneuverable helicopters for the Army's future needs. *Courtesy of US Army*

BuNo 147978 was the eleventh production UH-2A, which was modified to an NUH-2B with the J85 engine and wings from a Beechcraft Queen Air. The wings served as an auxiliary lifting surface, which, in combination with the jet engine, unloaded the main rotor. *Courtesy of US Army*

of wings would assist the rotor by reducing the lift it provided, in effect making the rotor act as if gross weight were lower. The Army anticipated useful data for designing fast, maneuverable, vertical-takeoff aircraft, with focus on performance, stability, and high-speed rotor stress. Thus, in June 1964, Kaman received from the US Army Transportation Research Command (TRECOM) a contract to add wings to the jet-augmented Seasprite.

In keeping with the program's simplicity and cost, outboard wing sections from a Beech "Queen Air" were bolted on a strengthened lower fuselage. Fuel storage lost by removing the aft fuel tanks under the cabin was regained by using the Beech wing tanks. To change wing lift at a given speed, the UH-2's tailplane was altered to allow the pilot to vary its incidence angle and, consequently, aircraft attitude. Testing at Kaman's Bloomfield facility began in September 1964 and was completed by year's end. The combination jet and wing expanded the speed envelope, which was limited only by rotor blade drag caused by high rotor tip speed. The compound Seasprite provided valuable data for technological advances in Kaman's proposed model K-800 "Seacat" helicopter. BuNo 147978 reportedly was returned to the Navy in 1968 as an NUH-2B permanent test platform.

SEACAT

Ever mindful of the need to provide optimum air rescue operations in the ongoing war in Southeast Asia, military planners and aircraft manufacturers worked to improve equipment and techniques. Encouraged by Army experiments with jet-augmented and gunship versions of the Seasprite, Kaman in 1969 proposed its model K-800 high-speed helicopter for combat rescue and fire support. Named "Seacat," the compound version of the twin-engine UH-2C reflected Kaman's philosophy that stated, "Retain that which is proven, and incorporate the latest technology to obtain a vehicle with the maximum potential for recovering downed personnel."

The Seacat would retain the UH-2's compact size, allowing it to operate from small ships and confined areas. Although the transmission and shoulder-mounted engines were lowered and faired into the fuselage to reduce drag, cabin space was adequate to adapt to a variety of missions in addition to search and rescue. The latest technology planned for the Seacat included all-weather navigation and avionics. Power would be derived from twin GE-T58-16 1,870 hp engines turning a four-blade main rotor and a 10-foot-diameter, three-blade pusher propeller. This arrangement worked in conjunction with the rotor to provide forward thrust. The only additional control in the familiar Seasprite cockpit was propeller pitch control to vary thrust. A 27-foot wing augmented lift and provided

NAVY titles had yet to be replaced during Army desert tests of the UH-2A at US Army Yuma Proving Ground, Arizona. Tests of BuNo 149786, named "Desert Fox," found the turbine engine arrangement and wheeled landing gear inadequate in the desert environment. *Courtesy of US Army*

During US Army evaluation of the Seasprite as a potential utility and transport helicopter, a UH-2A was able to lift an M38AIC Jeep with a 106 mm recoilless rifle but was unable to lift the jeep with a quarter-ton trailer. This photo dispels the notion that BuNo 149778 was involved in Army testing, since an identical photo with Navy markings appears to have been doctored with Army markings to promote use by multiple services. *Courtesy of Kaman Aerospace Corp.*

Crewmen pose with the statistics following achievement of high-altitude tests with the UH-2A BuNo 149786 on August 8, 1963. The Seasprite excelled in high-altitude performance, hovering in ground effect atop Pikes Peak's 14,000-foot height with a useful load of 2,568 pounds. *Courtesy of US Army*

mounts for weapon stores. Additional firepower for the combat search-and-rescue mission would come from a chin-mounted TAT-102 7.62 mm minigun turret.

With a crew of four, armor, armament, and full fuel load, it was estimated that the Seacat could cruise at 213 mph and attain a top speed of 247 mph; at cruise speed, mission radius was 300 nautical miles.

A US Air Force version of the Seacat was to be named "Firecat." Although seen as a promising concept with great potential for combat rescue, the Seacat did not go beyond the design stage.

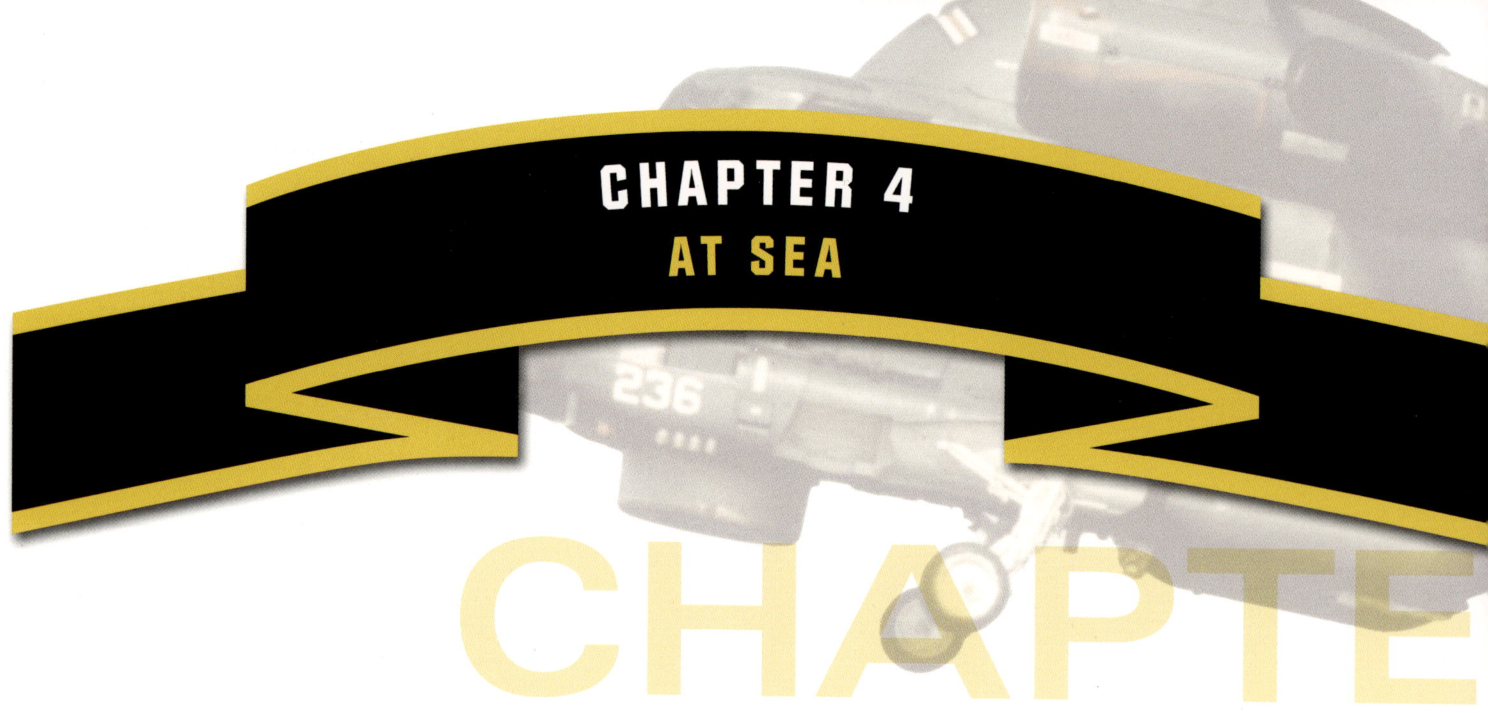

CHAPTER 4
AT SEA

"Any man who goes to sea must consider the possibility that sooner or later he will find himself in the sea."

Until the Seasprite's arrival, helicopter rescue, especially at sea, was a daunting task. The pilot had to fly the aircraft and maintain his horizon reference while maneuvering to position the rescue hoist—which he couldn't see—to the survivor. Further complicating the rescue was the independent motion both of helicopter and wave-tossed survivor, often in storms that created the emergency. Concurrent with Seasprite production, the Naval Air Systems Command awarded Kaman a research-and-development contract to investigate ways to improve helicopter rescue equipment and techniques. Although a relatively small contract, it paid huge dividends with development of the open-sea rescue boom, a rescue net, and the loud hailer.

"Fish pole" was an apt description for the open-sea rescue boom. First tested in 1962, the boom was a curved, 3-inch-diameter aluminum tube, 8 feet, 10 inches in length, that was rated to lift two soaking-wet, fully equipped survivors from the water. The fish pole was used in conjunction with the hoist; when stowed, its tip was directly under the hoist over the cabin rescue door. For its use, the crewman threaded the hoist cable through an eye and pulley at the tip of the fish pole. When extended, the pole swung forward 110 degrees, protruding 8 feet into the pilot's field of vision. He could then lower the hoist to a survivor and view the rescue without having to turn around, which might have caused him to become disoriented or lose his reference to the horizon. Use of the fish pole minimized constant communication between pilot and crewman when the pilot's attention was on flying the rescue. When the survivor reached the end of the boom, a microswitch tripped to swing him to the rescue door, to be brought into the cabin. After testing, which included open-sea trials in 8-to-10-foot waves, the fish pole was installed on UH-2A/Bs and was carried over to twin-engine HH-2Ds and a number of UH-2Cs.

Versions of a rescue net and rescue seat were first developed by members of HU-2 during the late 1950s. Kaman refined the designs to produce equipment that became standard on rescue helicopters. The rescue net was a foldable, 5-foot-diameter tubular frame with a nylon cord net. Although often called a "scoop net," it was best utilized as a platform to lower a crewman to the water to help the survivor into the net.

The rescue seat, after undergoing various design changes, became the standard device attached to helicopter rescue hoists. The seat evolved from a two-paddle seat to a tapered device with three fold-down seats, flotation collar, and protective head shield. During the Vietnam War, the seat would become known as the "jungle penetrator."

For lighting a search area, the UH-2A/B had two floodlights and a searchlight totaling 1,800 watts. The floodlights were aimed forward and down, while the third illuminated the water in the rescue hoist area.

Kaman also conducted research of motor-driven platforms attached to the hoist cable, to be remotely steered to a survivor by a crewman.

R 4: AT SEA

Having shown some measure of unreliability, the Seasprite's emergency flotation system was tested beyond the prototype stage. The fifth production aircraft, BuNo 147976, seen here practicing with the system, ditched in September 1963. Although the aircraft capsized, it remained afloat and was retrieved, only to be written off six weeks later. *Courtesy of US Navy*

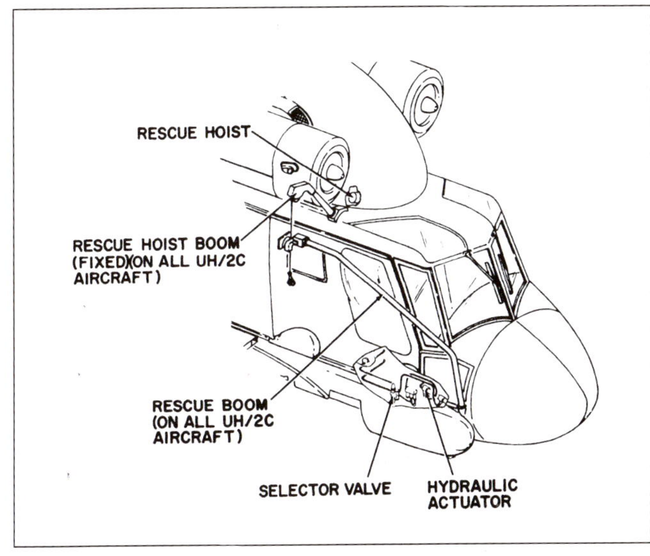

The rescue hoist of twin-engine Seasprites was hydraulically operated and electrically controlled. The purpose of the open-sea rescue boom, or fish pole, was to allow the pilot to observe and control the rescue operation without looking over his shoulder. *Courtesy of US Navy*

Paramount in any rescue situation is communication with survivors. If radio communication is not possible, aircrews are faced with the difficulty of voice contact with survivors. Finding existing loudspeakers inefficient, Kaman engineers concentrated their efforts on developing a powerful amplifier with directional-type loudspeakers. These were mounted to project sound forward and away from rotor and engine noise, generating a cone of sound covering 0.5 square miles away and at an altitude of 2,000 to 3,000 feet. The system, designated the K-250, reflecting its 250-watt power output, was so loud on the ground at full gain that persons within 50 feet were required to wear ear protection to avoid injury. During tests, the dual speaker K-250, also called the loud hailer, was installed on the outside of the aircraft nose but was soon recessed into the Seasprite's nose doors.

All-mission safety factors for overwater operation included flotation features to provide buoyancy for a period of time sufficient to allow the crew to escape in the event of an emergency water landing or rescue. The hull was designed to provide a 4-degree nose-up attitude in water. Despite the claim that the Seasprite's hull was watertight, the aircraft could take on water through seams and antennae ports. To

This 1963 US Navy photo was used by the Timken Roller Bearing Company to advertise its manufacture of the UH-2A's steel transmission support structure. Shown to good effect is the scoop net used in conjunction with the rescue fish pole. BuNo 147204 was one of four prototype YUH-2As. *Courtesy of US Navy*

The Billy Pugh helicopter rescue net, which incorporated a sea anchor and flotation collar, was capable of supporting multiple persons. The reliable device is seen here during the early 1960s in use with Helicopter Combat Support Squadron 2 (HC-2). *Courtesy of US Navy*

One of the major drawbacks of rescue by helicopter has been the pilot's inability to view the rescue operation. On the Seasprite, this was alleviated by placing the cabin door and hoist directly behind the pilot. The fish-pole rescue boom completed the arrangement by giving the pilot both control and full view of the rescue. A white angel and the inscription "Fleet Angel" were painted on the auxiliary fuel tank of this UH-2A aboard USS *Shangri-La* (CVA-38/CVS-38) in April 1967. *Courtesy of Franco Saya*

The practice of painting US Navy helicopters in overall International Orange began with Operation Deep Freeze during the mid-1950s. Both HC-4 and HC-5 supplied Seasprites for ongoing Antarctic operations. Seasprite crews flew ice recon ahead of icebreakers, hauled cargo, resupplied research stations, flew medical evacuation, and rescued scientific teams stranded by ice crevasses. Some helicopters assigned to SAR duty also wore the high-visibility scheme. *Courtesy of US Navy*

The UH-2B BuNo 150141 of HU-1 recovers a BQM-34 drone released from a DP-2E Neptune of Utility Squadron 3 (VU-3), based at NAS North Island. Drone recovery by Seasprite, and drone camera recovery by rescue swimmers, was a common occurrence throughout the Seasprite's life. *Courtesy of US Navy*

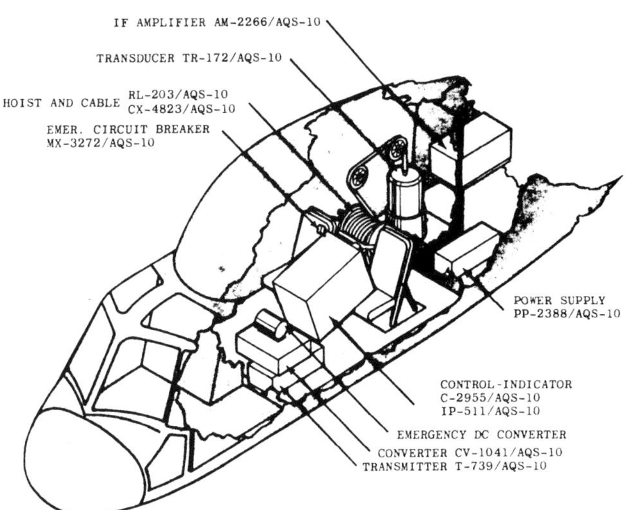

The proposed dipping-sonar installation tested on the UH-2A. *Courtesy of US Navy*

counter rolling up to sea state 5 (rough), two inflatable rubber airbags were contained in sponsons that were forward extensions of landing-gear fairings. These were inflated by solid propellant fired through a liquid ammonia cooling agent to inflate the bags in 2.5 seconds. Since the propellant was ignited and burned, the gas produced was mixed with 200-proof denatured alcohol to cool the bags. Each bag was 45 inches in diameter and 30 inches long. Although the bags provided lateral stability up to 30 degrees of roll, Seasprites had an affinity for rolling over in water. Thus, water landings were advised only for rescue, mechanical failure, or ditching. Landing, or even hovering close to the water, could result in ingested-salt accumulation on turbine compressor blades, resulting in compressor stall. James R. Gore reflects:

> I flew the H-2 while attached to NAS Miramar. The H-2 that I flew was a new single-engine one right from the factory. With only a few hours on the aircraft I had a flame-out during an autorotation. A full autorotation ensued with no problems. Single-engine H-2s had a terrible reputation for engine failure. It would ingest salt in the engine intake during a hover and build up until a flame-out occurred. It was said that HC-1, which had the H-2, was proficient only at holding memorial services. One night flying an H-46 off Ream Field, NAS Imperial Beach, we rescued three or four crew members of an H-2 that had gone in several miles off the beach. One pilot was killed.

Despite the danger of open-sea rescue, Seasprite crews displayed great skill and fortitude when facing seemingly insurmountable tasks. For example, in mid-September 1966, the British ore carrier SS *August Moon*, driven onto Pratas Reef in the South China Sea during a typhoon, was in imminent danger of breaking up. Ships were standing by, but heavy seas and shoal waters made their approach with lifeboats impossible to rescue the forty-four men aboard. A desperate call to the carrier USS *Oriskany*, 70 miles away, prompted the carrier to launch two UH-2As, call signs "Angel 2-5" and "Angel 4-7," from HC-1's Detachment Golf. Upon arrival, the two crews knew there was no time to waste, since gigantic waves slammed against the ship. Despite powerful winds, Angel 2-5 came to a hover and hoisted five crewmen. Angel 4-7 then moved in to hoist more survivors, with both Seasprites taking turns until twenty-four were taken to safety on an island. Dangerously low on fuel, both UH-2As headed for USS *Oriskany*, while a third Seasprite (BuNo 152196) of Det. Golf arrived. As its crew positioned to hoist survivors, without warning, a giant 65-foot wave engulfed the helicopter, killing the engine and dropping the aircraft into the raging sea. The aircraft was slammed against the rocky bottom, 20 feet below the surface, and rolled over. Both pilots and the crewman managed to escape the battered Seasprite. A frantic call from a British destroyer on scene had Angels 2-5 and 4-7 turning back to the scene, despite their fuel status. The pair rescued the three injured crewmen, flew them to *Oriskany*, refueled, and went back to rescue twenty remaining survivors from SS *August Moon*. Det. Golf's tally that day was forty-seven saves, including their brother Seasprite crewmen.

Shortly after risking their lives on this mission, three of the rescue crewmen, along with two other Det. Golf pilots, died in a fire aboard the carrier *Oriskany*.

The fire and explosions that wracked the carrier USS *Forrestal* in Vietnam's Gulf of Tonkin on July 29, 1967, led to numerous heroic feats as the plane guard UH-2A crew, "Angel Two-Zero" of HC-1 Det. 34, saved the lives of *Forrestal* sailors. The pilot, Lt. David Clement, the copilot, Ens. Leonard Eiland, and crewmen Albert Barrows and James James rescued five burned sailors from the water and then began shuttling fire equipment and medical supplies from USS *Oriskany* to *Forrestal*. When the hospital ship *Repose* reached the area about midnight, the Seasprite crew transferred critically injured sailors to her landing pad.

THE "TWIN CHARLIE"

A study of accident reports involving the Seasprite made obvious the benefits of twin-engine helicopter operations, especially at sea, where the extra engine could be a life saver. Accordingly, on January 2, 1964, Kaman received a contract for a twin-engine version of the Seasprite, designated the UH-2C. To meet the additional fleet requirements for reliability and safety, modification became a byword with the H-2. Kaman engineers came up with the twin-engine variant, with BuNo 147981, the tenth production UH-2A, selected for the mockup and prototype in October 1964 (soon after it left production, no. 981 embarked on a career as a permanent test platform, undergoing multiple modifications and associated designations).

Every effort was made to retain the original configuration to preserve the UH-2A/B cockpit, with which fleet pilots were familiar. Although changes were necessary to complete the conversion, the general overall dimensions of the twin remained unchanged from the UH-2A/B. In the mockup role, no. 981 was fit with wood-and-fabric cowlings and fairings for Navy evaluations in September 1965. In November, the Navy, pleased with the results, gave approval for the switch from research to further development. The first UH-2C flight was accomplished on March 14, 1966, with the second prototype (believed to be BuNo 149741) phased into flight test on May 20. Besides the increased twin-engine safety factor, signs of success appeared quickly in the form of increased takeoff gross weight to 11,614 pounds, and hot and high-altitude performance characteristics. The modification contract for forty conversions received the go-ahead in August, then evaluation by the Naval Air Test Center at NAS Patuxent River (shortened in Navyspeak to "Pax River"), followed by three-month Board of Inspection and Survey trials. The UH-2B, BuNo 150139, assigned to HC-2, was the first UH-2A scheduled for production line conversion to the "Twin Charlie." It left NAS Lakehurst for the Kaman factory on November 29, 1966. The modification process began in December, with fifty-seven Seasprites converted to the twin-engine UH-2C, six of which became the armed and armored HH-2C. Seasoned Seasprite pilot LaRon Stoker offers insight on his role in the process:

> My return home from Vietnam meant a new beginning for me. I had now received my promotion to lieutenant commander, and my new assignment was to be fleet project officer for the development of the UH-2C. I made many trips from HC-1 at Imperial Beach to the main Kaman factory in Bloomfield, Connecticut. In early 1967, I went TDY (temporary duty) to NAS Pax River, where they had placed the prototype UH-2C. I was to be the fleet test pilot to fly with test pilots through the BIS trials, which would qualify the helicopter for fleet operations. My first couple of test flights flown with the Navy test pilots were unbelievable. One of them started one of the engines while I was still doing the preflight on the rotor head. After that, I went to the captain in charge and related my experience with his test pilots, and I told him I refused to fly with them. The next day he called me into his office and gave me a letter designating me the official test pilot for the entire program. Two weeks later, I stopped the program after I had been flying a profile flight and developed severe tail rotor vibrations. When I returned to the flight line and inspected the tail rotor, I found the bearings had disintegrated. They brought in the engineers from Kaman, who agreed that a new tail rotor would have to be developed. I returned to HC-1, and Kaman began work on a new tail rotor. It took almost three months to get this completed. In the meantime, the Navy had decided that they wanted to deploy the first detachment on the carrier USS *Ranger*, which was to sail in November 1967. They had also designated me to be the officer in charge of that detachment.
>
> In early June of that year the UH-2C program was back on track, and I went back to Pax River to finish the BIS trials. It was mid-July when I completed all profile flights and agreed with

> Kaman that the helicopter was ready for fleet operations. Kaman had three helos near completion, and I needed them as soon as possible since the *Ranger* was starting precruise training and they wanted me on board to train with them. The first two helos were ready at the end of August, and I took the three-best-qualified pilots of my new detachment to Kaman to pick them up.

Stoker and crew of HC-1 Det. 61 aboard *Ranger* did not have to wait long to test their new "Charlie" under actual conditions. On September 26, 1967, ten minutes after takeoff for the afternoon plane guard mission, the crew received word that a pilot was in the water after ejecting from his aircraft 11 miles from the carrier. Sixteen minutes later, pilot Lt. (j.g.) Richard R. Mason and crew had the pilot safely back on deck. Two days later, Lt. Cmdr. LaRon Stoker and crew performed the first UH-2C night rescue in the Pacific Fleet, when a pilot ejected due to a collapsed landing gear. Stoker added, "The true value of the UH-2C's extra power and speed may mean the difference between a successful rescue or the loss of a pilot. You can gauge 'Charlie's worth on that fact alone.'"

Technically, the transformation from UH-2A/B to UH-2C was accomplished mainly by removal of the domelike section above the fuselage. The engines were shoulder-mounted on each side of the transmission, which had engine output shafts driving aft into a combining gearbox, from which a shaft led to the transmission. The UH-2C then had twice the power—2,500 shp, 800 of which was reserve—of the UH-2A/B with the same rotor system. Empty, normal gross, and takeoff weight of the UH-2C easily exceeded those of the UH-2A/B by more than 1,000 pounds. The speeds of the twin and its predecessor remained basically the same; however, the UH-2C saw dramatic increases in rate of climb and service and hover ceilings. Typical of the compromise found in most aircraft designs, due to increased fuel consumption the range of the UH-2C was 425 miles, considerably less than the 670 miles of the UH-2A/B. And like its single-engine predecessor, the twin was prone to ingesting salt water in a hover, causing corrosion and, at worst, engine failure. The three-blade tail rotor was retained; however, it wasn't sufficient to compensate for the vast power increase, requiring that pilots use power judiciously to avoid the loss of tail rotor authority or risk overtorquing the combining gearbox or transmission. A streamlined fairing was contoured around the transmission and engine nacelles and incorporated ample access panels, some of which doubled as work platforms. The twin's engine nacelle inlets were designed and tested at NASA's icing research tunnel at Cleveland to provide maximum engine anti-icing by using a chisel-like leading edge, heated bellmouth inlet, and heated bullet-nose engine starter.

Directional control and longitudinal stability were improved by extending and cambering the lower portion of the tail rotor pylon to port. This step-cambered tail fin was the optimum design for hover and higher forward-flight speeds. The narrow chord portion of the fin improved tail rotor effectiveness during hover and sideward flight, while the cambered portion acted like a rudder as airspeed increased above 92 mph. Outwardly, other changes included relocation of the pitot tube from above the right-side pilot's cockpit to beneath the copilot's station. The earlier retractable rescue hoist gave way to a hoist arm fixed to the twin's fuselage, with the winch and motor contained within the front cowling.

During conversion to the UH-2C, Kaman experimented with other modifications on the prototype BuNo 147981. "Bear paw" skis, which became standard on Kaman's H-43 Huskie helicopter, then in production, were attached to the Seasprite's main landing gear to broaden its landing footprint. Drawing from its experience with the Army Tomahawk, during late 1968 Kaman modified one aircraft (no. 981, then designated NUH-1C) with stub wings to carry fuel and a wide range of external stores, including torpedoes, auxiliary fuel tanks, and weapon systems. With fuel in the wings and mounting 60-gallon auxiliary tanks, the UH-2C's range was extended to 560 miles and nearly five hours of endurance. Rugged, dual-wheel Dowty landing gear was considered in lieu of Cleveland landing gear to handle the UH-2C's takeoff weight, which was 1,600 pounds more than that of the UH-2A/B.

DIPPING SONAR

In 1949, the Committee for Undersea Warfare, convinced that the solution to detecting submarines was with sound detectors, sponsored Project Hartwell during the Korean War. Hartwell worked under this premise: "The helicopter, as a vehicle invulnerable to torpedo attack, with a high search rate against submarines, the ability to operate with task forces, convoys, and fast independents, and to destroy submarines once contact is made, seems the most promising single weapon system for antisubmarine warfare."

Accordingly, little time passed before the versatile Seasprite's introduction to the world of antisubmarine warfare. Given the Seasprite's open-sea habitat, Navy engineers believed that UH-2s equipped with sonar could augment antisubmarine protection of the fleet. Besides

Lt. Cmdr. LaRon Stoker and Lt. (j.g.) Curtis Huffman inspect the tail rotor of BuNo 149741, the first UH-2C, during preflight for cross-country delivery to NAAS Ream Field, California. Huffman's hand rests atop the step-cambered tail rotor pylon. Obvious is the tail rotor driveshaft offset to port. *Courtesy of US Navy*

Prior to the cross-country delivery flight of the first UH-2Cs from Kaman to NAAS Ream Field, Kaman vice president Robert D. Moses gives Lt. Cmdr. LaRon Stoker a "bon voyage" handshake. Although an optimistic, expert pilot, Stoker's flight helmet wore the name "Jinx." Shown to good effect is the fish-pole rescue hoist connection, and the relocation of the pitot tube from above and forward of the UH-2A/B's left cockpit door to beneath the twin's right-seat rudder pedals. The new location eliminated airspeed indicator fluctuations during the twin's greater rate of climb and high-speed rotor downwash. *Courtesy of US Navy*

The arrival of the first UH-2Cs at NAAS Ream Field, home of HC-1, in August 1967. Three weeks later, a third Seasprite joined BuNos 149741 and 150139 in HC-1, with a total of twenty-five delivered to Ream Field, all of which were slated for carrier duty. *Courtesy of US Navy via Rod Stoker*

Besides rescue, the fish pole was useful for transferring personnel and delivering equipment. Seen here is BuNo 150164 of HC-1, assigned to USS *Bon Homme Richard* in 1969. Helicopter Combat Support Squadron 1 (HC-1) was a 1965 redesignation of Helicopter Utility Squadron 1 (HU-1), which formed at NAS Lakehurst in 1948. HC-1 was the Navy's largest helicopter squadron until 1967, when it was divided into four squadrons: HA(L)-3, HC-3, HC-5, and HC-7. *Courtesy of US Navy / National Naval Aviation Museum*

When photographed at Phoenix, Arizona, in late September 1969, this UH-2C of HC-1's Det. 7 recorded thirteen hoist saves on its scoreboard. After service with a number of US Navy units, no. 154 served the Royal New Zealand Navy. *Courtesy of Grady Cates collection*

providing warning for the attack carriers on which they were deployed, sonar-equipped UH-2s could operate from smaller naval and merchant vessels unable to accommodate larger helicopters. In 1965, three UH-2As—BuNos 149769, 149770, and 149771—underwent design and fabrication by Kaman for installation of the Bendix-Pacific AN/ASQ-10 sonar. The multicomponent system was heavy, and some said installation couldn't be done; however, Kaman engineer Anthony Rita designed a rail system for loading and unloading the cumbersome layout. Nine major components formed a modular package that could be quickly installed or removed for rapid conversion for other missions. In time trials, a four-man crew completely removed the sonar package in fourteen minutes and reinstalled it in thirty-one minutes; it functioned perfectly. The sonar operator's seat faced forward on the left side of the cabin, with a second seat and the sonar hoist on the right. The right doorway was left clear for rescue. Pilots had controls for positioning the aircraft for a sonar hover, and for monitoring sonar equipment.

Kaman then turned the aircraft over to the Navy for a six-week evaluation with Air Development Squadron 1 (VX-1) at NAS Key West. The tests proved the system successful, with the exception of single-engine marginal power under hot day conditions. That limitation was expected to disappear with the switch to the twin-engine UH-2C then in development. Dipping sonar, however, would not become an operational fixture in Seasprites in lieu of success with other systems.

THE "TWIN CHARLIE" JOINS THE FLEET

On July 1, 1965, helicopter utility squadrons were redesignated helicopter combat support squadrons; HU-1, HU-2, and HU-4, therefore, became HC-1, HC-2, and HC-4. Delivery of the first UH-2C took place on August 11, 1967, to HC-1 at NAS Imperial Beach.

For all the safety features the twin Seasprite promised, mishaps were inevitable, and they befell the UH-2C early in its existence. The tragedy that resulted in the largest loss of life in a single H-2 incident dampened enthusiasm for the Twin Charlie. Foreshadowing that fateful flight was the delivery flight of the first two UH-2Cs from Kaman to NAS Imperial Beach. Concern mounted when the helicopter with skilled H-2 pilot LaRon ("Ron") Stoker and crew was overdue, having made an emergency landing in the Arizona mountains due to severe vibration. Applying the rotor brake upon landing only intensified the vibration. Installed in the UH-2C was a new rotor brake disc with cooling slots. Cracks appeared at the slots, so the crew removed the damaged unit, allowing Stoker to complete the delivery flight. Some felt that the incident should have been a wake-up call for Kaman to fix the problem.

Ten months later, on July 10, 1968, UH-2C BuNo 150176 of HC-1, which was embarked aboard the carrier *Bon Homme Richard*, was flying in the vicinity of Clark Air

Base, Philippine Islands, when it crashed into a rice paddy. The six US Navy personnel aboard were killed. Among the dead were the commanding officer of Attack Squadron VA-93 and the officer in charge of the HC-1 detachment aboard the carrier *Bon Homme Richard*. Filipino locals scavenged parts from the crash site, which impeded the investigation. Kaman offered to buy back the parts, per pound. Among the parts returned were the rotor brake disc and a broken rotor blade. The disc had been thrown from its hub and flew upward, severing a rotor blade. The resultant vibration caused the transmission to separate from the fuselage. The newer style of rotor brake disc with cooling slots was deemed the cause—all H-2s were grounded and old-style rotor brake discs were reinstalled. After the crash, Kaman then knew that the rotor brake disc had separated much like it did on Stoker's delivery flight.

The new arrival would be joined by twenty-four Twin Charlies assigned to the "Fleet Angels" to replace UH-2As aboard carriers in the Pacific. Detachment 61, aboard USS *Ranger*, became the first UH-2C West Coast detachment. Three months later, the squadron's Detachment 63, aboard USS *Kitty Hawk*, became the first to fly the UH-2C in Vietnam, performing its first combat rescue on December 27, 1967, in the Gulf of Tonkin. The pilot of an Air Force F-4C Phantom that was shot down was rescued, but, tragically, the second crewman slipped from the rescue sling as he was hoisted and was lost.

The introduction of the twin Seasprite was not without growing pains. Scott Milner explains:

Helicopter Combat Support Training Squadron 16 (HCT-16) grew out of the USS *Lexington* / NAS Pensacola CVT SAR Detachment, which became operational on June 1, 1970, with three Seasprites, five officers, and twenty-nine enlisted personnel. The detachment became HCT-16 on November 1, 1974, with UH-2A/Bs for SAR coverage of NAS Pensacola's training complex and as plane guard training center on board training aircraft carrier USS *Lexington* (CVT-16). In 1972, the unit traded its single-engine Seasprites for UH-2Cs. In spring 1977, these were returned for LAMPS conversion and replaced by HH-46As, and the unit was redesignated HC-16 "Bullfrogs." The UH-2C BuNo 149775 seen here crashed off the Texas coast in December 1975. *Courtesy of US Navy*

Tests determined the optimum contour around the twin's transmission and rotor shaft housing, which raised level-flight airspeed by 5 knots. The streamlined airflow along the top surfaces of the engine nacelles and aft cowling eliminated turbulence from the tail rotor. *Courtesy of US Navy*

> From its introduction into fleet operations, the H-2 had a very poor maintenance record. Attack carriers were deploying in the early to mid-1960s with a detachment from either HC-1 or HC-2. Each detachment was assigned three H-2s. Although a "sports car" for pilots, the H-2 was underpowered and ran out of tail rotor authority very quickly. Many were lost in accidents. Kaman produced the twin-engine UH-2C; however, the maintenance issues that plagued the UH-2A and UH-2B continued. Parts were in short supply. Detachments were being deployed with three aircraft and finding that regularly only one or, at most, two were operational. In 1967, Western Gear Company manufactured nine main transmissions with alignment holes misdrilled. As a result, at least two UH-2Cs suffered "alpha damage" (totally destroyed). In November 1967, HC-1's Detachment 63 embarked on the *Kitty Hawk* with three of these transmissions. One Seasprite was lost at sea, while the other two were grounded due to unusual flight characteristics. Commander of Task Force 77, RAdm. Ralph Cousins, became irate that his carriers could not fly its helicopters. In early 1969, he ordered all UH-2C aircraft to be removed from his carriers and replaced with SH-3Ds from various ASW squadrons assigned to ASW carriers. This

action was short lived, but it spelled the end to the UH-2C being used for its designed purpose as a carrier-based search-and-rescue helicopter.

The nine faulty transmissions, which took the Navy far too long to find, should have been a wake-up call for Kaman and the Navy Safety Center, but the tempo of operations in the Gulf of Tonkin contributed to it being "just another accident caused by a less than thorough preflight."

On September 23, 1968, BuNo 151311 was the first UH-2C assigned to HC-2. The Seasprite is seen here displayed with major panels open three weeks after its arrival. The squadron's first UH-2Cs deployed with Det. 60 aboard the carrier USS *Saratoga* (CV-60) in the Mediterranean. HC-2 provided helicopter detachments to all Atlantic Fleet aircraft carriers for plane guard and rescue duty. *Courtesy of Roger Besecker via Norm Taylor*

Scott Milner, fellow pilot and good friend of LaRon Stoker, was assigned to the second UH-2C detachment, which went aboard USS *Kitty Hawk* in the Gulf of Tonkin in 1968. During a night mission, Milner's UH-2C crashed into the water. Although the crew survived, Milner was badly injured.

The UH-2C had become a helicopter with no mission, but luckily, as the versatility of the Seasprite increased, so did the demands for its services. As the largest and most active helicopter squadron in the Navy in 1967, HC-1 flew a wide variety of missions well beyond its core mission of safeguarding human life. For example, flying from US Coast Guard icebreaker USS *Staten Island* (WAGB-278) in 1967, HC-1's Det. 53 was the first US Navy detachment to fly the Seasprite in Antarctica. The UH-2A/Bs alternated with Coast Guard Sikorsky HH-52A Seaguard helicopters. To ease the workload of HC-1, HC-2, and HC-4, on September 1, 1967, HC-1 was divided into four different squadrons: Helicopter Attack (Light) Squadron 3 [HA(L)-3], flying former US Army Bell Hueys, and HC-3, HC-5, and HC-7, all of which flew Seasprites. HC-5 was commissioned at NAAS Imperial Beach, California, and its primary responsibility was to train pilots for other helicopter combat support squadrons. Equipped with the UH-2C, the squadron deployed three detachments aboard US Coast Guard icebreakers in the Arctic and Antarctic, along with non-aviation-type ships and eastern Pacific carriers. The squadron also conducted combat crew training for pilots destined for the South China Sea, along with various ground and survival schools. Also based at NAAS Imperial Beach, the "Merlins" of HC-3 was the Navy's sole vertical-replenishment squadron for the West Coast Fleet. HC-6 at NAS Norfolk, which originally was a detachment of HC-4 flying the UH-2A/B, split from the oversized squadron to become a VertRep squadron flying the UH-46D.

The HH-2D BuNo 149017 of HC-4, Det. 44, lifts off from the afterdeck of the heavy cruiser USS *Newport News* (CA-148) during US Second Fleet operations in European waters in October 1971. The crowded flight deck was between the ship's stern and aft 8-inch gun turret. Stenciled figures on the Seasprite's auxiliary fuel tank represent the ship's European port visits during a two-month deployment. *Newport News* was the Navy's last all-gun heavy cruiser. *Courtesy of US Navy*

On September 23, 1968, UH-2C BuNo 151311 took off from Kaman's Windsor Locks facility, headed for HC-2's home base at NAS Lakehurst, marking the first delivery of a Seasprite twin to the East Coast squadron. No. 311 would then be assigned to newly commissioned USS *John F. Kennedy* (CVA-67). As additional UH-2Cs arrived, they would be assigned to East Coast carriers to relinquish UH-2As of plane guard, rescue, and utility duty.

With its landing gear retracted, the UH-2C BuNo 151300 of HC-1 hovers and uses its cargo hook to lift equipment from the deck of USS *Coral Sea. Courtesy of US Navy*

The leading edge of the twin-engine Seasprite's engine air inlet was designed to prevent ice accumulation. The chisel-like leading edge kept air moving, while the circular bellmouth was heated along with the bullet-nose engine starter. Upper engine nacelles were covered with antiskid walkway strips. This SH-2F is chocked and chained, having landed on the no. 2 deck of the destroyer USS *Peterson* (DD-969) in the Atlantic in February 1990. *Courtesy of US Navy*

CHAPTER 5
THE SEASPRITE GOES TO WAR

5: THE SEASPRIT

While the first UH-2Cs were beginning flight trials, conflict in Southeast Asia was escalating, with the air campaign growing in scope and intensity. Rescue of aircrew downed in the South China Sea and overland in the high-threat environment drove the need for adapting the UH-2 to a combat environment. In the meantime, single-engine, standard-configuration Seasprites, UH-2Cs when they became available, and SH-3 Sea Kings aboard four ASW carriers shouldered the load of Navy combat rescue in Vietnam. Pilots of attack aircraft knew that their best chance of rescue was to eject over the sea, a goal termed "feet wet." Since this was not always possible, it was only a matter of time before ship-based helicopters had to make the perilous dash inland to attempt rescue.

From 1964 until 1973, twenty-one aircraft carriers from both the Atlantic and Pacific Fleets served western Pacific combat cruises; fifteen were attack carriers, the remainder being antisubmarine carriers. When airstrikes against North Vietnam began under Project Rolling Thunder in March 1965, HC-1 Det. M was directed to forward-deploy a Seasprite from the carrier USS *Ranger* (CVA-61) to the cruiser USS *England* (DLG-22). Equipped with flak jackets and a .30-caliber machine gun, the Seasprite crew remained aboard until the end of *Ranger*'s line period in mid-April. A Seasprite crew of HC-1 Detachment A aboard USS *Midway* (CV-41) then took over the mission and later embarked on the light cruiser USS *Galveston* (CLG-3). On September 20, the crew accomplished the first US Navy sea-based helicopter combat rescue in North Vietnam. With covering fire from a pair of VA-25 Skyraiders, the crew located and rescued the pilot of an A-4E Skyhawk that had been shot down.

Beginning in mid-May 1965, a carrier would serve on Dixie Station off South Vietnam before relocating north to Yankee Station, where Task Force 77 (TF 77) was the operational command. A SAR coordinator under TF 77 oversaw Navy operations from a North SAR Station destroyer. The normal complement of three Seasprite helicopters aboard carriers was effective in plane guard and utility roles, but they were all that TF 77 had available for combat search and rescue.

On November 7, 1965, a UH-2A/B of HC-2 Det. 62 was sent from the carrier USS *Independence* (CV-62) to the frigate USS *Richmond K. Turner* (DLG-20) as backup for a SAR mission that had gone bad after an F-105 had been shot down. Two A-1 Skyraiders and an Air Force CH-3 of the rescue force had been shot down, and an SH-3 Sea King that had run out of fuel crash-landed on a mountaintop. The Seasprite crew rescued two SH-3 crewmen, while an Air Force helicopter snatched the remaining two. Although the UH-2A/B had staged aboard *Turner* for a single mission, it gave further rise to the idea of placing the small, fast UH-2s aboard smaller, more-maneuverable ships that could operate closer to Vietnam's shore. Thus, the same day of the F-105 mission, a UH-2 of HC-1 aboard the carrier *Oriskany* (CV-34) was sent to the guided-missile cruiser USS *Gridley* (DLG-21) in the Gulf of Tonkin. After the ship touched down on *Gridley*'s fantail, its captain greeted Seasprite pilot Lt. Tom Saintsing with "I know

GOES TO WAR

BuNo 149774 was one of two UH-2A/Bs destroyed when fire ravaged the carrier USS *Oriskany*, stationed off the coast of Vietnam, on October 26, 1966. During the fire, HC-1 detachments flew equipment and medical evacuation missions to the hospital ship *Repose*. No. 774 had been assigned to HC-1, Det. 1, Unit Golf, aboard *Oriskany*. The aircraft's fuselage markings had yet to be changed when HU-1 was redesignated HC-1 in 1965. *Courtesy of US Navy*

nothing about helicopters. You're going to have to tell me what to do and how to do it." With no combat rescue time under their belts, Saintsing and crew barely knew what to do themselves. The second night they were aboard, they were awakened to locate and rescue Lt. Cmdr. Paul Merchant of VA-152, who had ditched his Skyraider a mile offshore after taking ground fire. The Seasprite's approach was met with enemy fire, but the crew's only defense was two Thompson submachine guns that had been hastily tossed aboard. The Seasprite got to the downed Spad pilot before enemy boats, hoisted him aboard, and touched down on *Gridley* with the low-fuel light flashing. The concept of operating Seasprites from smaller ships had taken hold, but more had to be done—much more.

In August 1966, Dixie Station was discontinued in lieu of maintaining two or three carriers on Yankee Station to position strike groups closer to North Vietnam targets. The placement of Seasprites aboard small boys continued, with valiant crews carrying out rescues of downed aircrews, often under fire. Without the benefit of adequate equipment and training, the mission was difficult, with a mission's success dependent on crew performance. Duty aboard DLGs in the Gulf of Tonkin called for rugged men and equipment. Pilots, aircrewmen, and maintenance personnel became skilled in operating on the open afterdecks of fast-moving ships, often in unforgiving weather. Engine and transmission changes were made with the UH-2's special hoist assembly. Corrosion control due to salt spray and the ship's corrosive stack smoke was a never-ending task. Landing on small deck platforms designed for smaller drone helicopters required skillful flying and precise timing as pilots competed with rolling, pitching sterns, often in turbulence. Their experiences highlighted the need for an armed and armored version of the Seasprite, prompting Kaman to draw upon its experience with the Army's proposed Tomahawk gunship to develop a suitable Navy version. Besides its poor survivability in combat, the single-engine UH-2A/B had limitations, but help was on

Since no official camouflage directive had been issued for US Navy helicopters in Southeast Asia, Seasprites in the war zone appeared in a variety of schemes, most of which were based on unit policy. Squadrons adopted a basic pattern, using various shades of gray, black, tan, and green. This UH-2A/B of HC-1, Det. 17, is seen on the fantail of USS *Reeves* (DLG-24) on South SAR in the Gulf of Tonkin in 1966. For two years, beginning in July 1966, *Reeves*, a Leahy-class destroyer leader, was stationed in the gulf for combat search-and-rescue support. *Courtesy of Michael J. (Mick) Rigby*

A naval aviator deplanes aboard missile frigate USS *King* (DLG-10) after he was rescued by the ship's helicopter detachment. During *King*'s on-station in the Gulf of Tonkin during 1966, HC-1, Det. 23, made twelve combat rescues. In the Seasprite's doorway is the crewman's M60A machine gun. Helicopter-landing facilities had been installed on *King* just prior to its departure for the WESTPAC cruise. *Courtesy of US Navy*

the way. In November 1965, the SH-3A "Sea King" was authorized for combat search and rescue. The Sea King's two engines, greater range, and larger size and payload meant greater survivability than with the UH-2. Sea Kings, which were stripped of their ASW equipment, were assigned to Helicopter Antisubmarine Squadrons (HS) 2, 4, 6, and 8, embarked aboard attack and ASW carriers in the gulf. Despite their size, Sea Kings periodically operated from the fantails of small boys. By the end of November 1965, HC-1's Det. 9 was formed and trained for combat SAR, although its aircraft were not yet fully configured for that mission. The unit's Seasprites were powered by the "Gold Stripe" version of the T58 engine, which had finer tolerances and fault-free components, thus raising maximum operating limitations to provide an additional 100 horsepower. The special engine, which got its name from the yellow stripe that encircled its storage container, was authorized only for CSAR helicopters. Meanwhile, at Cubi Point, Philippines, HC-1 Det. 5 was preparing for its role as the second HC-1 CSAR detachment to deploy to the Gulf of Tonkin. David J. McCracken, in his 2009 article, "The Adventures and Tribulations of a Helo CSAR Pilot in Vietnam," described the events that followed:

> In 1965, I was a newly frocked lieutenant commander serving as training officer with Helicopter Combat Support Squadron One (HC-1) based at Ream Field, Imperial Beach. Late that year I became the officer in charge of HC-1 Detachment 5. The detachment consisted of a single UH-2B helicopter and a complement of 13 men. We were scheduled to relieve Detachment 9 early in 1966. We were to deploy aboard the USS *Coontz* (DLG-9). This ship was fitted with a small helicopter platform, a legacy from the failed DASH ASW Drone helicopter program. Our detachment would be the first to be equipped with a combat-configured UH-2B helicopter. In preparation for the deployment, HC-1 maintenance personnel removed from the helo all the equipment that was not necessary for the CSAR mission and installed a Gold Stripe T-58 engine. Additionally, they installed self-sealing fuel tanks, M60 7.62 mm machine gun platforms on the cabin doors, bolted ceramic armor plating around the engine, transmission, tail rotor gearbox, pilot seats, and oil lines, and painted the fuselage in camouflage colors. This was the first time a camouflage paint scheme would be applied to a UH-2, and there were no instructions whatsoever on how to do it. The painters tried different ideas, but none seemed to

Lt. (j.g.) W. H. Natter of VA-52 is assisted by AMS2 Laron Hammon following his rescue from the Gulf of Tonkin after his A-1H Skyraider was shot down on November 27, 1966. This marked the first rescue of HC-1, Det. 5 "Flying Bears," stationed aboard USS *King*. Pilots of this UH-2A/B sacrificed downward vision for protection by replacing chin windows with armor. The pilot, Lt. Cmdr. M. T. Legare, sits in an armored seat comprising a swing-out armor panel. *Courtesy of USS King (DLG-10/ DDG-41) Association*

produce a satisfactory result. Finally, running against the deadline, I ran out of patience, grabbed a can of green spray paint and painted the contours of different fields around the entire airframe, and then directed the painters to fill those fields with green, tan, and gray paint. The result gave the Hooky-Two a very concealing appearance and became the standard for future CSAR-configured H-2s.

The 28th of January 1966 we flew our UH-2B to the naval station and hoisted it aboard USS *Coontz*. The next day we departed San Diego en route to Hawaii. The success we anticipated at the beginning of our deployment could not have been more shattered. Our helo was tied down to the helo deck on the 01 level at the fantail of the ship, right in front and above the aft missile launcher. The 30th of January, while exercising the missile launcher, its crew ripped the tail pylon off our helo, the only CSAR-configured UH-2 in the Navy inventory. All the hard work done at Ream Field had been lost. Upon our arrival in Pearl Harbor, the damaged helo was transported to NAS Barbers Point for further transfer to Naval Air Rework Facility (NARF) North Island to be overhauled. Before its transfer, we had removed all the armor plating and the M60 platforms from the damaged helo and retained those items with us aboard USS *Coontz*.

A UH-2A of HC-1 departs USS *Forrestal* after the fire aboard the carrier on July 29, 1967. During the 1965 to 1967 period, HC-1 deployed thirteen detachments to the Gulf of Tonkin. BuNo 149744 met its end when it crashed aboard USS *Voge* off Jacksonville, Florida, on July 17, 1984. *Courtesy of National Naval Aviation Museum*

Wearing an unusual scheme of overall green with large black markings while assigned to HC-7, Det. 101, UH-2A BuNo 149744 serves as backdrop for a Sunday "smoker" aboard Seventh Fleet flagship USS *Providence* (CLG-6). During the ship's 1966 to 1968 WESTPAC cruise, the detachment and UH-2A, with two pilots and eight enlisted personnel, were embarked aboard as VIP transport for commander of the Seventh Fleet (COMSEVENTHFLT). *Courtesy of US Navy*

We proceeded by air to NAS Cubi Point, arriving there the 11th of February. Another UH-2B that had been sitting at HC-1 Detachment Cubi in a dreadful state of neglect was quickly assigned as our replacement bird. With deep apprehension I was forced to accept this helo. Maintenance personnel worked tirelessly for many long hours to rebuild this "hangar queen" into an operational helo. At that time a Gold Stripe engine was installed.

LaRon Stoker poses with his camouflaged Seasprite aboard USS *King* in the Gulf of Tonkin in the 1966–67 time frame. Stoker named his UH-2A "OMYASSIS DRAGON." Life rings on the scoreboard of the black armor panel represent saves, while those with a crescent moon represent night rescues. The loud hailer was in the recessed area under the nose. *Courtesy of Rod Stoker*

During a water rescue in November 1966, the pilot of this UH-2A of HC-1 has swung the fish pole with survivor rearward to the cabin. *Courtesy of US Navy*

The 22nd of February we reported back aboard USS *Coontz*, which had arrived in Subic. The 23rd we flew the helo aboard and departed for the North SAR station, 50 to 60 miles southeast of Haiphong. We learned that fishing boats and junks along the North Vietnamese coast seemed to respond to a downed aircrew incident in a coordinated fashion. We knew that North Vietnamese fishermen were rewarded monetarily for each airman they could capture or kill. We noticed that many fishing boats tied up to bamboo poles sticking out of the water some distance from shore fished from there, returning to shore at the end of the day. We had the hair-brained [*sic*] idea that, if we could pull the poles out, we would disrupt the fishermen's system and force them to launch from the beach, thus slowing them down. The poles had bright-colored rags tied to their tips. We were just coming into a hover to give a pole a try when suddenly mortar rounds started to fall nearby. We immediately departed the area as fast as we could. We returned to USS *Coontz* and reported our training flight completed as scheduled. We didn't mention this incident to anyone. We saw no need to advertise our foolishness. We were new kids on the block but were learning fast what not to do. These poles were range markers for shore batteries.

The first call to perform a rescue under hostile fire came three days later. The 14th of March, late in the afternoon we were alerted to a rescue situation that was developing near Hon Ngai Island. An Air Force F-4 had been hit by AAA (anti-aircraft artillery) and its crew ejected about a mile off the heavily fortified island. An Air Force 33rd Air Rescue Squadron HU-16 Albatross, call sign Crown Bravo, had landed near the two survivors and had come under attack by 130 mm AAA fire from the emplacements on the island, and by small[-]arms fire from numerous sampans in the area. Before Crown Bravo could bring the first survivor aboard, a 130 mm shell hit the plane. Of its six crewmen, two were killed instantly and two were severely wounded. The F-4 pilot was also wounded. With six men in the water, three of them injured, the urgent call went out for assistance. Two SH-3As of HS-4 arrived and a Navy A-1 arrived and began to suppress the AAA fire from the island. One H-3 picked up the three uninjured survivors and departed the area. The second H-3, braving a hail of fire, was able to pick up two of the injured survivors, but after two failed attempts to pick up the last survivor, was chased away by the 130 mm shells exploding all around the helo. I dashed toward the survivor while a crewman manned the M60 and engaged the sampans. With the raft trapped within the rotor wash, after long and agonizing moments in a dreadfully vulnerable hover, a crewman was able to place the horse collar right on top of the survivor. As soon as the crewman announced, "Man on the sling, weight coming on the helo," I broke hover and departed toward the open sea and away from that infernal island and the threatening sampans.

Six days later, almost immediately after transferring from USS *England* to USS *Worden* (DLG-18), McCracken and crew were alerted to a SAR mission for a Navy F-4 that was on fire and trying desperately to reach "feet wet" off the coast. An Air Force HU-16 Crown Bravo was inbound to the area. The pilot and RIO (radar intercept officer) had to eject from the uncontrollable Phantom, landing close to shore, where the RIO was quickly captured. The pilot came down 1,000 yards off the coast, fired a flare at the incoming Albatross, and came under fire from an approaching junk. Shore batteries firing at the Albatross scored hits that damaged the amphibian's hull, making it unseaworthy. McCracken dropped down to 20 feet above the waves and was able to squeeze out 145 knots from the UH-2B. As they closed the distance to the survivor, the Seasprite was bracketed by gunfire from sampans and from shore. A crewman manned his M60 while copilot Robert Clark added to their defensive fire with a .45-caliber Thompson submachine gun. A flight of A-4 "Scooters" made continuous runs on approaching junks as McCracken and crew hovered among impacting mortar rounds to snatch the F-4 pilot. McCracken continues:

> As Chief Davis grabbed the survivor and pulled him into the cabin, a mortar round hit the water just behind us. The force of the explosion lifted the tail of the helo way up. I found myself looking straight at the water right in front of my eyes as the aircraft entered an un-commanded transition to forward flight. Since that was what I was about to do anyway, I just went with the flow. Getting out of there as fast as I could was my intention, but not with such a violent maneuver. As we began to move forward[,] another round exploded right in front of us. We had no choice but to fly through the ominous geyser of falling water. Shrapnel from the first mortar round damaged the rescue hoist, fortunately after the survivor was already in Davis's arms. Shrapnel also sieved the tail section. Miraculously, no vital component was damaged.

In the Gulf of Tonkin in December 1967, a UH-2C of HC-1 departs USS *Oriskany*, while a UH-2A/B remains aboard. Both were embarked aboard USS *Ranger*. BuNo 151333 began life as a UH-2B, was rebuilt to an HH-2C following a crash in 1968, and then became the first SH-2D in the Pacific Fleet and was later converted to an SH-2F, finally ending its career in the Royal New Zealand Air Force. *Courtesy of National Naval Aviation Museum*

Until the end of May 1966, Detachment 5 maintained its regimen of missions, at times flying with an unarmored UH-2B, and flying from various ships, earning it the nickname "Froggy Five." Detachment personnel worked under tremendous pressure for sixteen to twenty hours a day, performing repairs and routine maintenance, often in the weather on open decks of ships with unfamiliar accommodations, personnel, and commanders. Even worse, to the crew, was that their mail seldom caught up with them. McCracken offered this view:

> We continued doing our job, as we saw it. During those days, relatively early in the war against North Vietnam, CSAR rules, tactics, and procedures were somewhat fluid. We made them up as we went along, getting away with things that later would be more tightly controlled. For example, early in May somehow we got hold of an M-79 grenade launcher and a box of 40 mm shells. My guys rigged the launcher with an aluminum tube attached to the stock to allow the crewmen to shoot grenades straight down from the helo door. We flew a few training hops to test the rig and make sure we could shoot at the junks without blowing ourselves out of the sky. Then we went after the junks that had been giving us so much trouble on every rescue. We would make passes above the junks and lob a few grenades into them. This went on for about two weeks. We were getting

> good at the game, improving our score and really slowing them down. Somehow, the word got to Commander, Seventh Fleet (COMSEVENTHFLT), about what we were doing. Shortly thereafter, the skipper of USS *Worden* received a message ordering the immediate termination of unauthorized activities. Our anti-junk campaign came to a screeching halt.

Froggy Five ended its tour having logged forty-eight SAR sorties, five rescues under enemy fire, and four rescues of sailors gone adrift in a carrier's disabled small boat. On June 5, the detachment was transferred from USS *Worden* to USS *Enterprise*, which sailed to Cubi Point. There the UH-2B and supporting equipment awaited its next SAR detachment.

When Dixie Station was terminated, two combat SAR stations, labeled "North SAR" and "South SAR," were then officially established. Each had a guided-missile frigate (DLG) with TACAN and a combat SAR UH-2, and a "shotgun" destroyer (DD). The UH-2s then changed their name from "Angel" to "Clementine 1" for North SAR, and to "Clementine 2" for South SAR. As various ships reported on station for combat cruises, Clementine detachments periodically cross-decked. In May 1966, armed and armored Sea Kings, designated SH-3As, known as "Big Mothers," arrived in the Gulf of Tonkin. As lessons in combat rescue were being learned, a flight of A-1 Skyraiders, A-4s, or A-7s escorted each Seasprite and Sea King on rescue missions. To extend the endurance of helicopters operating independently of carriers, a technique called helicopter in-flight refueling (HIFR), termed "High Drink," was developed, which had a helicopter using its hoist to retrieve a refueling hose from destroyers that retained 7,000-gallon fuel tanks from DASH operations. The fueling procedure for the H-2 was the brainchild of pilot LaRon Stoker; he explains:

> During the online period in 1966 while aboard USS *King* (DLG-10) on North SAR, we had a situation that we had thought about and acted upon. The combat control staff would send up one of their SH-3 helicopters every day as backup rescue. Sometimes they would be there six to eight hours, approximately 100 miles from the carrier task force. During this time, they would come alongside our ship every two hours, and we would pass them a fuel hose so they could in-flight refuel. I thought, what if something happened on one of those flights and they had to make an emergency landing? My helo pad was all that was available, but where would I go? If I departed immediately, I could fly to the carrier, but if I was out flying, I would not have enough fuel to get there. I did not have the in-flight refueling that the H-3 had. I had my maintenance crew check where the fuel went into the helo, and I came up with the idea that if I had a special spanner wrench, my crewmen could open the fuel tank inside the aircraft. I could then hover alongside the ship, lower my hoist, pick up the fuel hose, bring it up, and pump fuel into my tank. I tried it and it worked great, so I sent a message to the fleet commander explaining that I had figured out a way to in-flight refuel my helo. It was the wrong thing to have done. They came back and blasted at me that it was a safety violation. However, a few days later the SH-3 developed a major hydraulic leak and had to land immediately before their transmission failed. We launched and they landed and discovered that they needed a hydraulic line from their ship, which was located 200 miles from us. I headed for the nearest carrier, 100 miles away, where I landed and refueled, then went on to the SH-3's carrier, where I picked up the hydraulic line and again refueled. On the return flight I again stopped at the carrier, refueled, and flew back to my ship. I hovered alongside and dropped the line, and they passed up the fuel hose so I could take on more fuel. It took two hours to fix the SH-3, so if I had not been able to in-flight refuel, I would have run dry. In the next message from the fleet commander, he gave me a "Well done" for my ingenuity. What happed to safety? Hell, I prevented the loss of a helicopter!

Since most rescues made by Seasprite crews had a rescue swimmer enter the water to assist survivors, lessons were also being learned stateside at SAR/Swimmer schools at various naval facilities. Swimmers, usually called "second crewmen," displayed courage and efficiency in braving heavy seas, entangled parachute lines, enemy fire, and other hazards. These specialists acquired skills and confidence through training furnished by the Navy's Paramedic Rescue Team 1 at NAS Cubi Point, Republic of the Philippines. This training was conceived in 1962 by two doctors stationed at Cubi, and the team staff comprised volunteer doctors and medical corpsmen who taught search-and-rescue aircrew parachuting, jungle survival, medical techniques, and management of difficult rescue conditions. Beginning in March 1967, HC-1's Det. Cubi, and later HC-7's Det. Cubi, underwent the intense six-day training course. The specialized training at Cubi and at other schools paid dividends for UH-2 rescue swimmers stationed aboard ships off North Vietnam.

Along with the 1967 division of HC-1 to more effectively meet global commitments, all Seasprite-equipped squadrons were kept busy on many fronts, with some flying combat rescue with the expansion of the Vietnam war, while supplying carriers with plane guard detachments. Others assumed the VertRep mission, while some embarked on icebreakers at the poles. All squadrons were well traveled, such as NAS Lakehurst–based HC-4. Nicknamed the "Invaders," HC-4 UH-2 crews lived up to the Navy's recruiting slogan: "Join the Navy and see the world." Seasprite crewmen of the squadron served at many places across the globe—from the Mediterranean to the South Pole, and from the eastern Atlantic to the North Pole.

'GATOR AVIATION

In Vietnam, the Invaders crews and their Seasprites filled the vital SAR role, operating with various ships of the amphibious ready groups (ARGs), commonly called the 'Gator Navy. The helicopter added so much flexibility to amphibious operations that amphibious vessels, once classed as nonaviation ships, were redesignated aviation facility ships. Major ARG ship types were landing ship, tank (LST); amphibious transport dock (LPD); and landing platform, helicopter (LPH). While older LSTs offered little more than a landing spot, LPDs featured a hangar, often dual landing spots, an air department complete with maintenance support and servicing capabilities, and a flight deck certified for day-night operations. Detachment 36 of HC-4 provided VIP Seasprites for four amphibious group command ships of Task Force 76 (TF 76), Seventh Fleet Amphibious Force, which rotated through the western Pacific. Among the four ships, USS *Mount McKinley* (AGC-7) served as flagship, with the commander of Amphibious Forces Pacific aboard, and typically anchored at Da Nang Harbor. At sea, Det. 36 consisted of three pilots and ten enlisted men; their VIP Seasprites were called "Gray Ghosts." Det. 36 also provided mail and passenger runs to helicopter pads in and around the major ports along South Vietnam's coast. Eventually, aviation facility ships had mainly HH-2Ds embarked for long periods, and later antisubmarine Seasprites as key elements of 'Gator Aviation.

In similar fashion, HC-4's Support Detachment 31 supported the Sixth Fleet commander in the Mediterranean Sea, homeported at Gaeta, Italy. A priority of the detachment was staying abreast of the admiral's busy schedule as the fleet commander. Then lieutenant Gordon I. Peterson recalls:

> My commanding officer informed me that I had been selected to report in late February 1972 to the US Sixth Fleet's flagship, the light guided-missile cruiser USS *Springfield* (CLG-7), to serve as the officer in charge (OIC) of the squadron's detachment. The detachment's missions also included personnel, cargo, and mail transfer; surveillance and photographic reconnaissance; search and rescue; and medical evacuation. The detachment's HH-2D helicopter was assigned on a twelve-to-eighteen-month rotation from NAS Lakehurst. USS *Springfield* alternated her flagship role every three to four years with her sister ship USS *Little Rock* (CLG-4). Both were nonaviation ships—they had no hangar. As I had learned on USS *Newport News*, the aircraft would be fully exposed on the flight deck to the very corrosive effects of the ship's stack gas and ocean salt spray. Special attention was devoted to keeping the helicopter clean—every day—to prevent corrosion.

Scott Milner explains the differences in the helicopter capacity of various ships:

> A single-spot ship refers to any ship that has only one spot to launch and recover a helicopter. During Vietnam, the LSTs were used by HA(L)-3 in the Mekong delta area. Although they frequently put multiple helicopters on the decks, only one was turning. Cruisers, destroyers, DLGs, and frigates are other examples of ships that could launch and recover only one helicopter at a time, even if the ship's hangar could hold two helicopters. LPDs have two spots and can simultaneously launch/recover two helicopters. Hospital ships have two spots. Coast Guard ships, including icebreakers, typically have single spots. Of course, the LPH, LHA, and CVN ships have multiple spots for multiple simultaneous launch/recovery operations.

Pilots seldom found taking off and landing a Seasprite aboard a small boy easy. Some, in fact, stated that they found it as difficult as making an approach for a rescue pickup. Teamwork, skill, reflexes, and heightened senses all came into play to accomplish takeoffs and landings from within a 24-foot-diameter circle on a small, ever-moving deck. Aboard "the boat," prior to takeoff, with flight operations imminent, the signal flag for "F," or "Foxtrot," was hoisted in a time-honored procedure called

"Foxtrot at the dip." When flight operations got under way, the flag was "two-blocked," or hoisted fully up the lanyard. Then, clearly heard over the loudspeaker system was "Now on the flight deck, stand clear of all jet intakes, propellers, and rotor blades—flight quarters, flight quarters!" Officers of the deck ensured that the boat was turned so that wind was in an optimum direction across the flight deck. Flight deck safety nets that surrounded the flight deck were lowered. Chocks and chains—two of each for each main landing gear—were undone, and tie-downs were removed from main rotor blades.

VISUAL LANDING AIDS

Seasprite pilots agree that night landings aboard small boys were challenging, especially before deck-lighting systems were developed. Often, during the Vietnam War, pilots returning to land aboard after making an inland rescue found that the ship had no lighting systems. As the helicopter was inbound, flight quarters was called and manned, which included a yellow-shirted landing signalman, enlisted (LSE). The helicopter was radioed a "Green Deck" for landing, and officers of the deck ensured that the ship was turned for optimum wind across the deck. Flight deck safety nets were lowered, and sailors kept clear of the deck. Scott Milner continues:

> The aircraft windscreen was usually clouded with salt spray. We approached the ship from 20 to 30 degrees starboard of the ship's landing course. Our approach usually began at 1 to 1½ miles aft of the ship, using TACAN and, later, the LN-66 radar for range. We were at 70 knots and wheels down. Some pilots used their landing lights. I did. As we closed to the ship and the red light on its mast became a ship, we slowed to about 40 knots and stayed above transitional lift speed. The ship usually provided us with 20 knots of wind across the deck from about 330 degrees. When in close, the salt spray from the rotor wash was around us. Visibility was not great, and we crept over the deck edge at about 30 feet on the radar altimeter. We lined up on the landing line, which was 30 degrees starboard to port. Our crewman then told us when our tailwheel was clear of the deck edge. We hovered, timing the ship's movement cycle of pitch (front to rear) and roll (sideways)—we landed after watching a cycle or two and seeing that there would be a stable time to land. Four deck crewmen came out; two chock men and two chain men, who expertly attached chains and chocks to the main mounts, while the rotor brake was applied. We could then relax and shut down.
>
> More than several times after we landed, the officers of the deck on the bridge would immediately turn the ship toward its assigned course. After tense moments and harsh words with the bridge team, they learned that the ship had to hold its turns until after we had shut down.

DASH-equipped FRAM II (modified) destroyers had flight decks on the 01 level, which was the first level above the main deck. When cruisers and DLGs took helicopters aboard in the early 1960s, most decks were on the main level, having very little freeboard and rarely a hangar. When the DLG-26 Belknap-class guided-missile cruisers went into service during the mid-1960s, most decks were on the 01 level, which afforded space for lighting systems. This consisted of a vertical string of clear lights (called drop-line lights) that were extensions of the center lineup line on the flight deck. If the pilot was on the lineup line, he would see one line of lights, and split lines if he was too far to either side.

Innovative H-2 pilot LaRon Stoker, aided by pilot Scott Milner, contributed greatly to the development of deck lighting systems. When Stoker returned from his SAR detachment in 1967, he persuaded the Navy to allow him to test deck-edge lights. Aboard an early San Diego–based DLG, Stoker and crew rigged white lights around the ship's main-deck landing pad. To dim the overly bright lights, brown paper bags were fastened over the lights. Stoker persisted, and months later a light system with rheostat was implemented. When Knox-class ships joined the fleet in 1969, they were furnished with deck lighting, centerline lights, and drop-line lights. Stoker and Milner also illuminated the hangar face with floodlights on tripods. Lighting was later added to Garcia-class and Belknap-class ships. Milner adds:

> Small ships, especially older vessels with no stabilization fins, were very unstable, being subject to 20-to-40-degree pitch and roll. The ship's movement could be so severe as to make the deck lineup lights disappear for helicopters approaching at night. Someone at NADC came up with an idea to install a 6-foot-long, bright-red or [bright-] green light bar atop the hangar and stabilize it gyroscopically so that it was always aligned with the horizon. The bar was a valuable aid during the approach if visibility was sufficient to see it

from a half mile or more. It was also a wonderful aid when over the deck in a hover while waiting for the ship to go through a cycle of rolls and finally stabilize to allow a safe landing.

In the continuing effort to increase the number of nonaviation ships from which helicopters could operate, the CNO in early 1971 ordered an evaluation of visual landing aids and deck lighting for helicopter operations. A simulated Knox-class flight deck with hangar was built on the taxiway at NATF Lakehurst. It supported all visual landing aids and featured movable lights to test various lighting patterns. After helicopter test pilots flying HH-2D Seasprites, H-46 Sea Knights, and AH-1J Sea Cobras evaluated numerous systems, the most-effective combinations of deck lights and glide slope indicators were selected for installation aboard ships.

THE "SEADEVILS" AND THE HH-2C

Combat search and rescue sometimes was a collaborative effort involving other services, particularly land-based Air Force Air Rescue units. The lessons learned in Navy CSAR by multimission HC and HS squadrons culminated with Helicopter Combat Squadron 7 (HC-7), named "Seadevils." Formed at NAS Atsugi, Japan, from the 1967 division of HC-1, HC-7 would grow substantially during its first eighteen months of operations. The squadron initially was an outgrowth of HC-1's CSAR/VertRep/VIP detachment. HC-1, which had operated eight detachments in the Gulf of Tonkin from December 1965 to August 1967, continued to supply detachments for plane guard and other duties, including combat SAR, aboard carriers. On October 1, 1967, HC-7 acquired HC-1's Clementine detachments, which became HC-7 Detachments 104 through 109. At the changeover, HC-1 had forty-nine UH-2A/B and two UH-2C Seasprites. Also on that date, HC-7 inherited the SAR responsibility at home base Atsugi, Japan. During the two-year period after its inception, HC-7 absorbed eight additional HC-1 detachments, including the maintenance, training, and station SAR detachment at Cubi Point, Philippines. As a result, the Seadevils flew not only CSAR missions, but VertRep, VIP (nicknamed "Blackbeard"), and mine-countermeasure missions with three helicopter types: the H-2 Seasprite, H-3 Sea King, and UH-46 Sea Knight. The squadron's seventeen detachments extended operations beyond Vietnam into the Philippines, Japan, and California.

Cmdr. Lloyd Parthemer became the first commanding officer of HC-7, the Navy's only squadron dedicated to combat search and rescue. Relying on training and the experiences of Clementine crews, the squadron began developing its own CSAR doctrine. Above all, Parthemer admonished his crews, "You will wait for ResCAP," that being "Rescue Combat Air Patrol," the armed escort aircraft available from all services. Parthemer admitted that his dedicated rescue crews, "if they had their way, they'd have gone in yesterday." Another rule dictated that if conditions allowed, a swimmer would enter the water. "Crossing the beach," or heading inland to attempt rescue, was a decision made in the cockpit. Did the pilot stay high and risk the deadly dance with missiles, or go in low and duel with ground fire? Neither was a viable option, but the crews pressed on. Flight personnel slated for combat duty with HC-7 rotated through Cubi Point, where they became familiarized with their respective specialty as pilot or crewman; pilots were required to qualify in small-deck landing. At its outset, the squadron suffered the loss of two Seasprites to operational causes, one of which crashed into Subic Bay, Philippines, during swimmer training. Successes too came quickly. On October 21, 1967, HC-7's Cubi Point SAR UH-2 accomplished the detachment's first rescue when an A-3 Skywarrior crashed into the water on takeoff.

Assignment rotations involved three detachments on the line in the Gulf of Tonkin: South SAR Station, North SAR Station, and PIRAZ (Positive Identification Radar Advisory Zone), whose call sign was "Red Crown." The zone was defined by the air search radar coverage of a ship patrolling a designated PIRAZ station. Such ships were armed with long-range surface-to-air missiles to defend their stations. A PIRAZ station was established in the westernmost portion of the Gulf of Tonkin, where air search radar coverage might extend over North Vietnam and US airstrike routes. This was the most important assignment given to the ships of the cruiser/destroyer force, since it was responsible for control of Navy, and frequently Air Force, airstrikes in North Vietnam. Since one of the ship's functions was CSAR assistance, an HC-7 Seasprite detachment was assigned to PIRAZ, usually a cruiser, a destroyer leader (DLG), or a guided-missile destroyer (DDG).

HC-7's UH-2 Clementine detachments had little time to prepare for combat rescue. Just three days after HC-7 acquired HC-1's Clementine detachments, Detachment 108's UH-2B BuNo 150153, aboard the frigate *Coontz*, left its pre-positioned orbit after its crew volunteered to head inland to locate and rescue Air Force major Robert W.

Members of Helicopter Combat Support Squadron 7 (HC-7) pose with some of their aircraft (Boeing Vertol H-46 Sea Knight, Sikorsky H-3 Sea King, and Kaman H-2 Seasprite) at NAS Atsugi, Japan. The "Seadevils" rotated out of either Atsugi or NAS Cubi Point, Philippines. *Courtesy of US Navy*

At the zenith of its operations, when HC-7 had fourteen detachments performing six distinct missions, three were deemed primary—combat search and rescue, vertical replenishment, and mine countermeasures. To highlight the threefold responsibility, the squadron chose the name "Seadevils," and the mythological three-headed dog "Cerebrus," the guardian of the gates of Hades. *Courtesy of HC-7*

Barnett after a SAM (surface-to-air missile) downed his F-105. Lt. (j.g.) Timothy S. Melecoski and crew, call sign "Clementine 1," were told to hold position while ResCAP attempted to locate Barnett. Clementine 1 then received a call from "Steel Hawser," a destroyer in the gulf coordinating SAR operations, to divert to Haiphong Harbor, where Lt. (j.g.) Allan D. Perkins had ejected from his flak-damaged A-4B. Barnett was evading the enemy, so Perkins, having landed amid anchored ships in the harbor, became the higher priority.

Weaving just a few feet above the water between merchant ships in Haiphong Harbor, Melecoski spotted Perkins squatting down in the shallows just 60 yards from a ship. Unbeknown to Clementine 1's swimmer, ATN3 John H. Bevan, the very tall Perkins was squatting to make a smaller target. When Bevan jumped from the Seasprite he became stuck in the mud. Helping each other through the quagmire, the swimmer signaled and then hooked himself to Perkins, and both were hoisted aboard the helo as it was taking fire. The Seadevils' celebration of their first rescue was tempered, since Barnett was still out there. With night closing in, Steel Hawser told him to "hole up" and await rescue in the morning. At daybreak, Clementine 1 launched, again with Melecoski and copilot Lt. (j.g.) James P. Brennan at the controls. With a pair of Skyraiders covering, Melecoski radioed Barnett to activate flares and signal smoke. During four approaches, the chopper took heavy fire until Clementine radioed, "Mayday, mayday, mayday." As fuel streamed from punctured fuel tanks, the crew threw out everything possible to lighten the aircraft, which made it to water, where it was ditched. A Sea King of HS-2 rescued the crew, and Barnett was left to spend another night in the jungle. While a second rescue attempt was underway, Barnett was captured, and for two days the enemy used him to summon

Seen at Da Nang Air Base in mid-1967, UH-2B BuNo 150153, when later assigned to HC-7, Det. 108, accomplished the squadron's first CSAR mission but was shot down and ditched on October 4, 1967. *Courtesy of Jerry Arruda via Don Jay*

In December 1967, a ferocious-faced UH-2A/B nears USS *Wiltsie* (DD-716) on North SAR as a crewman readies equipment to be lowered on the hoist to the destroyer. *Courtesy of Jack Long via Rick Burgess*

overhead rescue aircraft. Barnett, however, using deceptive techniques, was able to warn the now-cautious rescue pilots of flak traps. The men of HC-7 were learning the hard lessons of wins and losses.

The year 1967 proved costly for the forces in the Gulf of Tonkin; 133 Navy aircraft had been lost, with forty-five airmen recovered from North Vietnam or the gulf, including six saved by HC-7. It wasn't until 1968 that a Navy contract called for conversion of twelve twin-engine UH-2Cs to HH-2Cs for combat rescue. Meanwhile, Seasprite crews, like their Air Force counterparts, wrote the book on combat search and rescue. Seldom was there the opportunity for Seasprite crews to train with protective escort aircraft. Nor was there a formal training program for crews to learn tactics. Night rescues were to be illuminated by flares dropped from escort aircraft; yet, most night rescues normally were accomplished by the use of the Seasprite's searchlights and landing lights, which made ideal targets for enemy guns (in September 1968, after an HC-7 crew was fired upon during a nighttime attempt to rescue the crew of an A-6 Intruder, Seasprite crewmen fashioned a cone from a soup can to fit around the aircraft's rotating beacon, making it visible only to aircraft above). The crews themselves simply did their best under the circumstances. The purest example of their mettle occurred on the night of June 19, 1968.

THINGS THAT GO BUMP [AND BANG] IN THE NIGHT

Shortly after midnight, an F-4J Phantom on a night interdiction mission 20 miles north of Vinh, North Vietnam, was destroyed by an SA-2 missile. Lt. Cmdr. John W.

A UH-2A/B practices open-sea rescue, using the rescue hoist and a rescue swimmer in Subic Bay, Philippines, in 1969. *Courtesy of US Navy*

Holtzclaw and his RIO (radar intercept officer), Lt. Cmdr. John A. Burns, ejected in a densely_inhabited area; Burns received severe leg injuries in the bailout. "For the first hour," recounted Holtzclaw, "we heard no airplanes overhead. We made our way up the hill to an extremely_dense section of jungle, where we first heard the sound of airplanes. We used our walkie-talkies and were told 'Clementine 2' was on the way to get us." The pair tried unsuccessfully to find a clear area for the pickup.

"Clementine 2" was the call sign for Lt. (j.g.) Clyde E. Lassen, flying UH-2A BuNo 149764 of HC-7's Det. 104 aboard USS *Preble* (DLG-15) on South SAR Station. Heading through the black, moonless night, Lassen's crew comprised copilot Lt. (j.g.) Clarence L. Cook and crewmen

Lt. Clyde E. Lassen became the first naval aviator to be awarded the Medal of Honor for bravery in Southeast Asia. *Courtesy of US Navy*

The HC-7 Seasprite crew that rescued the crew of F-4J BuNo 155546 of VF-33 on the night of June 19, 1968. *Left to right,* Lt. (j.g.) Clyde Lassen, AE2 Bruce Dallas, ADJ3 Donald West, and Lt. (j.g.) Leroy Cook. Symbols representing night rescues are painted on the Seasprite, and in the cabin doorway is a hinged armor panel. *Courtesy of US Navy*

AE2 Bruce B. Dallas and ADJ3 Donald West. Two SAMs streaked past the Seasprite before the pilots spotted the flaming wreckage. Lassen landed about 600 feet from the survivors, but gunfire drove him off. Task Force A-7s arrived and began dropping flares. Despite tall trees in the area, Lassen decided to attempt a pickup under flare light. When he brought the chopper to a 50-foot hover between the trees, Dallas began lowering the rescue sling. Suddenly the flares burned out, leaving Lassen in blackness with no visual ground reference. Lassen vividly recalled:

> Dallas yelled that we were going to hit a tree. I added power and was starting to climb when I hit it. The jolt was terrific. The helo pitched nose down and went into a tight starboard turn. I regained control and waved off. I then told the rescue aircraft orbiting overhead that we had struck a tree and that I was experiencing heavy vibration. We requested more flares and were told that no more were available, but some were on the way. Also, I told the survivors that they would have to get down off that hill and into the clearing.

Dallas added:

> I started retracting the hoist as fast as possible, and in the process the helo hit a tree on the right side. I was leaning out of the open door at the time, and I was hit on the face as the tree went by. As soon as the limb hit me, I yelled, "Get up! Get up!"—and we were out of there and climbing. Nothing but Mr. Lassen's skill and experience saved us from crashing.

The tree strike caused a heavy vibration and damaged the horizontal stabilizer, tail rotor, antenna, and cabin door. With the Seasprite low on fuel, badly damaged, and taking heavy fire, no one would have faulted Lassen and crew for leaving the area, but they knew they were the survivors' last chance of avoiding capture or death. Shaken but undeterred by the collision, Lassen made several passes over the airmen so that Dallas and West could fire at enemy troops nearing the survivors. Holtzclaw and Burns made it down to a rice paddy, where Lassen again landed. Too far from the survivors and taking increasing fire, Lassen went around and landed closer to the pair. A missile streaked underneath the Seasprite, and enemy troops aggressively maneuvered to reach their

Clyde Lassen, *far left*, proudly poses with dedicated and determined aircrew of HC-7, Det. 104, in 1968. Tom Hitchcock, standing next to Lassen, holds an M60A machine gun, the standard armament for Seasprite crews. *Courtesy of US Navy*

Lassen and crew's UH-2A, BuNo 149764, "Clementine 2," aboard USS *Worden* (DLG-18) on South SAR in 1967. Lassen credited the camouflage for averting some enemy fire. *Courtesy of Jack Long via Rick Burgess*

Lassen and crew's UH-2A in better days, when assigned to HU-1, embarked aboard USS *Ranger* in October 1964. High-visibility orange flight suits and aircraft markings eventually gave way to low-visibility colors on WESTPAC cruises as war intensified. *Author's collection*

prize. For three minutes, the Seasprite hovered under renewed flare light while Holtzclaw and Burns struggled through mud and over paddy dikes to reach their ride out. When the flares burned out, Lassen turned on the spotlight, which immediately drew heavy fire. With Dallas, West, and copilot Cook exchanging fire coming from three sides, Lassen immediately lifted off when the exhausted Holtzclaw and Burns clambered aboard.

Near the coast, the Seasprite encountered heavy flak and gunfire, and during evasive maneuvers the damaged door was torn off. Short of fuel and with the helo badly damaged, Lassen headed for the nearest ship and landed aboard USS *Jouett* (DLG-29) with only five minutes of fuel remaining; *Jouett*'s captain already had reversed direction and sailed at flank speed to close the distance to the battered Seasprite.

One year later, Lt. Lassen was awarded the Medal of Honor. Cmdr. Kenneth J. Davis, pilot of the A-6 Intruder on the night interdiction mission, after witnessing Lassen's rescue, stated, "Lassen was equipped like the proverbial brass monkey, and his crew wasn't far behind. He deserved the medal. His copilot received the Navy Cross, and he deserved that as well. On my list the aircrewmen were up for all they could drink." Dallas and West received Silver Stars. Lassen became the first naval aviator to be awarded the Medal of Honor in Southeast Asia.

Of interest is Lassen's comment regarding the paint schemes of wartime Seasprites. Despite the Navy's attempt to standardize the helicopter paint scheme with Gunship Gray or Engine Gray, aircrew camouflaged their aircraft to give them an edge when flying inland. Lassen seemed certain that camouflage had spared him and his crew from withering gunfire on the mission. He stated, "It seemed that the dark paint scheme and Vietnamese gunners trained to lead fast-moving targets had spared the Seasprite from most of the ground fire." Maybe so, but it was Lassen's courage and skill that saved the lives of Holtzclaw and Burns and earned him the Medal of Honor.

Lassen's legacy is held by the guided-missile destroyer USS *Lassen* (DDG-82), named in his honor, plus training buildings at South Whiting Field, Florida, and NATTC Millington, Tennessee, and the Clyde E. Lassen State Veteran's Nursing Home, St. Augustine, Florida. Lassen and his crew's Seasprite was denied its future as an honored museum display when, six months after the daring mission, it was ditched off North Vietnam due to fuel starvation.

THE PURE CSAR SEASPRITE

The 1968 Navy order for one dozen HH-2C combat search-and-rescue-configured Seasprites (often referred to as the "Gunship Seasprite") was downgraded to six aircraft, reportedly due to the expected replacement of UH-2s by H-3 Sea Kings and the winding down of the bombing campaign. Navy officials were encouraged by extensive Army tests with Kaman's Tomahawk gunship several years earlier. The Navy brass was confident that the combination of consistent point-target weapon accuracy—which showed no effect on stability and control of the aircraft—and the Twin Charlie's dual power plants was the answer to survivability and a high probability of successful combat rescues.

Beginning with newly configured UH-2Cs, an uprated transmission was installed, along with a Gold Stripe T58-GE-8F engine to handle the added weight of weapon systems and armor. The gunship's level speed was 150 mph with a hot-day flat rating capability. A four-blade tail rotor allowed safe use of the additional power from the second engine, and dual-wheeled main landing gear became necessary for operations at 12,800 pounds gross weight. Extensive armor was added to protect the pilots, crew, and vital areas such as engine and controls and gearboxes. A 200-foot hoist cable, which was a provision of a previous Navy contract, made possible rescues in Vietnam's jungle and karst terrain. Other features included self-sealing oil lines and fuel tanks, explosion-suppressant foam around fuel cells, an enlarged starboard doorway, acrylic shatter-proof windows, and dual UHF electronics for homing in on survivors. Crew-served M60 machine guns in enlarged cabin windows were added, with a spare kept in the aircraft. Gunship identity took the form of a chin-mounted TAT-102K turret with 7.62 mm GAU-2B/A "minigun." Driven by a hydraulically operated motor and electrically controlled, the six-barrel gun fired at a low rate of 1,300 rounds per minute (rpm) and a high rate of 4,000 rpm. The gun could be fired from the copilot's sighting station, or by the pilot in stowed, forward-firing position. Typical armament carried was 4,000 rounds for the turret and 1,600 rounds for the M60s, plus ammunition for M-16 rifles and other personal weapons.

A number of systems were removed to accommodate the HH-2C package and keep the aircraft within weight limits; they included cabin heater, rotor-deicing system, cabin seats, flotation gear, loud hailer, and fish pole unit. Approach and hover electronics were removed, leaving the pilots with manual approach procedures for nighttime rescues. Installation of the turret required that the UHF-DF antenna, normally on the forward under-nose section, be incorporated into the lower aft portion of the turret. The crew complement for the HH-2C comprised pilot, copilot, and two crewmen, one of whom was the swimmer; all were volunteers.

The first HH-2C was scheduled for delivery to the Navy in February 1969, and testing with the first model (BuNo 149773) began in the fall of that year at NATC, Patuxent River. On April 21, 1970, HC-7's Det. NAS Cubi Point received its first two HH-2Cs, BuNos 149773 and 150164, via Air Force C-133 from HC-5 at Imperial Beach. At Cubi the HH-2Cs were assembled and crew training was conducted, followed by final testing. On June 11, BuNo 149773, along with two officers and eight enlisted crewmen, went aboard the guided-missile cruiser USS *Bainbridge* (DLGN-25) with Det. 107 in the Gulf of Tonkin. Ten days later, HC-7's last UH-2A/B was relieved of its CSAR duties and was replaced by another

This view shows to good effect the offset position of the minigun turret, and the position of the retractable landing light and two searchlights. The starboard light was aimed somewhat sideward to illuminate rescue hoist operations. *Courtesy of US Navy*

The armed and armored HH-2C in its original configuration with a chin-mounted minigun turret. The "blister" on the forward engine / transmission cowling made room for the HH-2C's 200-foot rescue hoist cable. The pitot tube was relocated from the cockpit roof to under the copilot's station. *Courtesy of US Navy*

HH-2C. Equipped with their new armed and armored Seasprites, the Seadevils continued its nomadic existence of sixty-day rotation throughout the gulf. The first rescue by HH-2C occurred on August 12, 1970, when Cmdr. M. Wright left his F-8H Crusader when it developed fuel problems over the Gulf. The HH-2C was airborne before Wright hit the water.

Although the HH-2C was both more powerful and more survivable than the single-engine Seasprite, operations revealed deficiencies. The second engine of the heavy helicopter doubled fuel consumption, which reduced range and endurance. The most prominent feature of the HH-2C, the minigun turret, proved troublesome from the outset. When the turret-equipped HH-2Cs arrived, the guns had yet to be delivered. Further complications arose when the system was found unreliable since it couldn't be properly safed; periodically, unexpected firing from the jolt of deck landings spelled a quick end to the turrets. Before they saw combat use, the turret's guns were removed and their ports taped over; however, that did not deter some units from using broomsticks to simulate gun barrels to retain the gunship mystique. Since fuel and CSAR equipment were priorities, the entire TAT-102 system was removed as a weight-saving measure. Crewmen welcomed removal of the ammunition storage trays, which occupied a large portion of an already small cabin. A 1970 field service report stated, "Pilots are willing to give up anything but fuel." Phil Poisson, a seasoned Seasprite pilot, reflected on the HH-2C:

> After having flown about 1,500 hours in the UH-2A/B and having been in four major accidents, it was a pleasure to climb into the HH-2C. The A/B was quite underpowered. When they added the Gold Stripe engines to the A/B for SAR missions, that was good, but it was still underpowered. We got the first HH-2C without the gun turret, as that function was quite dangerous.
>
> After a few flights in the HH-2C, one could figure this baby had a massive amount of power and could haul ass. Though it was rated at 140 knots, it flew 158 knots in a dive and still was very smooth. The first time I hovered an HH-2C at 2,500 feet in the Philippines, I knew we had a beast that could do it all. We had flown them for two years before they were all taken back to be switched into SH-2Ds. Damn, what a waste.

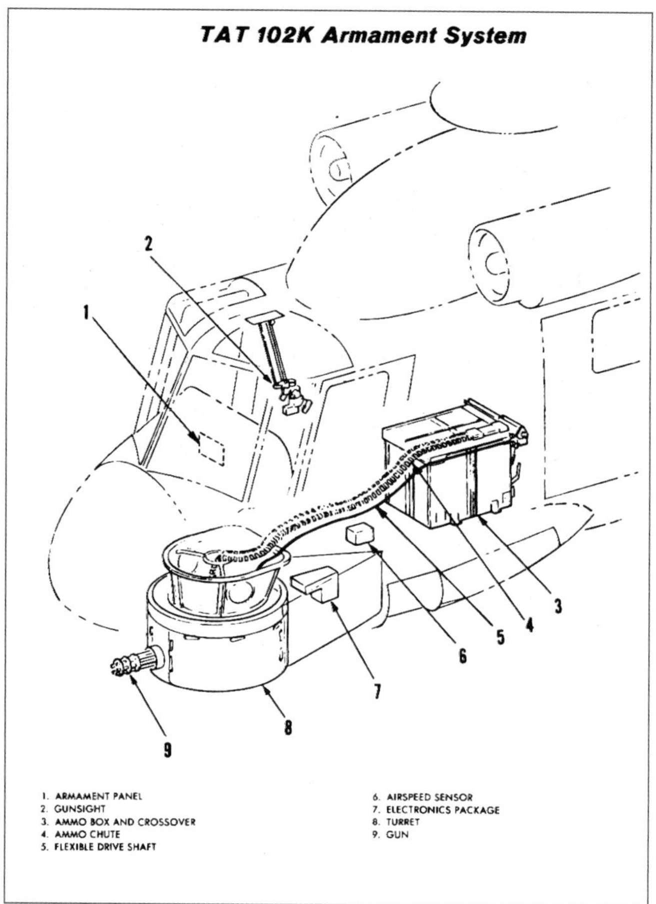

The arrangement of the complete TAT-102K armament system. *Courtesy of US Navy*

Aviation Electrician Second Class (AE-2) Eric Oxendorf of HC-7 poses with the HH-2C BuNo 150179 at Det. Cubi, Philippines. The minigun had been removed from the turret and the openings taped over. Eventually, the entire system was removed from the aircraft. *Courtesy of Eric Oxendorf Collection*

The Seasprite was quite nimble compared to the battle-worn, underpowered (and overloaded) UH-1B/C Hueys I flew on 515 mission with HA(L)-3 in Vietnam. With its hydraulic boost flight control and automatic in-flight rotor-tracking systems, the HH-2D was a responsive helicopter. It handled smoothly and was sensitive to flight-control and power inputs. The helicopter's comparatively small size and footprint made it nimble to fly and allowed landings in more-confined areas, especially for shipboard operations. Two auxiliary fuel tanks extended our range considerably. I transitioned smoothly from flying single-engine Hueys to the more complex HH-2D.

HC-4's motto was "Service to the Fleet." The squadron's threefold mission included ASW, replacement air group training, and deploying both HH-2D and SH-2D detachments to nonaviation ships operating in the Atlantic Ocean and Mediterranean Sea. In September 1971, I deployed as Det. 44's second pilot aboard USS *Newport News* for a two-month North Atlantic NATO / Northern European deployment. Our detachment's enlisted complement consisted of nine men. Our crew leader was a chief petty officer who was well qualified and experienced in maintaining the HH-2D. The enlisted mens' ratings included aviation electronics, electrical systems, jet engines, and hydraulic systems. We operated as a one-aircraft squadron.

HC-4 regularly provided single-helicopter detachments to support commanders of the Second and Sixth Fleets. The deployment was also a "show-the-flag" cruise in western Europe at a time when anti-US sentiment was running high in many countries owing to the Vietnam War. This NATO cruise was important, as our flag officer explained: "The Soviets are increasing their warship population in the Atlantic by tremendous amounts and are putting in all kinds of new ships, submarines, light cruisers, and destroyers. The admiral advocated increasing the number of ships from NATO-member nations to the Standing Naval Force Atlantic, as well as increasing the number of ships in their own navies to protect their shipping routes. This was the first time I had experienced coming nose to nose with the Soviet navy at sea. As I would learn during my two-year assignment on the US Sixth Fleet flagship in the Mediterranean Sea, it would not be my last."

Beginning in 1972, HH-2Ds of HC-4 (which the following year became HSL-30) were assigned to hydrographic survey ships. Later, Seasprites of HSL-30 joined the Marine Coast and Geodetic detachments. On the ground, shrouds that protected equipment in the nose from water often were seen unfastened and hanging from the aircraft. The HH-2D BuNo 151327 notes its ship assignment on auxiliary fuel tanks. *Courtesy of US Navy*

After service as the station aircraft at NAS Jacksonville, BuNo 151310 got its feet wet while assigned aboard survey ship USS *Chauvenet* with HSL-30, Det. Alpha. *Courtesy of US Navy*

Like the ship to which it was assigned, the HH-2D BuNo 151300 in 1981 wore white livery with the "Double Nuts" (double zeroes) on the flotation gear fairing, signifying the squadron commander's aircraft. Lettering above the small national insignia reads: "USNS HARKNESS—CAPT. HARRIMAN MASTER." A Navy Meritorious Unit Commendation ribbon was applied to the rescue door. *Courtesy of David Balcer via Rick Morgan Collection*

The HH-2D BuNo 149750, pictured here at Bahrain, Persian Gulf, in 1974, was assigned to HSL-30 Support Detachment Middle East aboard command ship USS *La Salle* (AGF-3). Painted white with a Gull Gray bottom, no. 750 reflected *La Salle*'s diplomatic role, having sailed in 1972 to its home port at Mina Sulman, Bahrain. The ship, which is noted on the Seasprite's tail boom, was nicknamed "the Great White Whale" and later became known as "the Great White Ghost of the Arabian Coast." *Courtesy of US Navy*

Nose art depicting Snoopy riding a camel identified BuNo 149750's Middle East support role aboard USS *La Salle* in Bahrain. *Courtesy of US Navy*

BuNo 149031 was rare in that, as an HH-2D, it was not converted to a LAMPS platform. Although upgraded with the 101 main rotor system and T58-GE-8F engines, it retained the rearward tailwheel. While assigned to HSL-31, Det. Bravo, no. 031 periodically alternated assignment aboard survey ships *Chauvenet* and *Harkness*. It is seen here during survey work in Indonesia, Indian Ocean, during the late 1970s. The white-painted *Chauvenet* lies in the distance. *Courtesy of Timothy Jara*

The mud-caked crew and HH-2D of HSL-30, Support Det. 31, aboard USS *Forrestal* (CV-59) in March 1973. The detachment staged from the carrier during search-and-rescue and humanitarian work in Tunisia's flooded Medjerda Valley. *Courtesy of Capt. Gordon Peterson, US Navy (ret.)*

The crew of 031 prepares to lift a sling load with its cargo hook from a cruiser's fantail in the late 1980s. Det. B of HSL-31 called itself the "Bad Boys of Bravo." On the Seasprite's port cargo door was painted the devious cartoon character "Snidely." The legend "SHAKA" on the lower tail rotor pylon was pidgin for a Hawaiian-based friendly gesture. *Author's collection*

With its upper fairings removed and open, BuNo 149031 undergoes maintenance on the helicopter spot of the survey ship *Chauvenet* in January 1981. Maintenance personnel often worked in harsh conditions on decks without hangars. *Courtesy of US Navy*

In spring 1971, Helicopter Combat Support Squadron 4 conducted the Navy tradition of piping retiring shipmates "over the side" when it bid goodbye to the UH-2A. The UH-2A/B's replacement, such as "Scooter 6-4" (*seen here*), was the HH-2D. HC-4's mission entailed support of Atlantic Fleet combatant helicopter facility ships and providing every variety of helicopter support with ship detachments in almost every ocean, sea, and gulf in the world. *Courtesy of Doug Slowiak*

With the conversion from HH-2D to SH-2F, BuNo 149021, an early production UH-2A, saw a change in mission from search and rescue to extending the search and attack capabilities of destroyers and escort ships. Its primary mission then became antisubmarine warfare and antiship surveillance and targeting. No stranger to the testing circuit, during the 1980s no. 021 wore the emblem of the Rotary Wing Aircraft Test Directorate of the NATC. *Courtesy of Jim Burridge*

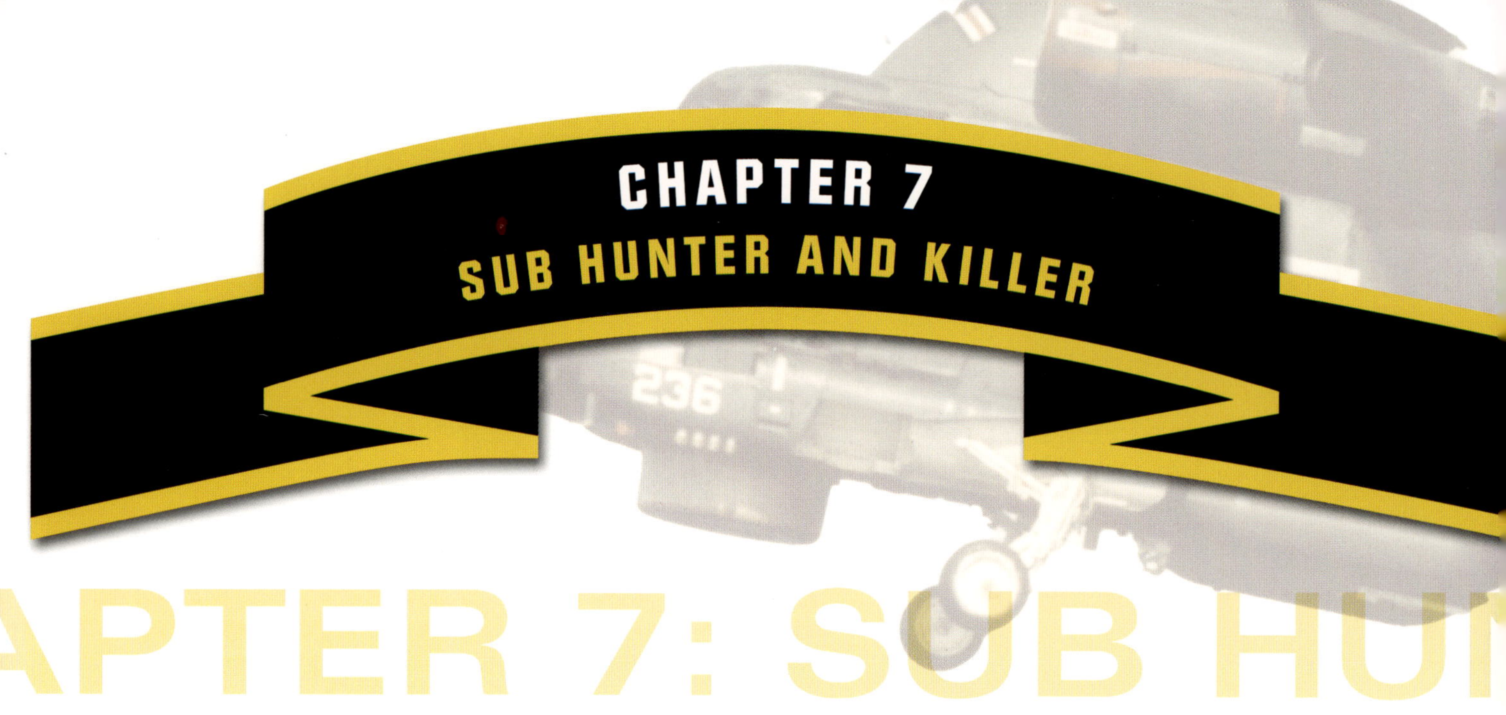

CHAPTER 7
SUB HUNTER AND KILLER

APTER 7: SUB HU

Despite the US Navy's lagging development of the helicopter and its integration into the fleet during the Cold War, the Seasprite lived up to its reputation for versatility, having helped shape the Navy's modern helicopter force. Although deck space aboard ships was, and remains, prime real estate, torpedo-armed helicopters would become vital components of the surface fleet.

A brief look back in history reveals the differences that existed between commands over the subject of shipboard helicopters. Unquestionably, the new helicopter was expected to spend a great deal of its service aboard ship, but to what extent had yet to be determined. The concept of aircraft operating from ships was nothing new. Beginning in the 1920s until the late 1940s, fixed-wing aircraft were flown from nonaviation ships—battleships and cruisers—for spotting gunfire and scouting ahead of the fleet. These dangerous operations were the subject of many heated arguments over the value of aircraft aboard nonaviation ships. Although opponents agreed that shipborne aircraft could observe gunfire and fly antisubmarine patrol, their gasoline and doped fabric were not worth the fire hazard they presented, particularly when mounted amidships close to smokestacks, which emitted burning scale and embers. With the advent of radar during World War II and the increase of carrier aircraft, the role of the battleship and cruiser scout plane reverted from long-range scouting to rescuing downed airmen. With no further need for scouting planes after the war, observation squadrons were removed from ships by 1950.

Since these floatplanes were catapulted off battleships and cruisers and could be taken back aboard only with boom and tackle, the assistant secretary of the navy for aeronautics, David S. Ingalls, ordered three Pitcairn autogyros, small aircraft with rotor blades that could take off and land on small ship decks. On September 23, 1931, one of the trio was successfully tested on the carrier USS *Langley* (CV-1) off Virginia, marking the first time a rotor craft landed aboard a ship at sea. Jubilation over the tests fizzled when one of the autogyros, after combat testing by the Marines in Nicaragua, was labeled "an exasperating contraption not fit for military use." Undaunted, military leaders in 1938 pressed Congress for funding to conduct research on rotary-wing aircraft, which was approved. The Allies had already begun protecting merchant shipping with aircraft and blimps in the effort to locate the elusive, grimly effective U-boats. In late 1943, Cmdr. Frank A. Erickson, a Coast Guard helicopter pioneer, implored Navy officials to consider the helicopter for antisubmarine and search-and-rescue work. Merchant ships were being torpedoed in the Atlantic, forcing even the skeptics to admit that the helicopter might have a place in antisubmarine warfare. Yet, the Navy brass, despite the insistence of several Coast Guard officers, remained steadfast in its belief that the helicopter had few, if any, applications that would benefit its operations. They deemed research of the helicopter costly and not essential to the war effort. Adding to their skepticism was the apprehensiveness that helicopter production would interfere with the production of fixed-wing aircraft. Coast Guard officers Cmdr. Watson A.

TER AND KILLER

Burton, commanding officer of Air Station Floyd Bennett Field, Brooklyn, and Cmdr. William J. Kossler, chief of the Aviation Engineering Division at Coast Guard Headquarters, on the other hand, envisioned unlimited use of the helicopter. Cmdr. Erickson emphasized the helicopter's role in protecting convoys against submarine attacks, adding that any vessel that could mount a 30-by-30-foot platform could accommodate a helicopter. These men pointed out other uses of the helicopter that foretold of future applications: they could bomb submarines with more accuracy, they could be refueled by lowering a hose to the smallest patrol boat, and they could rescue persons from torpedoed vessels by lowering a rubber boat or harness. Erickson felt that the helicopter could be equipped with radar and sound-ranging gear to detect submarines. They could be the eyes and ears of the convoy escorts, since the Navy's greatest problem was not killing submarines but finding them.

Despite the Navy's limited enthusiasm for the helicopter, not to mention the dislike of the fling wings by the fixed-wing community, Navy admiral Ernest King, commander in chief, US Fleet, and chief of naval operations (CNO), was convinced otherwise. On February 19, 1943, he imparted to the Bureau of Aeronautics the need to exhaust every practicable means for combating enemy submarines, and that meant immediate testing of helicopters. King arranged through the Army Air Force for three Sikorsky HNS-1 (R-4) helicopters, which had entered production months earlier. Setbacks were ongoing, some of which stemmed from the administrative assignment of helicopters to the battleship/cruiser community, which had shown strong opposition to rotary-wing aircraft. It didn't help that shipboard trials met with marginal results. Adm. King stepped in to create a workable program and establish a board combining the agencies involved in evaluation of the helicopter in antisubmarine warfare.

Based aboard destroyers, it was surmised, the helicopter could carry a 200-pound Mk. IX fast-sinking depth charge that could be dropped after surface contact had been made. To make helicopters more proficient as sub hunters, a project began in April 1944 to equip them with "dipping sonar" similar to those carried by blimps. In October a rescue harness was devised and tested. As the submarine menace decreased and the helicopter showed promise in the lifesaving role, its antisubmarine role gradually diminished. The Coast Guard, which was largely responsible for evaluating the helicopter, found their enthusiasm for further development dampened by the difficulty in shifting national policy, not to mention the Navy fixed-wing mindset. The antisubmarine role they envisioned was replaced by long-range bombers and planes aboard escort carriers.

Naval authorities could no longer ignore the success with the helicopter enjoyed by the US Army, Coast Guard, and British air arms. Showing lesser attitude and more confidence in those successes, the Navy in 1946 established its first helicopter unit: Helicopter Development Squadron 3 (VX-3) at Floyd Bennett Field, Long Island, New York. Its mission was to study the helicopter for fleet and land use. Two years later, the squadron's assets were divided to form Helicopter Utility Squadrons 1 and 2 (HU-1 and HU-2). Finally convinced of the helicopter's ability to counter the submarine threat with dipping sonar and air-dropped torpedoes, on October 3, 1951, the Navy established Helicopter Anti-Submarine Squadron 1 (HS-1) at NAS Key West. The difficulty in detecting nuclear-powered submarines, which appeared after the Korean War, prompted the Navy to place high priority on the evaluation of sub-hunting aircraft. Having proved its worth in Korea, Sikorsky's HO4S (H-19) helicopter was equipped with a torpedo and rudimentary detection gear. The underpowered HO4S was replaced by Sikorsky's S-58 model, known in Navy parlance as the HSS-1 "Seabat." Deemed the first effective ASW helicopter, the Seabat worked as a hunter/killer team, one having dipping sonar, and its partner a Mk. 43 torpedo. Despite the Seabat's success, the capability to locate and destroy submarines had yet to be devised for nonaviation ships.

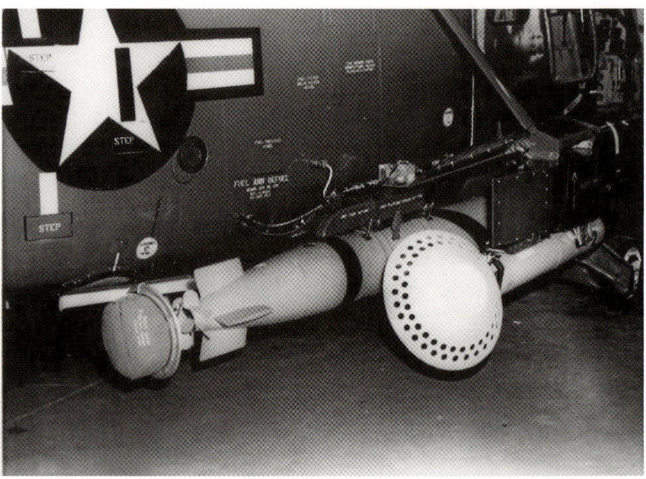

Seasprites were highly adaptable to varied mission loads, such as this torpedo mounted to the auxiliary fuel tank support. Attached to the torpedo's tail was the drogue parachute container. *Courtesy of US Navy*

DASH

The story of how the Seasprite became the Navy's efficient submarine hunter-killer cannot be told without first examining the controversial DASH program. Although interest in pilotless aircraft existed in the days of the autogyro, the lessons for unmanned aircraft began two decades later, during the early 1950s. Mindful of the growing number of Soviet submarines after World War II, Charles Kaman brought the drone concept to the forefront. Driven by a keen interest in antisubmarine warfare, Kaman convinced a reluctant staff of the Office of Naval Research (ONR) that the drone helicopter was a fresh approach to countering the Soviet submarine threat. Kaman asserted that a rotary-wing drone with listening sonar and torpedoes could serve as the eyes and ears of a ship far beyond its horizon. From Kaman experiments came the realization that a helicopter with electronic-assisted control systems could be flown pilotless—an unthinkable feat during the early 1950s. Kaman's success opened the door for Navy staff to announce an industry-wide competition for a Drone Anti-Submarine Helicopter, or DASH. The firms of Bell, Kaman, and Gyrodyne submitted proposals. Bell Helicopter's research and development of torpedo-armed helicopters during the 1950s included a Bell HUL-1 carrying two torpedoes conducting takeoffs and landings on the stern of the destroyer leader USS *Mitscher* (DL-2), thereby justifying the concept of torpedo-armed helicopters aboard nonaviation ships.

BuNo 150171 began life as a UH-2B and is seen here in 1972 as an SH-2D assigned to the NADC, Warminster, Pennsylvania, testing a sonobuoy launcher and related equipment for the LAMPS program. The launcher bore the name "The Buoy Boy." *Courtesy of US Navy*

Still at NADC Warminster in 1973, BuNo 150171 was converted to HH-2D with AN/APS-115 nose radar to serve as the test platform for Phase C electronics systems. *Courtesy of Bill Carmody*

In November 1972, the SH-2D BuNo 151328 of HSL-30 aboard guided-missile frigate USS *Standley* (DLG-32) tracks a Soviet submarine 60 miles east of Gibraltar. This was the first photograph of an SH-2D with a Soviet sub. *Courtesy of US Navy*

Standing on the antiskid surface of the auxiliary fuel tank, Petty Officer Third Class Bridge preflights an SH-2D of HSL-31 at NAS North Island in 1977. The first female Seasprite plane captain was AA Judith A. Booth of HSL-32 in 1974. *Courtesy of US Navy*

The SH-2D BuNo 150157 of HSL-30 on the helo deck of the Knox-class frigate USS *Bowen* (FF-1079). Aft of the flight deck is the eight-cell Sea Sparrow missile launcher. *Courtesy of Capt. David W. Moulton Sr., US Navy (ret.)*

Above: BuNo 152206, the last production UH-2B, as an SH-2F keeps company with the Royal Netherlands Navy Kortenaer-class frigate HNLMS *Philips Van Almonde* (F823) in October 1984. The ship served the NATO Standing Naval Force Atlantic. *Courtesy of US Navy*

Left: The SH-2F "Seasnake One-Zero" of HSL-33, BuNo 151326, was retrieved after crashing into San Diego Bay on July 15, 1976. *Courtesy of US Navy*

The SH-2F BuNo 152190 of HSL-32 uses the Helicopter In-Flight Refueling (HIFR) system. HIFR permitted fast refueling without having to land aboard ships and refueling from ships with no landing deck. This Seasprite was stationed aboard the Knox-class frigate USS *W. S. Sims* (FF-1059), which in November 1970 was the first Knox-class ship to have a manned helicopter land on her deck. *Courtesy of US Navy*

Chock-and-chain men clear the deck as BuNo 151316 of HSL-32 prepares for takeoff. Visible above the squadron emblem on the forward landing-gear fairing is the Mk. 25 smoke float ejector, which replaced the emergency flotation system. *Courtesy of US Navy*

BuNo 150164 of HSL-31 after crashing at NAS North Island on November 19, 1985. Extensive damage required that the Seasprite be written off. Shown to good effect is the tail rotor driveshaft's position left of the centerline. *Author's collection*

Having been converted to an HH-2C, BuNo 151333 was rebuilt as an SH-2D following a crash in 1968. In December 1971 it became the first SH-2D in the Pacific Fleet, assigned to HSL-31 aboard USS *Sterett*. The Seasprite is seen here in November 1972 at NAS Imperial Beach, California. *Courtesy of Frank Roos via Norm Taylor*

In 1958, Gyrodyne won the DASH competition. Despite being passed over, Kaman Aircraft Corporation remained steadfast in drone helicopter development, with many of its proven concepts adopted for future remotely piloted vehicles (RPVs). Kaman and the Navy maintained an active partnership in helicopter development, conducting tests during the 1960s that gave rise to the DASH program.

Peter J. Papadakos, the founder of Gyrodyne Company of America, at Flowerfield Airfield, New York, perfected his coaxial helicopter design, which first flew in 1951. Gyrodyne was then awarded a Navy contract to study applications of the coaxial rotor configuration. The study yielded positive results that led to a follow-on contract for a small one-man helicopter for use by the Marine Corps as a reconnaissance vehicle. Impressed with the machine, called the XRON Rotorcycle, the Navy approached Papadakos to submit a design proposal for a torpedo-carrying, remote-control version of the Rotorcycle to meet the requirement for ASW operations beyond the limited range of ship sensors and torpedoes. Navy officials saw in the Rotorcycle a less costly and simpler alternative to earlier plans for placing large ASW helicopters on modified World War II–era ships. A small, unmanned helicopter that could take torpedoes to the target seemed the ideal solution.

Gyrodyne came up with a 1,000-pound helicopter with an automobile engine built into a tubed skeleton frame topped with 20-foot counterrotating rotors. The "stacked" rotors dampened vibration and allowed operations from the tight stern space of destroyers. Tucked between elongated skids were a pair of Mk. 44 torpedoes, and later, a more capable Mk. 46 torpedo.

Being pilotless and low cost, and lacking redundant and fail-safe systems, the machine was expendable. These features, however, coupled with a poorly organized and managed parts-and-logistics system put the machine out of commission for long periods or, at worst, at the ocean bottom. The resultant lack of proficiency due to inexperience and rising accident rate foreshadowed numerous pitfalls that plagued the DASH program. Expendability was assumed, since the DASH was intended for delivery of a nuclear depth bomb and would not survive the blast. The high risk of storing the weapon aboard ships, however, ruled out its use, resulting in the dual torpedo load. That ruling, unfortunately, did not move officials to pursue, much less order, upgrades of the machine's design.

While American sonar technology improved dramatically, weapon development lagged, prompting the Navy to explore an antisubmarine rocket (ASROC) capable of delivering a conventional torpedo. Since developmental problems of the ASROC made the DASH a more promising venture, especially in view of the rapid expansion of the Soviet submarine fleet, attention turned to extending the life of World War II destroyers to accommodate both the DASH and ASROC. Greater emphasis was placed on the need for an attack helicopter in view of the ASROC's limited range. Besides, the DASH could be recalled after launch, an obvious bonus.

After World War II, Kaman's reputation for innovation ensured his company's place at the forefront of technological advances in ASW. Charles Kaman was convinced that rotary-wing drones with sonar could be positioned ahead of naval ships. The HTK-1 was chosen for experimental work. Progressive testing led to trials with an HTK-1 drone aboard USS *Mitscher* (DL-2) off Key West, Florida, in 1951. Here, the drone is winched down to *Mitscher* under the direction of a shipboard operator during ASW trials. *Courtesy of US Navy*

The chief of naval operations at the time, Adm. Arleigh Burke, who declared ASW the Navy's top priority, is credited with implementing both ASROC and DASH. In mid-1958, Burke had ordered the Navy to develop a drone helicopter that could be operational by 1962. Since the destroyer was central to Navy ASW operations as the DASH platform, Burke instituted the Fleet Rehabilitation and Maintenance (FRAM) program to extend the life of 240 destroyers. Meanwhile, on January 31, 1958, the Navy ordered twelve DASHs: nine DSN-1s (QH-50A) and three DSN-2s (QH-50B). In January 1960 the DSN-1 made the world's first free flight of an unmanned aerial vehicle (UAV) at NAS Patuxent River. On July 1, 1960, the DASH, with a safety pilot aboard, landed aboard USS *Mitscher*. More aviation history was recorded when on December 7, the DASH made the first unmanned landing on a ship at sea, USS *Hazelwood* (DD-531), which served as the DASH trials ship from 1958 to 1965. The US Navy now had the ability to counter a submarine threat before it could approach within striking distance of a US Navy ship. In November 1962, a QH-50 launched from San Clemente, California, to land on the destroyer USS *Buck* (DD-761), signaling the beginning of DASH deployments. Late the following year, Secretary of Defense Robert McNamara approved budgeting for mass production of DASH to provide three for each FRAM destroyer—two plus a spare. Peter P. Papadakos, son of Gyrodyne's founder, states, "We built 378 QH-50C models and 395 QH-50D models, and over 200 spares, roughly 1,000 aircraft."

DASH units would be subordinate to a parent utility squadron on each coast. During takeoff and landing, the DASH was remotely flown by the destroyer's DASH officer from a control station near the small flight deck built onto the ship's stern. Once it was airborne, control of the DASH was handed over to an operator in the ship's Combat Information Center (CIC). Its effective range, about 30 nautical miles, was determined by the radar range of its destroyer.

Challenges from the outset of production surfaced both on technical and operational fronts. Since the gasoline that powered the DASH Porsche engine was deemed too dangerous to have aboard ships, the switch was made to turbine power. Fuel for the Boeing 270 hp T50-BO-4 turbine engine then was compatible with the jet fuel becoming standard throughout the fleet. Turbine power increased the gross weight of the drone, designated DSN-3 (later the QH-50C), which made its first flight on January 15, 1962. Next was the more powerful QH-50D, which was ordered into production in April 1964, followed, finally, by the QH-50E, with an Allison T63-A-5A turbine engine, only three of which were built before the program was terminated.

The life (and death) of the DASH is checkered with success and failure that stir controversy to the present day. Operationally, some ships launched and recovered their drone helicopters hundreds of times, often in rough weather, without mishaps. The skipper of USS *Steinaker* (DD-863) emphasized, "The success of our system hinges on its continual utilization." Gyrodyne's Papadakos concurred:

Production of the DASH began with the QH-50C model, which was powered by a turboshaft engine in place of a piston engine, allowing it to carry two Mk. 44 torpedoes totaling 860 pounds. The platforms of most ships were designed to support the 6,000-pound DASH. During the 1960s, the Navy operated QH-50 drones from about 130 destroyers and destroyer escorts. Here, a DSN-3 (redesignated QH-50C in 1962) comes aboard USS *Hazelwood* (DD-531), a World War II–era Fletcher-class destroyer, the fastest in her day, which was modified by removing two aft guns to accommodate a hangar deck. *Courtesy of US Navy*

"The system is successful when in the right hands." Crews that found it easier not to fly their DASHs for fear of breakdowns recorded low proficiency ratings, and higher accident rates when they did fly. Some ship captains viewed drones as "career death" since DASH losses reflected upon their command history, which was another reason to keep them grounded. Discord over the drones also existed in the aviation community, where fliers not only felt their careers threatened by drones but feared flying into DASHs that sometimes went wayward. Carrier pilots often expressed their dislike for drones operating in "their" airspace.

When surface elements found it difficult to pinpoint targets, DASH was blamed even though targeting was the problem, not weapons engagement. True, to minimize costs, DASHs used 1940s-era off-the-shelf electronic control systems, but the Navy's reluctance to upgrade the system only contributed to sounding of the drone's death knell. Resistance to drone development came early in the Navy; however, it was the Navy that pushed the DASH into the fleet too early, purportedly as an attempt to keep pace with the FRAM modification schedule. The fleet acted as test directors, with almost all training done on actual aircraft by nonaviation personnel . . . and drones crashed. Compounding the problem was the rapid turnover

To visually identify drone helicopters, left-side components were painted red, with right-side areas painted green, in accordance with the colors of running lights of vessels and aircraft. Lacking strong advocates and ever vexing to the Navy fixed-wing community, the crash-prone drone DASH served eight years on obsolescent ships. *Courtesy of US Navy*

of technicians and controllers before valuable experience could be gained. As failures mounted, so did the DASH's incorrigible reputation. No single incident could have added more fuel to that fire than what became known as "the DASH that torpedoed the Bennington."

The incident occurred aboard the ASW carrier USS *Bennington* (CVS-20) as it sailed off Long Beach, California, in November 1964. Aboard was the secretary of the navy and associated dignitaries, being shown the ship and its various operational capabilities. A demonstration of the DASH was to cap the tour. The DASH was launched from a nearby destroyer and turned to make its flyby between *Bennington* and the destroyer that had control of it. As it passed between the two ships—too close to *Bennington*, observers noted—it crashed into *Bennington*'s mast and bridge overhead. Debris and flaming fuel slid down into the sea; broken rotor blades and parts skittered across the deck. The DASH's dummy Mk. 44 torpedo crashed through the bridge overhead and came to rest in the navigator's position, which erupted into flames. The fire was quickly extinguished, and injuries were minimal. *Bennington* was the only ship ever to return to port with a torpedo protruding from its bridge roof. A sailor who had witnessed the mishap probably said it best: "That had to be the final nail in the coffin of what was already on shaky ground."

But the list of factors that led to the decline of DASH got longer. War in Southeast Asia created budget restraints, which incurred realignment of priorities despite a multitude of wartime uses for the DASH other than ASW. Since submarines were not an issue in the war, modified DASHs were sent ashore for naval gunfire spotting, reconnaissance,

The UH-2A BuNo 149035 of NAS Norfolk–based HU-2 overflies a DSN-3 operated by NAS Norfolk's Utility Squadron 6 (VU-6), which provided target drones for the Atlantic Fleet. The dual-torpedo-armed QH-50C saw the most use by the fleet during the 1960s. *Courtesy of US Navy*

and even gunship trials; visionaries considered the DASH's role in rescuing downed fliers. But the Navy and Congress turned a deaf ear to such enormous potential. In addition, improvements in rotary-wing technology and power plants promised success for manned helicopters small enough to operate from ASW surface ships.

Despite the dedication of those involved with the DASH program, its fate was sealed from the beginning. Mismanaged by the Navy, devoid of advocates and responsible owners, and victimized by bureaucracy and clashing Navy cultures, the DASH program limped toward its end. The Navy acknowledges the loss of 411 QH-50C/Ds of 746 built for the DASH program. Of these, 5 percent were combat losses, while 80 percent were the result of failed electronic systems. As defunding loomed, their removal from ships began in late 1969. In November 1970, fifty-two QH-50Cs went to the Naval Air Rework Facility North Island, California, followed by thirty-one QH-50Ds during the next two months. The CNO struck QH-50s from the inventory on January 31, 1971. Most began second careers with the army at White Sands Missile Range and at the Naval Air Weapons Center, China Lake. There, the DASH proved itself, providing the impetus for development of modern drone aircraft. DASH was ahead of its time; with its parent destroyer, it was the most capable ASW system of its time.

CHAPTER 8
LAMPS

In the mid-1960s, the Navy reverted to its earlier plan for a manned helicopter as an alternative to the DASH. Not only had the office of CNO become aviation oriented, with Adm. George W. Anderson at the helm and VAdm. Paul Ramsey as deputy chief of naval operations for air, both of whom were career aviators, but larger destroyers were being built that could accommodate helicopters. When the Navy reduced the number of DASH-modified destroyers in mid-1966, Ramsey stated that manned helicopters should perform the DASH mission because "in robots you can't build judgment." Especially of interest was the reverse of the sensor-weapon mismatch that gave birth to DASH. Advances in ASW technology opened the door for a manned attack helicopter, since the massive SQS-26 sonars being built into ships' bows created a shortcoming for which the DASH had no solution. The new sonar, which could detect submarines at the first convergence zone (approximately 26 miles), could not provide a precise torpedo release point to catch a fast Soviet submarine, whereas the DASH depended on the ship's sonar to achieve release accuracy. The inability of the ship to provide a precise release point meant that it fell upon the helicopter crew to accurately acquire the target. Only a manned helicopter with the right equipment and skilled crew could do the job. The helicopter would provide expanded ASW capability with a combination of surface search radar to detect a sub's snorkel or periscope, a magnetic-anomaly detector (MAD) to localize a sonar contact, electronic intercept equipment, sonobuoys, and a data link to feed sonobuoy data to the destroyer, with a crew that could operate the equipment beyond a ship's line of sight. The Seasprite could either attack the target or mark it for other aircraft or surface vessels. A manned, pure ASW helicopter was deemed insufficient, since the Navy requirement called not only for ASW capability, but Anti-Ship Missile Defense (ASMD) and Anti-Ship Surveillance and Targeting (ASST), along with SAR and utility capability. In the ASMD role, the Seasprite could not only extend the radar range of its mother ship to detect vessels with ship-to-ship missiles but could, with its onboard electronics, confuse the missile's guidance systems or create decoys. The tall order was labeled Light Airborne Multi-Purpose Systems, or LAMPS.

Regardless of how Navy officials viewed the DASH's record—which included verification that helicopters could operate from small ships—they were resigned to the fact that helicopters would be a mainstay of the fleet, with ships of all sizes operating helicopters from their decks. Carriers could easily accommodate ASW helicopter detachments, but smaller ships also needed the protection that only helicopters could provide. More than 150 ships, many of which had deck platforms for DASH operations, did not have deck space, nor could they handle the weight of Sikorsky's large ASW SH-3D Sea King helicopter, which served aboard carriers. The size and strength of DASH platforms were key considerations in drawing up specifications for LAMPS. It was estimated that the 4,000-pound weight limit of a DASH deck would be required to handle a 12,000-pound LAMPS helicopter. The DASH deck limit was raised to 6,000 pounds in 1969, and ultimately, deck-strength tests conducted by Kaman engineers

R 8: LAMPS

In November 1970, the HH-2D BuNo 150186 of HC-2 operated aboard USS *W. S. Sims* (FF-1059) to confirm that decks built for DASH operations could handle 12,000-pound LAMPS Seasprites. *Courtesy of David Cox*

proved that much-higher gross weights were tolerable. Confirmation came in November 1970, when a deck-strength test was conducted utilizing a 12,500-pound HH-2D on board USS *W. S. Sims* (DE-1059). The HH-2D, BuNo 150186 of HC-2, operated from the deck with no problems. Since the H-2 was the only operational helicopter that could carry the LAMPS package yet fit and operate off the smallest platform, the Knox-class 1052 frigate, it was selected for the program.

The steadily increasing ability of submarines to launch missiles while remaining outside the range of ships' defenses lent a sense of urgency to LAMPS development. And Navy leaders were ever mindful of the hard lesson endured by Israel when that nation's destroyer *Eilat* was sunk by Soviet Styx missiles fired by an Egyptian warship in October 1967, the world's first surface-to-surface missile engagement.

The event most responsible for quickening the pace of helicopter research and development was the arrival in mid-1970 of Adm. Elmo R. Zumwalt Jr. as CNO. Immediately after taking the helm, Zumwalt cited the importance of helicopters aboard escort ships, making the LAMPS project his highest priority. What had long been deemed inconceivable had happened: a CNO wanted helicopters, and many of them. In his 1976 memoir, *On Watch*, Zumwalt made known his position as a strong advocate of LAMPS, which was one element of his "Project Sixty" plan to modernize and optimize the Navy and spotlight the Soviet threat. He stated that

> helicopters are coming into increasing use in naval warfare. Project 60 demonstrated that we could achieve high payoff if escort vessels carried one or two helos on their decks to use as aids in detecting incoming aircraft, cruise missiles, and submarines. We had available in our inventory over 100 SH-2s, a sort of all-purpose helo that was not highly satisfactory for the new mission, being too light to load with all the equipment the mission called for, but it was adequate and inexpensive and available, so we decided to adapt the SH-2 for the near term and at the same time begin research and development (R&D) on a more advanced machine. We called the new helo, together

with its embarked detection and kill equipment, LAMPS, for Light Airborne Multi-Purpose System, a combination of sensors to find submarines and equipment to fire Mark 46 torpedoes at them. Expediting LAMPS, which was already in the design stage, was one of the high-priority items in Project 60. The SH-3, the carrier rescue helo, which is bigger than the SH-2, is the one we planned to put on the sea-control ship.

This growing Soviet threat demanded a two-stage LAMPS program, with LAMPS I filling an interim role on the basis of an existing helicopter, while a more effective LAMPS II was sought. Proposals for the interim LAMPS were submitted by Bell (UH-1 Huey), Boeing (Bo-105), Sikorsky/Westland (WG 13 SeaLynx), and Kaman (Model K-820 Sealite). The HH-2D, however, already a familiar fixture in the Navy inventory and having demonstrated its compatibility with small boys, ranked high on the list of proposals. Concurrent with drafting of a test plan, Kaman was in final stages of preparing a full-size mockup of a proposed advanced multimission helicopter designated K-820 and called "Sealite." Early in 1969, Kaman had proposed to the Navy two versions of its UH-2C for the LAMPS mission: a LAMPS-configured UH-2C variant (called "SEA Lamp") for use on larger ships, and the lighter Sealite on smaller vessels. Although the Sealite would utilize many of the UH-2C's dynamic components, it would feature different landing gear, a new three-bladed rotor system, and a different power plant, in a vastly altered fuselage. The NADC, which was tasked with formulating the proposed technical aspects of the program, determined that completely different LAMPS helicopters for different-sized vessels without commonality of parts would increase costs and put a tremendous burden on logistic and supply systems, as well as on training.

SEALITE

Despite the use of HH-2D flight dynamic systems, the Sealite, from a dimensional perspective, was a new aircraft that would require an inordinate amount of refinement to fit the requirements as outlined in the LAMPS *Request for Proposals*. Lower and shorter than the HH-2D, the Sealite was designed to meet rigid space requirements and deck-loading limits of newly built DE-1052-, DE-1040-, and DEG-1-class ships. Kaman advertised that three Sealites, when folded into 31-foot lengths, would fit in the hangars of the series DD 963 Spruance-class destroyers, first ordered in mid-1970. The 27-foot DASH hangars of DE-1052-class destroyer escorts would require enlargement. Kaman planned three versions of the Sealite—ASW, ASMD, and general purpose—or offered interchangeable modules in a single airframe for multimission capability. In all three mission modes, weights remained constant: mission gross weight was 8,800 pounds, with a maximum takeoff gross weight of 9,500 pounds. Power would be derived from a light Pratt & Whitney Canada PT6T Twin-Pac (T400-CP-400) turbojet of 1,800 shp, familiar to the Bell twin Huey and Sikorsky S-58T. A foldable, three-blade main rotor would incorporate Kaman's new 101 rotor features. Fixed, quadricycle, wheeled landing gear was favored over skids for ease of deck handling.

On September 21, 1970, Kaman unveiled a full-size mockup of its K-820 Sealite. Despite the Sealite's many features, Kaman's HH-2D (slated for conversion to the SH-2D) was soon deemed the logical selection for filling the interim LAMPS requirement. The US Navy at that time had nearly four hundred ships with helicopter platforms, more than half of which were destroyers.

Four HH-2D Seasprites were assigned to the at-sea Development and Validation 98 program (DV-98), which had been initiated in 1968 by the CNO for management by the Naval Material Command and NADC. DV-98 was composed of three phases: Phase 1 was MAD; Phase 2 was ASMD, ESM (electronic support measures), and data link; and final phases tested SAR and logistics and introduced sonobuoys and continued testing of MAD and ASMD. The firms Texas Instruments, Sperry, and Raytheon came aboard the project for involvement with the first two phases. Project Iron Barnacle, although unplanned, was the 1970 combat evaluation mainly of Phase 1. Concurrent

The initial design of proposed "Sealite," which was to be powered by United Aircraft of Canada PT-6T-400 CP-480 engines, having a gross weight of 8,800 pounds for the ASW mission and 7,900 pounds for the ASMD mission. The concept was considered from August to October 1969. *Courtesy of Kaman Aerospace Corp.*

A more promising proposed version of the Sealite included a nose radome for housing search radar. This view illustrates the Sealite's low profile of 10 feet, 8 inches in height, achieved by installing the engines and transmission as low as possible. The standard Seasprite model was 13 feet, 7 inches to the top of the main rotor hub. *Courtesy of US Navy*

A major selling feature of the proposed Sealite was a 52-foot operating length that could be shortened to 31 feet with blade fold, a foldable tail rotor pylon, and raising the large, hinged nose section. Many of the aircraft's access panels doubled as work platforms. This mockup's fictitious BuNo was assigned to a T-28D of the South Vietnamese air force. *Courtesy of US Navy*

with the development of DV-98, the test H-2, BuNo 147981, was modified with an AN/ASQ-81 MAD at the NADC at Warminster, Pennsylvania. Phase 1 would test whether a helicopter could convert an SQS-26 sonar contact at the first convergence zone to a successful prosecution, using only MAD as the sensor. The MAD was nothing new to the Navy, having been in use with Navy patrol aircraft since World War II. The sensitivity of the detector to metal and electromagnetic interference required that it be towed distant from the aircraft, low over the target. The ability to operate helicopters independently for extended periods from small boys would also be evaluated. Aircraft involved with DV-98 included MAD-equipped HH-2Ds (BuNos 149756, 149766, and 152190) for ASW trials assigned to HC-4 aboard USS *Belknap* (DLG-26), and two configured for ASMD (BuNos 150169 and 151324) assigned to HC-5 to operate from USS *Fox* (DLG-33) and USS *Denver* (LPD-9). The latter pair of HH-2Ds was configured with AN/APS-115 radar, ALR-54 ESM equipment, and AKT-19 data link for Phase 2. First was evaluation of the AN/ASQ 81 magnetic-anomaly detector on a helicopter. Scott Milner offers his views:

> The MAD installations on the HH-2Ds, BuNos 149756 and 149766, were completed and ready for flight when Bob Clark and I went to NADC in January 1970. With us were fourteen enlisted members of HC-5, including four electronics technicians. Our task was to learn how to deploy the MAD bird and read the charts that were being produced. I was the officer in charge of what was then the first and only LAMPS detachment. As we got to know the systems and walked around the aircraft, Bob and I believed that a mirror would be needed on the starboard cockpit window to enable the pilot to see the MAD bird in its launch and recovery cycles. We selected the round mirror over the rectangular mirror, and that mirror became standard on all SH-2D and SH-2F aircraft.

There was no "pulling punches" in the acid test for the "MAD Bird," since it was quickly sent to Vietnam to join with a US Army hunter-killer helicopter team of the 1st Cavalry Division. In April 1970, President Nixon authorized an incursion into Cambodia to search for and destroy North Vietnamese Army (NVA) sanctuary sites. The operation began on May 1, with US forces allowed only two months in questionably neutral Cambodia. Infantrymen prodding with metal rods to sense hidden weapon caches was quickly found ineffective. Due to this short time frame, the commander of US forces in Vietnam sought from all services any technology that could aid in locating NVA weapons caches.

When the Army asked the Navy to assist with equipment that was used to locate submarines, the realization came that HH-2D crews of HC-5 were working under DV-98 to evaluate the MAD unit at the NADC at Warminster. An officer in the CNO's office explained, "We need pilots to fly the birds and can't think of a better group than the pilots already familiar with the equipment." Former

Since the Sealite's fuselage was 15 inches wider than that of the HH-2D, external stores mounts were kept as short as possible. The cabin could accommodate modular packages to adapt to a specific mission, or to seat six passengers. The upper portion of the rescue doorway incorporated the rescue hoist, while the lower section incorporated steps. A fourteen-tube sonobuoy launcher was located immediately above the starboard external stores mount. *Courtesy of US Navy*

Sparrow missiles could be mounted to both sides of the Sealite; however, interference with the rescue door made obvious the need for design changes. *Courtesy of US Navy*

Seasprite pilot Scott Milner recalls: "Clearly sonar wouldn't work. Sonobuoys wouldn't work. MAD was the only solution, and it had to be mounted on a helicopter to work from landing zones in Cambodia. That's how we got the call to join the team in Vietnam."

The pilots flew the two MAD-equipped HH-2Ds to Kaman's Bloomfield facility for minor modifications, and from there these were flown by C-5A transport to NAS North Island to load maintenance personnel and support equipment and then continued on to Vietnam. Former Seasprite pilot Robert Clark continues:

> The detachment was hosted by the 1st Air Cavalry Division at Phuoc Vinh located in III Corps. The army named the operation "Iron Barnacle." During June we flew on missions in Cambodia, always under the watchful eyes of an experienced Army hunter-killer team consisting of an AH-1G Cobra gunship and OH-6A LOH (light observation helicopter). Our mission profile was to fly at 300 to 400 feet at 90 to 110 knots above the triple canopy, with the AN/ASQ 81 deployed in order to have the maximum possible sweep width of the MAD.

Scott Milner added, "Our squadron mates who served in HA(L)-3 gave us zero chance of returning alive with that flight envelope."

To broaden their margin for survival, the HH-2D crews, which included young physicist and MAD expert Andrew R. Ochadlick, kept weapons handy, and they had painstakingly covered all of the aircraft's high-visibility markings with tape. With the MAD system continually tweaked and peaked during evaluation, the largest cache of weapons, ammunition, and equipment was found in Cambodia on June 25, 1970, exceeding all expectations of detachment personnel.

On July 17, Clark's Iron Barnacle crew of four in BuNo 149756 was assigned a search of a suspected enemy location off the Ho Chi Minh Trail. Late in the day and low on fuel, the equipment operator in the cabin got a MAD contact. A smoke grenade marked the location, and the Seasprite climbed to altitude to allow the LOH Scout crew to go down to investigate. Although the Scout crew soon reported strong signs of enemy activity, the three helicopters were low on fuel, so a strike mission was planned for the following day. That morning the HH-2D crew and the hunter-killer team returned to the scene. A MAD contact was again made, a smoke marker was thrown, and the Seasprite and LOH exchanged altitudes.

A few minutes later the LOH pilot, Warrant Officer Walker A. Jones, reported smoke in the cockpit, the result of a single bullet that had found his transmission. When the transmission seized, Jones autorotated down to the treetops and then thrashed through 300 feet of jungle, crashing upright in a stream, its three crewmen alive. Jones picks up the story:

One of two HH-2Ds of "Iron Barnacle" of HC-5, Det. 102, in Vietnam in 1970. The black "NAVY" title and national insignia on the tail boom were barely visible against dark gray. Iron Barnacle pilot Scott Milner reflects: "The subdued markings were done with 90-knot tape. Our crew spent hours taping over all the white markings on our aircraft." Armor plating is visible around the copilot's seat and in the lower half of the cargo doorway. *Courtesy of US Navy*

> It was clear that our Blues [infantry] could not rappel this deep, and we could not see much sky. So, I decided that we had to somehow climb through thick bamboo and trees to make it to higher ground. Upon moving out, I was stunned by a loud voice saying, "Do not move away. Stay where you are!" I thought at first, I was hallucinating and God was speaking to me. But it was that damn Navy Seasprite with a freaking loudspeaker. Scared the spit out of me. The Seasprite pilot had managed to open foliage to see down and soon started deploying their rescue hoist. I had not radioed that I had been hit, so the Navy guys didn't realize I had been shot down. And thank goodness, as their assholes were puckered up enough as they hovered over us for so long.

Since the LOH was down in the enemy's backyard, and the wait time for an Army hoist-equipped Huey to arrive was unacceptable, Clark informed the Cobra pilot that they were hoist-equipped and had rescue-trained crewmen aboard. The Seasprite crew skillfully lowered the HH-2D through trees, using a gunner's belt to extend their 90-foot hoist cable to reach Jones's crew.

Milner stated, "On July 1, the US pulled out of Cambodia, and we were extended to continue our operations in South Vietnam."

Seasprite pilot Lt. (j.g.) James Marsh, who served with the Iron Barnacle detachment in 1970, created this oil painting commemorating the "Mad Men" of HC-5, Det. 102. Marsh died in 1980 as a direct result of exposure to Agent Orange, which had been freshly sprayed over areas in which the unit flew low level in Vietnam and Cambodia. *Courtesy of Scott Milner collection*

Iron Barnacle was deemed a success, with the MAD having earned high marks, which led to development of its highly advanced offspring designated AN/ASQ-81(V)2. In August, HC-5 Det. 102, along with both HH-2Ds, returned to the business of validating LAMPS equipment in friendlier skies, and for which it was specifically designed: detecting submerged submarines. A less friendly environment existed aboard frigate USS *Truxtun* (CGN-35), where Phase 1 ASW trials got underway in the Pacific. The detachment was not well received by the skipper, and little was accomplished. Scott Milner elaborates:

> When we returned from Vietnam, the detachment got a new officer in charge, Lt. Cmdr. LaRon Stoker, who was the most experienced H-2 pilot in the Navy, with nearly three thousand hours. None of HC-5's DV-98 flight crew had ASW experience, but all had seen service in HC-1 and HC-5 operating off carriers, cruisers, and support ships. Since the H-2 was to test the LAMPS concept, it was only logical that all the pilots be experienced in flying the H-2, which had never

flown ASW missions. Worthy of note is that the LAMPS program was being managed by OP-05, the Air Warfare section of the Navy. It was considered to be an "ugly stepchild" to the leadership in OP-05, who wanted to dedicate all available resources to development and acquisition of fighter and attack aircraft. LAMPS and helicopters were not receiving much attention in OP-05 or from the aviation rear admiral who was given the task of managing the program. Noticing this, Admiral Zumwalt in mid-1971 transferred the LAMPS program to OP-03, the Surface Warfare section, where a surface rear admiral headed the program. Everything changed for the better—clearly, the surface warfare community needed LAMPS on its ships and wanted the program to succeed.

Later, LAMPS was evaluated in the Atlantic aboard the cruiser USS *Wainwright* (DLG-28), and Detachment 102 shifted to USS *Fox* (DLG-33), where supportive Capt. Robert McCabe was eager for LAMPS to work. Tests revealed that MAD alone, due to unsynchronized systems, could not convert a ship's sonar contact into the helicopter's direct contact with the submarine. Phase 1 came to an end.

Besides mounting the bulbous Texas Instruments AN/APS-115 radar, the pair of Phase 2 HH-2Ds was equipped with ALR-52 passive ESM sensors and an AKT-19 data link. The latter allowed the ship's personnel to "see over the horizon" and be a part of the events taking place distant from the ship. Scott Milner adds:

The bulbous nose radome of YSH-2E BuNo 150181 housed APS-115 and APS-122 radar antennas during the LAMPS evaluation period. The system was considered too bulky for the Seasprite's airframe and was replaced by the less effective LN-66 search radar. The LN-66 would occupy the "tub" immediately aft of the nose radome, seen here in November 1972, which, during trials, housed UHF, DF, and data-link antennas and associated electronics. *Courtesy of US Navy*

BuNo 150169 was one of two HH-2Ds of HC-5, Det. 33, that conducted at-sea antiship missile defense (ASMD) trials from the Belknap-class cruiser USS *Fox* (DLG-33) in the Pacific in mid-1971. Ships hangars that had been built for DASH aircraft later were enlarged to accommodate LAMPS Seasprites. *Courtesy of US Navy*

Because Phase 2 was solely dedicated to ASMD/ASST while the ultimate LAMPS aircraft would be capable of prosecuting ASW and ASMD simultaneously, an exercise was created to test the combined missions. USS *Cleveland* (LPD-7) was chosen because it had two landing spots. An SH-3D Sea King from HS-2 was assigned to the exercise along with HH-2D BuNo 151324. The two aircraft flew in proximity for about three to four days, searching for "aggressor" submarine and airborne threats. "Hostile" jets had simulators that emulated Soviet search radar and missile-homing radar. It was a successful exercise as we searched for evidence of a submarine snorkel and hostile air contacts while the Sea King dipped its sonar to search for submarines. Phase 2 proved to the surface warfare community that having a helicopter on board that was equipped with radar and passive ESM equipment richly enhanced the capabilities of the ship to protect itself and the task force group.

In view of Phase 2 successes, Adm. Zumwalt considered halting DV-98, declaring that LAMPS would become reality with "Interim LAMPS." Shortly thereafter, the term "Interim" was dropped, and the program became "LAMPS

The marriage had been a long time coming—the destroyer-type ship as the cornerstone of ASW operations, and the sub-hunting/sub-killing helicopter. Joining BuNo 150169 in ASMD tests with HC-5 was HH-2D BuNo 151324, seen here landing aboard Knox-class frigate USS *Cook* (FF-1083). *Courtesy of US Navy*

The LAMPS sensor operator, or senso, at his cramped workstation at the forward portside cabin area. *Courtesy of US Navy*

MK I." Selection of the proven Seasprite over Kaman's proposed Sealite was officially decided with Kaman in receipt of the contract for conversion of ten HH-2Ds to SH-2Ds in October 1970. Fully configured for ASW with the LAMPS suite, the SH-2D was powered by two 1,250 shp General Electric T58-GE-8B engines. The NADC contracted with IBM for the electronics-helicopter integration package. In the SH-2D, the copilot controlled launching of all stores, including torpedoes, sonobuoys, and smoke markers, and extending the MAD bird on its cable. He was also responsible for navigation, communications, and electronic countermeasures (ECM). A sensor operator, or "senso," was seated, facing forward in the aft left cabin to monitor and interpret displays, such as MAD readings, radar, and sonobuoy data. Avionics equipment modules were located mainly in the cabin, the fuselage, or the nose. The key piece of equipment for the ASMD mission was an off-the-shelf Canadian Marconi LN-66HP search radar, whose antenna was housed in a circular, tublike, honeycomb fiberglass dome under the nose. While not as effective as the bulbous AN/APS-115, the LN-66HP featured adequate surface search capabilities. The ASQ-81 towed magnetic-anomaly detector was mounted on a short, strut-braced sponson on the starboard side. Both stores' stations were moved slightly aft and "hardened" to carry Mk. 44 or Mk. 46 torpedoes on Mk. 8 Mod 5 shackles. In the ASMD role of lengthy radar surface search, torpedoes could be replaced by 60-gallon external fuel tanks; ASW equipment, including the AN/ASQ-81 MAD bird, sonobuoys, and smoke markers, could also be removed. The portside doorway was replaced with a panel with push-out windows to fit a fifteen-tube launcher for AN/SSQ-41 passive or AN/SSQ-47 active sonobuoys, ejected by small explosive devices. Ejectors of four Mk. 25 marine smoke markers replaced both flotation fairings in the lower forward fuselage. The 4,000-pound-capacity cargo hook and rescue hoist were retained, allowing the aircraft to retain its utility and rescue function.

The SH-2D's avionics suite included Doppler radar, radar altimeter, navigation computer, ARR-52 sonobuoy receiver and data link (with folding antenna under the fuselage), electronic-surveillance-measuring gear, UHF direction finding, and dual ARC-59 UHF communications.

When the first SH-2D contract was signed, Kaman was converting UH-2A and B models to HH-2Ds. It was then decided to cycle all single-engine models through rework into SH-2Ds. Robert Daniel recalls:

> In 1970, a group of us fixed-wing ASW guys were "volunteered" into the LAMPS program. They sent us to NAS Willow Grove, Pennsylvania, where we installed mostly P-3 Orion avionics in a couple of standard H-2s, making them the first SH-2Ds. When we finished, they took us to NAS Lakehurst as part of HC-4.

After March 16, 1971, when the first SH-2D, BuNo 151319, made its maiden flight, the CNO announced that all 115 Seasprites then in service would be committed to the LAMPS program. As the first ten SH-2Ds were being configured, a formal Bureau of Inspection and Survey (BIS) program was established at the NATC, with Lt. Robert Parkinson as lead test pilot. Parkinson was the only Test Pilot School graduate with H-2 experience in the program. In October 1971, after BIS trials, the first two LAMPS SH-2Ds underwent trials aboard USS *Wainwright* (DLG-28). Delivery of the twenty SH-2D LAMPS Seasprites had begun in September 1971. Two aircraft were bailed to Kaman for test purposes. Like with DASH assignments, LAMPS SH-2Ds were distributed among West and East Coast parent squadrons, each assigned nine aircraft. On December 7, 1971, the first operational LAMPS detachment went aboard USS *Belknap* (DLG-26) in the Mediterranean with HC-4, which was the designated LAMPS squadron for the Atlantic Fleet. BuNo 151308 was the unit's first SH-2D deployed. The designated LAMPS squadron for the Pacific Fleet was HSL-31 (formerly HC-5), based at NAS Imperial Beach, which deployed its first SH-2D, BuNo 151333, in January 1972 aboard USS *Sterett* (DLG-31). Detachment 1 from HSL-31 returned from a seven-month Pacific cruise with an outstanding record. Both detachments developed tactics and procedures to fully exploit system capabilities, noting especially the remarkable performance of the LN-66HP radar and MAD unit. All twenty SH-2D conversions were completed by the end of March 1972. So successful were initial trials that in early May, three complete LAMPS detachments, including personnel and spares support, were airlifted by C-5 to NAS Cubi Point, Philippines, for Seventh Fleet assignments. By year's end, twelve LAMPS detachments were aboard ships of the US Fleet: four were in the Mediterranean and five in the Gulf of Tonkin. Despite the successes, Seasprite pilot David Moulton noted that

> we lost a lot of people and aircraft on early LAMPS dets, mostly tail rotor problems for a design failure. The intermediate gearbox transmits torque and changes the angle of drive from the main transmission gearbox to the tail gearbox. It wasn't strengthened enough when they added the weight of the ASW equipment. As a result, the increased torque on the gearbox created from the additional power required caused the attach points to crack and sometimes led to a failure of the gearbox—hence a tail rotor failure. We learned a lot in those first few years of LAMPS. Improvements were made—most were changes written in blood.

To better reflect their main mission, on March 1, 1972, HC-4 and HC-5 were redesignated Helicopter Anti-Submarine Squadron Light Three-Zero (HSL-30) and HSL-31, respectively, with six more squadrons to be formed. Although tests demonstrated that the decks of DE-1052 Knox-class and DE-1040 Garcia-class ocean escorts were compatible with SH-2D operations, neither class of ships had hangars large enough to accommodate the aircraft. Plans to enlarge, or add, hangars aboard groups of ships led not only to additional LAMPS helicopter orders but plans to add to the program a helicopter haul-down system and deck-traversing system. Neither system was pursued until 1973, when the premier test Seasprite, BuNo 147981, was fitted with experimental haul-down

Following extensive service with the Marine Corps as a UH-2B, in 1970, on its second return to the US Navy, BuNo 150167 became the first SH-2D LAMPS conversion, seen here on a test flight in March 1971. She served HSL-31, followed by storage at AMARC in 1977. When returned to service with HSL-34 aboard guided-missile frigate USS *Fahrion* (FFG-22), on March 10, 1986, no. 167 crashed into the Indian Ocean. *Courtesy of Kaman Aerospace Corp. via James D. Dowd*

After multiple assignments to USMC base SAR units, and conversion to SH-2D, no. 167 served HSL-31, followed by storage at AMARC. Stored aircraft had all openings and glass surfaces protectively covered. *Courtesy of Larry Wielgosz*

systems for tests at NAS Lakehurst. In August 1972, the Navy contracted with Kaman to modify twenty-five additional Seasprites to SH-2Ds, with deliveries to begin in spring 1973. But change was in the wind.

After the four HH-2Ds modified for ASW and ASMD evaluations had completed their DV-98 assignment in late 1971, they were converted to SH-2Ds, two of which became experimental YSH-2Es for further exploration of LAMPS II configurations with advanced systems. The pair (BuNos 149033 and 150181), which made their first flights on March 7 and 28, 1972, respectively, technically accounted for prototype Mark II of the DV-98 program. Brian Stecher, then a newly minted lieutenant and helicopter aircraft commander (HAC), was one of the West Coast pilots on the DV-98 project, which was run at NADC, Warminster, Pennsylvania. His logbook states that in September 1972, HSL-31 formed a detachment to support DV-98, with aircrew and maintainers at NAS Imperial Beach. They received two aircraft from NADC: YSH-2Es BuNos 149033 and 150181. From December 1 to 7, 1972, he and Lt. Dan Ellision ferried BuNo 149033 back to NADC. Lieutenant Commanders Jackmon and Curtis ferried 150181. Originally, all LAMPS SH-2Ds after the first twenty examples were to fall under LAMPS II classification as better-equipped SH-2Es. The expanded ASW and ASST capabilities proven by the YSH-2Es had prompted CNO Zumwalt to cancel the LAMPS II program in late 1972 to advance to another model. Success with the YSH-2Es led to the SH-2F model, labeled the "Improved LAMPS I." Zumwalt ordered that LAMPS become operational in six months. Test results that had been gathered by HSL-31 with the YSH-2E during mid-1972 aboard USS *Fox* led to specifications for LAMPS Mark III, with improved subsystems. The term "Anti-Ship Missile Defense" (ASMD), which early in the program was called Cruise Missile Defense, then fell into disuse.

Prominent among the YSH-2E's expanded technological capabilities was a Texas Instruments AN/APS-124 (XJ-5) maritime surveillance radar housed in a large, spherical radome under the nose, replacing the SH-2D's LN-66. Like the LN-66 and AN/APS-115 surface search radar, the AN/APS-124 could detect small targets such as submarine periscopes and fliers' equipment. Knowledge gained in development of this radar was useful in development of advanced radar, which was adopted for future LAMPS helicopters. Both the AN/APS-115 and the MAD were standard equipment on Navy Lockheed P-3 Orion maritime patrol aircraft.

The marked change in the YSH-2E's interior was the absence of the sensor operator as the result of NADC's intensive program to evaluate a two-man concept that relied on a new instrument panel with a multipurpose function display. Five associated equipment racks in the cabin filled the former senso's position, but the cabin doorway was left clear for rescue operations. The YSH-2Es were updated with all the improvements slated for the SH-2F, with the addition of ripple-fire emergency jettison of the fifteen sonobuoys, plus prototype installation of bleed-air pressurization of external fuel tanks. As

The SH-2D BuNo 152190 served as a test platform assigned to HC-4. Fitted with a horizontally installed twelve-tube sonobuoy launcher and ASW test equipment on its starboard side, no. 190 comes aboard the guided-missile cruiser USS *Belknap* (DLG-26) in choppy seas.

Bob Daniel was among the crew that modified the first SH-2Ds into LAMPS helicopters. In 1970, the group was sent to NAS Willow Grove, Pennsylvania, where it installed mainly P-3 Orion avionics in two H-2s to become the first SH-2Ds. The group was then assigned to HC-4 at NAS Lakehurst and, in 1971, made the first LAMPS cruise aboard USS *Belknap*. One of the first LAMPS Seasprites, BuNo 152190 of DV-98, prepares for takeoff from *Belknap*'s helicopter deck. In the background is *Belknap*'s Mk. 42 5-inch gun. *Courtesy of Robert Daniel collection*

In 1971, extended evaluation of the ASW portion of LAMPS was conducted by NADC with two HH-2Ds. The two-helicopter, nineteen-man Det. 26 of HC-4 flew day and night for three weeks to prove the LAMPS theory of ASW tactics. One of the Seasprites occupies the ship's landing pad previously built for DASH aircraft. Hangars for DASHs eventually were enlarged to accommodate LAMPS Seasprites. *Courtesy of US Navy*

development of the SH-2F progressed, the YSH-2Es continued a busy test schedule, which included evaluating the performance of new systems and applying them to tactical procedures and ship interface tests off Cape May, NAS Norfolk, at sea, and at the Atlantic Undersea Test and Evaluation Center (AUTEC) in the Bahamas.

Evaluation of the Seasprite included arming the NUH-2C BuNo 147981 with the Sparrow III air-to-air missile to determine the effects of firing and guidance of the missile from a helicopter, as compared to launching from a fixed-wing aircraft. In mid-July 1972, four missiles were fired during a three-day test demonstration at the Pacific Missile Range–Sea Test Range, Pt. Mugu, California. The tests, which were conducted by the NATC and Raytheon Company, were successful. Although it was hoped that the attack weapons capability would add greatly to the LAMPS ASMD role, the concept received no further consideration.

Throughout years of intricate testing of Seasprite models by various agencies, model designation changes proved difficult to follow. The designation YSH-2E seems to have been used interchangeably with HH-2Ds; officially, two YSH-2Es existed, while six HH-2Ds are known to have been used for testing: four on the West Coast and two on the East Coast. Confounding accurate identification of specific aircraft were numerous equipment changes and modifications, numerous military and commercial testing agencies, and long delays in changing model designations painted on aircraft tails. Contradiction of model designations is abundant in published material, often at no fault of the writers, depending on the photographs and reports they referenced. Although the LAMPS program was very slow "getting out of the gate," the six-month deadline for completion following the cancellation of DV-98 left little time for deciding designation changes and developing multiple test-bed aircraft. In the following excerpts from his speech at the commissioning ceremony for HSL-32 on August 17, 1973, RAdm. Donald V. Cox summarized LAMPS:

> Commissioning of this squadron represents a real milestone to the Atlantic Fleet, to Naval Aviation, to the Destroyer Force, to the LAMPS program, and to the increase of our Naval capability to control the seas . . . times have been hard for the Navy in these years. While the Vietnam war was on, the Navy tightened its belt everywhere else to do what had to be done in Southeast Asia . . . with the decreasing funds available to us, everything which doesn't bear great future promise is being culled out—ships, aircraft, bases, and people. In LAMPS, a manned-aircraft program replaced a drone. The program took a utility aircraft which just happened to be available, and made into one of our most effective and respected tactical aircraft. Today these aircraft operate regularly in tactical environments from the decks of ships—known rather ignominiously in the aviation community as non-aviation ships. Ships whose designers had no idea such a thing would happen to them. In fact, the major class ship in the LAMPS program, the 1052 class destroyer escort, had been on the rocks. The 1052 was a beautiful new ship, still building in quantity, but it was being so roundly criticized that the very existence of the remaining ships in the program was in jeopardy. It was pictured as an expensive new ship—delivered in the seventies but built for World War II missions. LAMPS pulled this ship off the rocks—out of the past and into the future.
>
> What makes this program so important and so valued at all levels to the future of the Navy? The growth of the Soviet Navy, and we are reducing the numbers of our ships and aircraft—each will be expected to do more and do it more effectively. LAMPS certainly fills this ticket. The forthcoming SH-2F is pound-for-pound the most potent tactical ASW and surveillance aircraft in the business—combined with a ship it can reach any part of the world's waters. The system can cover many times more ocean in both looking for targets and attacking them than either could do alone. One of the 1052[-] class DEs with LAMPS can now do the job that formerly took three to four ships.

The "front office" of BuNo 149033 during LAMPS evaluation. The large screen is a tactical display. *Courtesy of US Navy*

A towed MAD does its work trailing an SH-2D by its cable. *Courtesy of US Navy*

Below: Evaluation of the Seasprite for the LAMPS role was expanded to include arming test aircraft NUH-2C BuNo 147981 with AIM-7C Sparrow III missiles, seen here at NAS Point Mugu, California, in mid-July 1972. Three days of test firing of the missile took place at the Pacific Missile Range. Fire control radar was housed in a nose radome reportedly fashioned from that of an F-4E Phantom. *Courtesy of US Navy*

BuNo 151332 was one of a number of HH-2Ds bailed to Kaman to test various LAMPS systems. A Sparrow missile was temporarily displayed alongside the aircraft in 1968 to simulate the missile's mounting location. Raytheon's radar-guided AIM-7C Sparrow III missile was 12 feet in length and weighed 500 pounds. *Courtesy of US Navy and Kaman Aerospace Corp.*

A torpedo on its dolly is loaded onto an SH-2D. *Courtesy of US Navy*

BuNo 150166 is chocked and chained to the deck, after which crewmen will fold the main rotor blades to prevent their damage in high wind. Navy regulations required that national insignia on aircraft top surfaces have the star pointing forward. *Courtesy of US Navy*

Prior to conversion to YSH-2E, the HH-2D BuNo 149033 served as test bed for the bulbous AN/APS-115 radar at NADC Warminster in mid-1972. The Mk. 25 smoke float ejector was also mounted to the aircraft for testing. *Courtesy of Stephen Miller*

Two YSH-2Es identified experimental development aircraft intended for LAMPS, with expanded ASW and ASST capabilities. Findings were incorporated into the SH-2F after the LAMPS II program was canceled for advancement to LAMPS III. Under-nose was APS-124 radar, while eight-unit Mk. 25 marine smoke markers occupied the area under both sides of the cockpit. The pitot tube was relocated above the windshield. *Courtesy of US Navy*

BuNo 149033 fully converted to YSH-2E for LAMPS II trials until cancellation of the program. White radomes atop the nose and on the ventral tail boom housed data-link antennas. Four square units on the nose doors corresponded to the ALR-47 ESM system. Visible on the trailing edge of the tail rotor pylon is an aft-facing AN/ALR-66 ESM antenna. *Courtesy of US Navy via Harold M. Troxell*

A Mk. 46 torpedo mounted to BuNo 151308 of HSL-30, the first SH-2D for the Atlantic Fleet. The lanyard for releasing the torpedo's parachute is visible, attached to the aircraft below the national insignia. *Courtesy of US Navy*

Lt. (j.g.) David W. Moulton Sr. is greeted by Capt. Robertson, skipper of USS *Wainwright* (DLG-28), in 1972. The occasion was the five hundredth landing aboard the guided-missile frigate, with Moulton flying the first SH-2D (BuNo 151308) of the Atlantic Fleet. *Wainwright* tested her new LAMPS system from January to September 1972. *Courtesy of Capt. David W. Moulton Sr., US Navy (ret.)*

Like its successor SH-2F, the SH-2D carried Mk. 25 marine smoke floats in place of emergency flotation bags. Square-shaped housings on the nose of BuNo 150166 of HSL-31 contained antennae for the radar-warning receiver system. The LN-66HP surveillance radar tub is painted the aircraft color, versus its usual bronze finish. *Courtesy of US Navy*

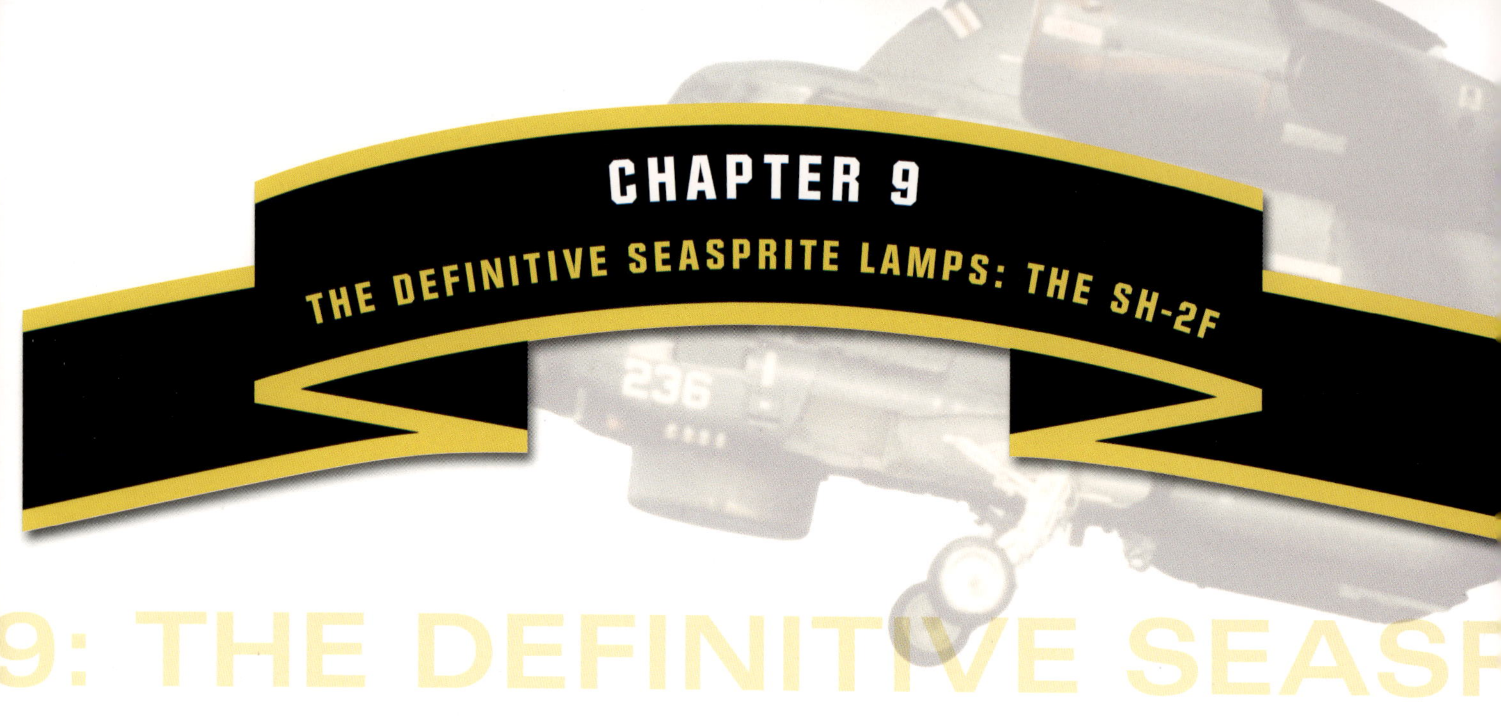

CHAPTER 9
THE DEFINITIVE SEASPRITE LAMPS: THE SH-2F

9: THE DEFINITIVE SEASP

Although the LAMPS MK II program was canceled, the valuable lessons learned from trials with the YSH-2Es led to the improved LAMPS MK I, designated SH-2F, the seventh model designation of the Seasprite. The YSH-2Es would be converted to SH-2Fs in 1976. The SH-2D BuNo 150159 served as the SH-2F prototype, which was first flown on September 5, 1972. The first Navy contract for SH-2Fs was let in February 1973. During the conversion period, SH-2Ds, which had performed stellar service since late 1971, would continue to shoulder the load, pending the arrival of SH-2Fs. Significant changes in the SH-2F were the new 101 rotor system, the latest avionics, and more-powerful twin T58-GE-8F turbine engines of 1,350 horsepower each. Takeoff gross weight then was 12,800 pounds, which was later certified for 13,500 pounds on the basis of a structural demonstration program conducted by Kaman. Significant increases in power through various models brought into question how the original fuselage carried increases in gross weight. In reengineering the SH-2F, the upper frame structure was beefed up not only to handle weight and maneuver stresses, but to ensure a lifetime without component fatigue. Kaman chose steel tubing from the Timken Company of North Canton, Ohio, to fabricate the main transmission support connecting the power plant to the fuselage.

The SH-2F's range was 340 nautical miles (391 statute miles), and it had a maximum speed of 153 mph (133 knots). To give pilots an edge in all-weather landings on small boys, the main landing gear was strengthened by increasing the aircraft's sink rate and improving its energy absorption capability. This was accomplished by replacing the liquid spring and axle and using a higher-capacity tailwheel. Pilots attempted to land when the deck was near level in a "null period." That was not always possible, especially in sea conditions of random rather than repetitious ship motions, requiring landing on rolling deck angles. The most noticeable change was relocation of the tailwheel 6 feet forward to shorten the Seasprite's footprint to 17 feet for additional deck-edge clearance on small flight decks. The pilot then could put the main gear anywhere in the 24-foot-diameter landing circle, while lined up on the approach line, with no fear that the tailwheel would miss the deck. The SH-2F could carry Mk. 11 depth charges or two Mk. 46 homing torpedoes in place of 60-gallon external fuel tanks. The Mk. 46 was the standard NATO antisubmarine air-launched torpedo. Advancements in Soviet submarine hull technology, however, would soon make the weapon almost obsolete.

Dimensions of the H-2 remained nearly constant through all models. The SH-2F's overall length, with main and tail rotor, was 52 feet, 7 inches. Folding all rotors and fully opening the clamshell nose doors reduced its length to 38 feet, 4 inches. The main landing gear spanned 11 feet, 7 inches, while overall width of the aircraft with the MAD installation was 12 feet, 3 inches. Main rotor diameter was 44 feet, and tail rotor diameter was 8 feet, 2 inches.

A total of 104 SH-2Fs were produced from earlier versions of the Seasprite between 1972 and 1982. Of this total, seventy-nine were converted from UH-2Cs, six from HH-2Cs, seventeen from SH-2Ds, and two from YSH-2Es. All

ITE LAMPS: THE SH-2F

The SH-2D BuNo 150159 served as the SH-2F prototype and became the first operational SH-2F. The 3-foot-diameter "tub" beneath the cockpit housed the Canadian Marconi LN-66HP radar, which had been introduced on the SH-2D. This surface search radar had a range of 36 miles and became the standard for US Navy LAMPS helicopters. An ESM antenna is located below the tail rotor warning band, while the blade antenna aft of the tailwheel corresponded to UHF radios communication. *Courtesy of US Navy*

surviving Seasprites, with the exception of BuNos 149031 and 147981 test aircraft, were converted to SH-2Fs. BuNo 149031 was the last HH-2D in the Navy. As part of HSL-31's Detachment Bravo, it was the only aircraft entirely officered by women naval aviators, who were allowed aboard USNS research ships to which Det. Bravo was assigned.

LAMPS GOES TO WORK

In contrast to the DASH program, the LAMPS program could be successful only with integration of the helicopter and surface ship communities. In the early days of LAMPS, fleet personnel were unreceptive to the concept. The sonobuoy had not yet been proven in an ASW community comfortable with the established dipping sonar. The culture clash that existed between a LAMPS aviation contingent aboard a nonaviation surface ship eased, since the senior pilot assumed responsibility for flight operations, basically unburdening the ship's captain in order for him to focus on ship operations.

The SH-2F was delivered to the Navy in May 1973, with HSL-33 making the first shipboard landing of an SH-2F on a Pacific Fleet destroyer on August 11, aboard USS *Bagley* (DE 1069); the squadron had begun service aboard *Bagley* in June. As more SH-2F LAMPS aircraft were delivered, additional HSL squadrons were established.

Prior to the SH-2F's arrival, on March 1, 1972, East Coast HC-4 had been redesignated HSL-30, and West Coast HC-5 had been redesignated HSL-31. Eventually the total force of SH-2Fs was distributed among eleven squadrons consisting of eight frontline units, two of which also functioned as fleet replacement squadrons, and three reserve units. Allocation of the LAMPS force followed the standard US Navy practice of East and West Coast assignments to service their respective fleets. Accordingly, four even-numbered squadrons with two-letter tail codes beginning with an H served the Atlantic Fleet, four odd-numbered squadrons with two-letter tail codes beginning with a T serviced the Pacific Fleet, and three squadrons, with eight Seasprites each, all using tail code NW, were assigned to the Naval Reserve. Their breakdown is as follows.

HSL-33 "Seasnakes" was the first squadron dedicated solely to providing LAMPS detachments for like-configured ships of the Pacific Fleet; HSL-32 did likewise for Atlantic Fleet ships. White strips painted on tail rotor blades made it easier to spot cracks during inspections. The strips were added after investigation of a crash in Italy in 1974 revealed tail rotor blade failure due to cracks as the cause. In addition, the stripes aided in avoiding mixing of metal and later fiberglass rotor blades. *Courtesy of US Navy*

ATLANTIC FLEET

HSL-30 "Neptune's Horsemen," call sign Scooter; tail code HT; motto was "Service to the Fleet" and "LAMPS to light the way"; established as HU-4 at NAS Lakehurst on July 1, 1960; first East Coast HSL squadron; by 1969

The SH-2F continued the Engine Gray livery for its family of Seasprites and followed the Navy practice of white wheel wells. Dual fuel fillers appear immediately aft of the rescue/pilot's door, while the single-point pressure fueling port for "hot" refueling is below the national insignia. *Courtesy of Don Brabec collection*

Following duty in the Persian Gulf aboard USS *LaSalle* in 1974, BuNo 149750 was converted from HH-2D to SH-2F, which meant another change in livery, from white to Engine Gray. *Courtesy of Ray Wilhite collection*

Noted aviation photographer Stephen Miller captured no. 750 with a change in assignment to the NATC at NAS "Pax" in September 1974.

After extensive service as a test platform and having undergone four model conversions, the last known assignment for SH-2F BuNo 150169 was HSL-37. No. 169 comes aboard USS *Fox* off Southern California in July 1977. *Courtesy of Rick Morgan*

flew only UH-2B, switching to HH-2D in 1970; provided dets for US Sixth Fleet and Middle East Force; redesignated HSL-30 on March 1, 1972, relocated to NAS Norfolk in July 1973, with squadron split to form HSL-32; primary missions changed to ASW/ASST and became training unit for SH-2D/F for Atlantic Fleet; as such, provided air and ground crews for Atlantic HSLs and VX-1; disestablished on September 30, 1993.

HSL-32 "Red Tridents," call sign Invader; tail code HV; formed from HSL-30 on August 17, 1973 at NAS Norfolk, with four each SH-2Ds and SH-2Fs; Det. 3 on June 5, 1975, was aboard USS *Joseph Hewes* (DE-1078) when it became the first US Navy ship to transit reopened Suez Canal, which had been closed due to damage and sunken ships resulting from the 1967 Arab-Israeli War; involved heavily in Cold War ASW operations, with surface surveillance and over the horizon the dominant mission; in 1977 tracked three Soviet submarines in Mediterranean for three days; in 1987 deployed the first specially modified SH-2Fs for Middle East combat operations; prior to that, the tridents evaluated the AN/DLQ-3A jammer; deployed five detachments during Desert Shield / Desert Storm; as the last East Coast LAMPS MK I detachment, the Invader's Det. 9 in 1993 supported CVN-71 battle group and United Nations operations; disestablished on January 31, 1994.

HSL-34 "the Professionals," call sign Green Checkers; tail code HX; established on September 27, 1974, at NAS Norfolk. Three days later, the squadron began flight operations with forty-two men and one SH-2D, making its first shipboard landing on December 6 aboard USS *Truett* (FF-1095). The squadron grew to full strength with fifty-one officers, 190 enlisted men, ten H-2s, and eight detachments. Detachments (which were first formed in March 1975) generally deployed to the Mediterranean and North Atlantic for four to six months; during the 1980s, participated in operations off Grenada, Central America, Lebanon, and Persian Gulf, along with deployments in the North Atlantic, South Atlantic, Southeast Pacific, and Baltic regions; disestablished on November 30, 1993.

HSL-36 "Lamplighters," call sign Lamplighter; tail code HY; established on September 26, 1975, at NS Mayport, Florida; by the second anniversary of commissioning, the squadron had operated in all oceans of the world while embarked on East Coast–based ships; in 1980, HSL-36 deployed the first detachments aboard a Spruance-class destroyer and a Perry-class frigate; in 1984, the Lamplighters was the first East Coast squadron to receive new production SH-2F aircraft; at one point in 1986, HSL-36 deployed nine of its ten detachments simultaneously in the region of Libya; disestablished on September 30, 1992.

An SH-2F of HSL-36 hoists a photographer's mate from the Dutch frigate HRMS *Callenburgh* (F-808) during FLEET EX 1-90 in the Atlantic. The Dutch navy does not permit foreign aircraft to land aboard its ships. Details clearly visible include the folded sonobuoy antenna on the belly, the surface search radar tub, and the oblique searchlight in the nose. The new tactical color scheme for SH-2Fs was Dark Ghost Gray (FS36320), with Medium Gray (FS35237) for top surfaces, and Light Gray (FS36595) for undersurfaces. *Courtesy of US Navy*

PACIFIC FLEET

HSL-31 "Archangels," call sign Archangel, later Copyright; tail code TD; redesignated from HC-5 on March 1, 1972, at NAS Imperial Beach to provide LAMPS detachments for the Pacific Fleet; became replacement training squadron on July 31, 1973, to train SH-2F pilots in ASW, ASST, and utility missions, plus maintenance; Survival, Evasion, Resistance, and Escape (SERE); and Deep-Water Environmental Survival Training (DWEST); also maintenance personnel in the SH-2F, and aircrewmen as ASW operators, Aircrew Swim School, MAD operation, radar detection and tracking, sonobuoy data, and weapons stems; HSL-31 provided a detachment for the oceanographic support ship USNS *Chauvenet* (T-AGS-29) with an HH-2D, rotating three officers and eight enlisted personnel every six months; disestablished on July 31, 1992.

HSL-33 "Sea Snakes," call sign Sea Snake; tail code TF; established on July 31, 1973, at NAS Imperial Beach with thirteen detachments; first West Coast fleet squadron after splitting from HSL-31; served multiple deployments off Vietnam, and in Persian Gulf, the Mediterranean-Lebanon, and Indian Ocean; in 1973 Det. 3 aboard USS *Cook* (DE-1083) with SH-2D worked with Japanese Navy Midshipman Program and Korean navy; Det. 2 participated in exercise "Longex 73," which included British, Australian, New Zealand, and Dutch naval forces; disestablished on April 29, 1994.

HSL-35 "Magicians," call sign Magus; tail code TG; established on January 1, 1974, at NAS Imperial Beach, organized into thirteen detachments of one SH-2F each with three officers and eight enlisted men; disestablished on December 4, 1992.

HSL-37 "Easy Riders," call sign Easy Rider; tail code TH; established at NAS Barbers Point, Hawaii, on July 3, 1975; on February 6, 1992, HSL-37 became first and only squadron to transition from SH-2F to the SH-60B Seahawk LAMPS MK III, then operated as composite LAMPS MK I/MK III squadron until October 1, 1993; unit received its first MH-60R in September 2013; redesignated HSM-37 in January 2014.

On February 8, 1973, Det. Cubi was commissioned to support LAMPS and other H-2 detachments deployed in the western Pacific (WestPac). Due to the small size of detachments, personnel with a wide range of maintenance experience were not always available. Det. Cubi was formed, therefore, as a forward unit with highly qualified technicians and supply personnel to expedite technical assistance and requests for parts.

Details made clear by this view are the Seasprite's landing-gear track, which was 11 feet, 7 inches. The LN-66 radar housing was mounted slightly off-center to starboard. Seasprite veterans agree that the offset resulted from the placement of other electronic equipment, or structural issues that required more-secure mounting. Dual Doppler antennas protrude from the aft tail boom. The trio of lights under the nose functioned as a retractable landing light, a floodlight on the port nose door, and an oblique spotlight to illuminate rescue hoist operation. *Courtesy of US Navy*

NAVAL AIR RESERVE

HSL-74 "Demon-Elves," tail code NW; redesignated from HS-74 on April 1, 1985, at NAS South Weymouth, Massachusetts; weekend training had four detachments flying the SH-2F, supporting several 1052-class frigates at Newport, Rhode Island; disestablished on April 1, 1994.

HSL-84 "Thunderbolts," tail code NW; redesignated from HS-84 (an SH-3D squadron) on March 1, 1984, at NAS North Island; received its first SH-2G in December 1992; The Thunderbolts in September 1996 led a battle group consisting of fixed-wing patrol aircraft, surface ships, and a LAMPS III helicopter to a simulated submarine kill in the "Wolfhunt" competition off the California coast; disestablished on June 30, 2001.

A LAMPS SH-2F comes aboard the destroyer and exercise flagship USS *Thorn* (DD-988) during Operation UNITAS XXV in June 1984. During the exercise, the Seasprite teamed with Brazilian forces to conduct ASW operations. The ubiquitous Playboy bunny adorned the LN-66 radome. The square nose-mounted fairing was an antenna that provided hemispheric coverage for the radar-warning receiver. *Courtesy of US Navy*

When the US Navy divested itself of its frigates (which were designated destroyer escorts until 1975) and Seasprites, thousands of sailors and naval aviators bid farewell to forty years of service performed by the landmark union of sub-hunter ship and helicopter. USS *Robert E. Peary* (FF-1073), seen here off San Francisco in October 1981, was loaned to Taiwan in mid-1992 and stricken from the US Navy register in November 1995. *Courtesy of US Navy*

HSL-94 "Titans," tail code NW; established on October 1, 1985, at NAS Willow Grove, Pennsylvania; in March 1994 the Titans began transitioning from the SH-2F to the SH-2G for a total of eight Super Seasprites; the following year, the squadron completed a six-month sea deployment as part of UNITAS joint exercises with Latin American navies; the Titans in December 1996 received two Magic Lantern mine detection systems; for annual training in 1997, went aboard USS *Stark* (FFG-31) to participate in NATO Naval Forces Atlantic exercises; disestablished on April 1, 2001.

Since September 1973, all LAMPS detachments were SH-2F equipped. Through August 1974, fifty-four LAMPS detachments had deployed on long cruises: twenty-four from East Coast squadrons and thirty from West Coast squadrons.

Parent to Helicopter Anti-Submarine Squadrons were various naval aircraft wings such as commander, Helicopter Sea Control Wing 1 (CHSCW-1), which oversaw the training, administration, and support of Atlantic Fleet LAMPS MK I squadrons. The commander, in turn, reported to commander, Helicopter Wings, Atlantic. During its nineteen-year history, which began in June 1973, CHSCW-1 has deployed units to every world ocean and directly supported operations such as the Iranian rescue mission; operations during the Lebanon-Israel war, Beirut; Operation Ernest Will; and Operations Desert Shield and Desert Storm in the Persian Gulf, plus support of Mediterranean, NATO, and UNITAS exercises; the latter were exercises with Latin American navies. Counter drug operations became a staple for the Seasprite, usually conducted with US Coast Guard cutters in the Caribbean. In February 1980, the "HSL LAMPS Mobile Support Detachment" was established as part of the HSL wing at NAS Sigonella, Sicily, to bolster LAMPS readiness within the European, Middle East, and Indian Ocean regions.

The "front office" of the SH-2F. The pilot's collective lever is at lower right, and the copilot's cyclic control stick is center foreground. *Courtesy of US Navy*

The sensor operator's position from the cargo doorway of SH-2F BuNo 151326. *Courtesy of US Navy*

The only test facility regularly assigned Seasprites was Air Test and Evaluation Squadron 1 (VX-1) "Pioneers," at NAS Patuxent River, Maryland (at NAS Key West prior to 1973). Since it was established on April 1, 1943, at Quonset Point, Rhode Island, VX-1 has maintained in its inventory at least two of each ASW aircraft type, both fixed wing and rotary wing, wearing tail code JA. Throughout its long history, the squadron conducted operational test and evaluation of ASW aircraft and maritime anti-surface-warfare systems and developed tactics and training for their use.

Although the primary missions of the SH-2F were ASW and ASST, various combinations of equipment, including torpedoes, fuel tanks, sonobuoys, smoke markers, and electronic systems, allowed numerous mission profiles, which included SAR, VertRep, Medevac, gunfire support, surveillance, personnel transfer, mine hunting, and utility transport. Beginning in the early 1980s, SH-2F crews, using the aircraft's tactical navigation system, were tasked more frequently with surface surveillance and over-the-horizon targeting for its ship's long-range Harpoon or Tomahawk surface-to-surface missiles. The Harpoon, which was introduced in 1979, had a range of 150 nautical miles, while the Tomahawk, introduced in 1983, could travel 1,500 miles.

An HSL typically supported ten single-aircraft detachments, each comprising three or four pilots, two sensor operators, and from six to eleven maintenance specialists. A detachment formed approximately one month prior to a planned deployment for training and preparation. As the host ship's aviation department, detachments were operationally responsible to the ship's captain, while the detachment remained under the control of the HSL for administrative and maintenance matters. The officer in charge of the detachment was a lieutenant commander or senior lieutenant with experience flying the SH-2F at sea. Requirements called for one pilot, other than the OIC, to be qualified as a helicopter aircraft commander (HAC), and to be qualified to perform postmaintenance checks. Officer ranks included a maintenance officer and operations officer. Among the enlisted crew, the two sensor operators were rated as aviation anti-submarine-warfare operators (AWs). Prominent among the ranks of flying ASW technicians, these "sensos" served as radar operators, acoustic analyzers, MAD trace interpreters, and helicopter crewmen, who doubled as trained rescue swimmers. All the corrective and preventive maintenance at sea was performed by detachment maintenance personnel who were specialists in airframe, hydraulics, turboshaft engines, electrical systems, avionics, and ASW mission equipment. Being distant from major maintenance facilities, they learned each other's trade to perform as a team, most desirably as a tight-knit, well-functioning group.

The AN/ASQ-81 magnetic-anomaly detector, unofficially called "the MAD Bird," was standard equipment on the SH-2F's starboard external mount. When towed on its cable 180 feet from the aircraft, the nonmagnetic unit detected disturbances in the earth's magnetic field caused by the presence of large metallic objects. Its effectiveness was determined to be secondary to sonobuoys. The cone-shaped, perforated skirt stabilized the MAD body. Inboard of the MAD was a 60-gallon auxiliary fuel tank. *Courtesy of US Navy*

The SH-2F BuNo 150164 of HSL-33, with markings on its fuel tank for USS *Hammond* (FF-1067). The Seasprite wears an "E" Efficiency Award on its nose. *Courtesy of Mike Wilson*

Members of HSL-94 aboard guided-missile frigate USS *Clark* (FFG-11) give a squadron SH-2F a freshwater wash-down in October 1990. Corrosion control was a never-ending task in the Seasprite's environment. *Courtesy of US Navy*

Beginning in 1983 with BuNo 161907, from the second batch of new production SH-2Fs, increases in gross weight were authorized, allowing 60-gallon external fuel tanks to be replaced by 100-gallon tanks. Named "Michelle," no. 907, in very dark-gray livery, served HSL-34 "the Professionals," which was home-based at NAS Norfolk. *Author's collection*

"Magus 3-8," SH-2F BuNo 149758 of HSL-35 "Magicians," flies over San Diego's Coronado Bridge in 1970. *Courtesy of Michael Coumatos collection*

This SH-2F lies on the flight deck of USS *Trippe* (DE-1075) after crashing aboard at Roosevelt Roads, Puerto Rico, in February 1978. *Trippe* was overhauled in 1973 to operate LAMPS helicopters. Dual oval-shaped navigational antennas are visible on the lower tail boom. *Courtesy of US Navy*

The spirit of HSLs, as with many small military groups, was evident by colorful unit and personal markings that embellished the aircraft.

Some HSLs began operations with a small number of SH-2Ds, eventually becoming all-SH-2F LAMPS MK I units as conversions left the factory. The first few years saw many growing pains as supply and maintenance problems were addressed and tactics were developed. Ship conversion and outfitting for LAMPS detachments usually outpaced manning and training of LAMPS detachments. As conditions steadily improved, an ample supply of spare parts were carried on board LAMPS ships, often with storekeepers responsible for those parts. Ships to which HSL detachments were assigned included frigates, guided-missile frigates, destroyers, guided-missile destroyers, cruisers, battleships, Coast Guard cutters, supply ships, and amphibious assault ships.

Of interest is this perspective on the SH-2F, and Seasprite in general, by Rich Jaeger, who not only spent the majority of his at-sea Navy flying career in all versions of the H-2 (with the exception of the SH-2G) but served simultaneously as test pilot for both Kaman and Sikorsky:

> One aspect of the H-2 community that is unique for a specific aircraft is how the H-2 was used when compared to other helicopters (alone vs. squadron). I'm addressing the relationship between the operators/maintainers with a specific aircraft. Much of the H-2 development was driven by the USN employment of the aircraft after the early 1970s—that being single aircraft detachment operations from the decks of small ships with limited spare-parts support, often on independent operations. The result was an unusual, intimate relationship between the aircraft and its crew, sometimes resulting with great readiness and performance throughout the six-month deployment; at times, unfortunately, just the opposite.
>
> The LAMPS MK I mission matured when maintenance training, parts supply, and shipboard facilities matured, and the small maintenance crew had to meet the readiness requirements of the mission from the back of a small ship with a flight deck close to the water.
>
> Once mastered by a detachment maintenance crew, their H-2 helicopter (in my opinion and that of Kaman test pilots) would be among the smoothest helicopters to fly in all regimes. That was particularly evident when I was assigned as executive officer to

the Navy office at Sikorsky in Connecticut. When I'd fly a government-acceptance test flight in a new H-60 Blackhawk from the Sikorsky plant, I would stop midway through the flight at the Kaman factory to fly a government-acceptance flight on a new SH-2F, then finish the Blackhawk acceptance flight on my return to Sikorsky. The Sikorsky maintenance folks wanted the government to accept the aircraft at the end of our acceptance flights, as did Kaman, but they were aware that after I flew the SH-2F, I'd be more sensitive to the vibration level in the Blackhawk on the return flight, occasionally causing a maintenance action prior to acceptance.

Based on my operational and testing experience, the H-2 was a much more superior aircraft than was generally believed, mostly because the demand for quality/trained/experienced maintenance people and supply support exceeded what was available.

Most SH-2F deliveries were completed by the end of 1975, with the final batch of ten converted from SH-2Ds joining the fleet in March 1982. After 1975, FRAM destroyers were replaced as ASW ships by Knox-class frigates and destroyer escorts, and Spruance-class destroyers. Both types featured improved ASROC systems and LAMPS helicopters.

THE SEASPRITE GETS BETTER

Citing a shortage of airframes to convert to SH-2Fs, Kaman, from 1982 to 1986, reopened the Seasprite line to produce fifty-four SH-2Fs from the ground up. This order came on the heels of a review of US armed forces by the new Reagan administration, which resulted in authorization of a large-scale military buildup, including more than doubling the number of Navy ships. After the SH-2F had been fully flight-tested at higher alternate gross weights, the Navy authorized an increased maximum takeoff weight of 13,300 pounds, which identified the ASW mission. The ASMD/ASST mission used the maximum fuel load of 3,509 pounds, but with fewer external stores, weighing in at 13,200 pounds. Gross weight for the search-and-rescue mission was 12,275 pounds. New gross weight allowances resulted in the switch from 60- to 100-gallon external fuel tanks, which increased mission endurance; this pushed the ASST mission up to two hours and twenty minutes. The F model's internal fuel capacity was 276 gallons in four fuselage tanks. The change also allowed the SH-2F to carry the Mk. 50 Barracuda torpedo, which, although labeled "lightweight," was 300 pounds heavier than the Mk. 46. Other improvements

The diagonal blue-and-yellow band on the tail rotor pylon of this new production SH-2F was a later marking of HSL-33 Seasprites. BuNo 161651 "Seasnake 1-7" crashed in the Persian Gulf in November 1988. *Courtesy of Gordon Permann*

Mounting a Mk. 66 practice torpedo, SH-2F BuNo 150142 of Task Force 14 flies over San Diego in April 1976. "Seasnake 1-4" wears bicentennial markings below the cargo door window. *Courtesy of US Navy via National Naval Aviation Museum*

This fixed-wing pilot, who likely was waiting to be transferred to his carrier by the SH-2F, wears a life preserver required for overwater flight. He grips one of two retractable steps of the bulkhead. *Courtesy of US Navy*

The AW of this SH-2F prepares to lower the rescue hoist cable. Forward-retracting landing-gear doors often were eliminated for ease of inspection and maintenance of the landing gear. *Courtesy of US Navy*

included simplified fuel and electrical systems, separate hydraulics for automatic stabilization equipment, an improved tail rotor, crash-resistant seats, improved doors, and ripple-fire sonobuoys that could be ejected in an emergency.

Of more than 170 cruisers, destroyers, and frigates then in the US Navy that were capable of operating LAMPS helicopters, seventy-two were configured for the LAMPS MK I, while eighty (frigates, cruisers, and destroyers) were, or were slated to be, configured for larger LAMPS MK III helicopters, two per ship. In addition, sixteen battleships, along with Coast Guard cutters, were planned for MK I modifications. The Navy order for fifty-four new airframes would provide a sufficient number of SH-2F helicopters to fill the requirements for the LAMPS MK I mission. New production was listed in the 1982 defense budget as an order for eighteen new-build SH-2Fs, plus eighteen additional in 1983, with orders to follow, totaling fifty-four aircraft. The latest airframe and avionics changes incorporated into fleet SH-2Fs were built into the new machines. These changes included AN/ALQ-66A(V)1 radar-warning receivers and AN/ALE-39 chaff/flare dispensers.

Subassemblies were begun at Kaman's plant at Moosup, Connecticut, in mid-February 1982, with airframe deliveries begun at the end of the year. Rollout of the new-build SH-2F, with BuNo 161641, occurred in June 1983, four months ahead of schedule. Deliveries began in early December, with the final example delivered in 1986. It was anticipated that the SH-2F would be in service alongside the LAMPS MK III until the end of the twentieth century and beyond.

Preparations are made to launch this well-secured SH-2F BuNo 151303 of HSL-34, Det. 8, from USS *John Hancock* (DD-981) off San Clemente, California, in February 1986. *Courtesy of US Navy*

United Technology Sikorsky Division's submission for the LAMPS III competition was its model S-70L, later designated SH-60B Seahawk. The Seahawk (based on the Army's UH-60A Blackhawk) was chosen over Boeing-Vertol's model 237 in September 1977, and in February 1978 the US Department of Defense awarded Sikorsky a contract for development of the SH-60B. IBM Federal Systems would continue development of the avionics necessary for the Seahawk to fulfill the LAMPS MK III role. Shipboard trials with the SH-60B mockup occurred in mid-1978, and five YSH-60B prototypes arrived at IBM's Oswego, New York, facility for trials in April 1980.

BuNo 152201, one of two SH-2Fs assigned to Air Test and Evaluation Squadron 1 (VX-1), which was located at NAS Key West, Florida, until relocated to NAS Patuxent, Maryland, in mid-1973. VX-1's main mission is test and evaluation of airborne ASW and maritime antisurface-warfare weapon systems, along with development of ASW/SUW tactics for fleet use. BuNo 152201 later became the aircraft of the commander, Seventh Fleet, at NAS Atsugi. *Courtesy of US Navy*

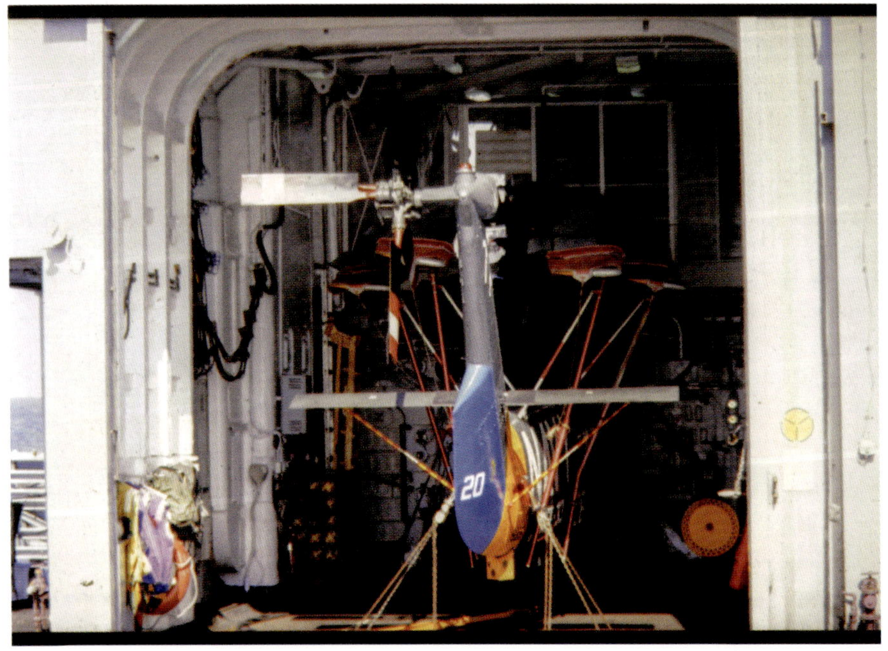

Tight squeeze for an SH-2F of HSL-30 aboard USS *Bradley* (FF-1041). Main rotor blades are folded back, and a tail rotor blade is folded inward to ensure door clearance. *Courtesy of Capt. David W. Moulton Sr., US Navy (ret.)*

An SH-2F of HSL-31 with its sonobuoy-sensing antenna deployed and armed with a Mk. 46 torpedo over the Pacific in February 1981. *Courtesy of US Navy*

Wearing artwork on its auxiliary fuel tank and sonobuoy cover, SH-2F BuNo 151321 of HSL-34, Det. 7, hovers above the carrier USS *Saratoga* in January 1986. *Courtesy of US Navy*

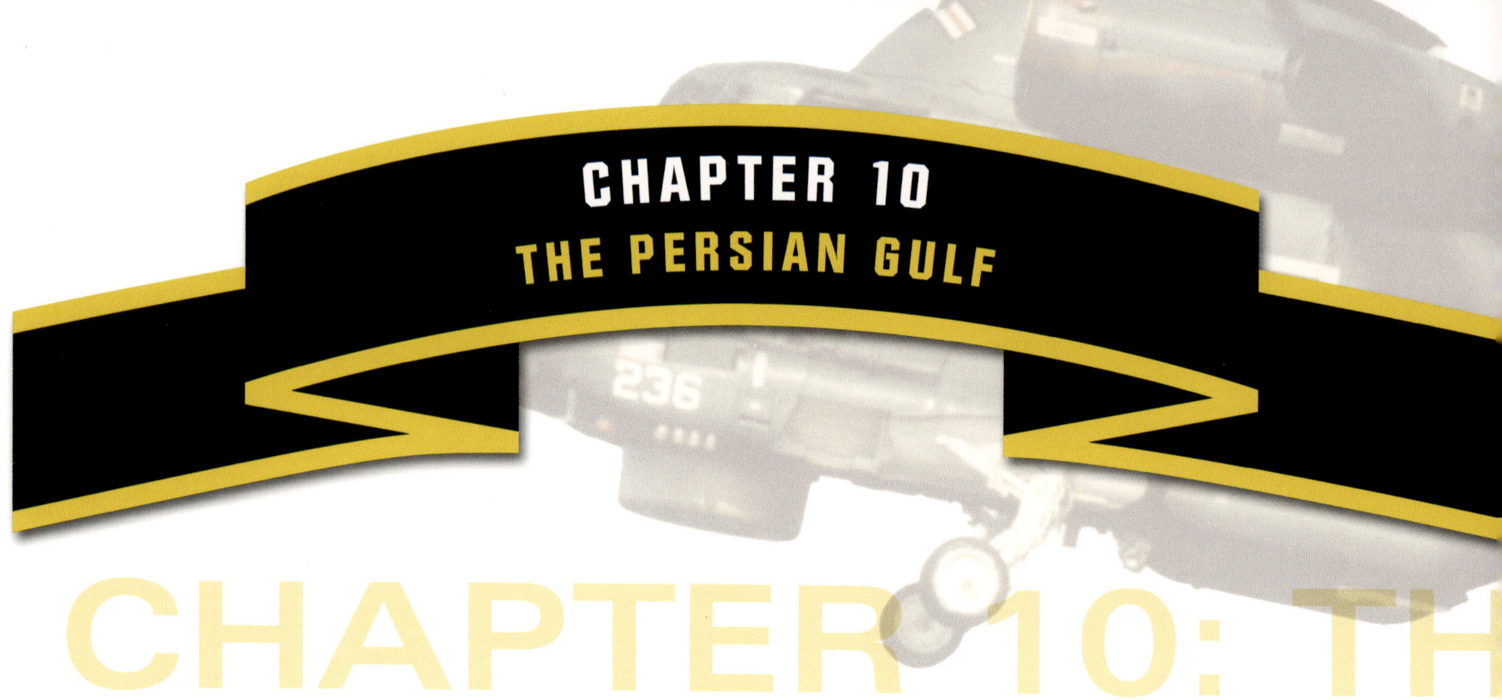

CHAPTER 10
THE PERSIAN GULF

To counter Iranian offensives in Iraq during the mid-1980s, in 1987 the Navy's SH-2F fleet was committed to enforce and support Operation Ernest Will, which identified military protection of Kuwaiti-owned tankers from Iranian attacks. The LAMPS MK I quickly proved a highly effective asset as over-the-horizon targeting and antishipping warfare became its dominant mission in the Persian Gulf. To adapt to surface warfare duty and combat support in these hostile environments, sixteen SH-2Fs were specially modified with systems called the "Middle Eastern Force" (MEF) package. Upgrades consisted of AN/ALQ-47 missile-warning and AN/DLQ-3A jamming equipment, AN/ALQ-144 IR guided-missile jammers, updated radios, twin AN/ALE-39 chaff /flare dispensers, and an AN/ALQ-16 forward-looking infrared radar (FLIR), which could detect targets at night and in low visibility. The AN/ALE-39 system was capable of launching sixty flares or sheet metal chaff to confuse and divert enemy missiles, both infrared and radar-guided. The AN/ALQ-44 IR countermeasures system was an always-on IR jammer against IR missiles. It can operate with a missile-warning system and flares. Armament consisted of door-mounted, crew-served 7.62 mm M60A/D machine guns. At least one MEF-modified SH-2F has been photographed mounting a 2.75-inch seven-tube rocket launcher.

On May 17, 1987, USS *Stark* (FFG-31) was on patrol in the Persian Gulf when it was hit by two Exocet missiles fired by an Iraqi fighter. HSL-32's Det. 3 was aboard *Stark* during the attack but was unharmed. Within three weeks after the attack, Detachment 3 had cross-decked to USS *Stephen W. Groves* (FFG-29) to evaluate the DLQ-3A Sea Force jammer. HSL-32 broke new ground for helicopter operations in the region by deploying Detachment 2 "Outlaws" with the first MEF-configured Seasprites, which went aboard USS *Jack Williams* (FFG-24).

Four days after USS *Samuel B. Roberts* (FFG-58) struck an Iranian mine in the gulf on April 14, 1988, Operation Praying Mantis got underway in retaliation for Iranian mining of the Persian Gulf. Naval forces, which had trained extensively for combat in the gulf, included three surface action groups (SAGs), each comprising three ships, some of which had SH-2Fs aboard. "SAG Bravo" included USS *Merrill* (DD-976), with one SH-2F of HSL-35, Det. 1, aboard; "SAG Charlie" included USS *Bagley* (FF-1069), with one SH-2F; and "SAG Delta" included USS *Jack Williams* (FFG-24), with HSL-32, Det. 2, aboard with two SH-2Fs, and USS *O'Brien* (DD-725), with two SH-2Fs of HSL-33, Det. 2. Detachments would fly airborne surveillance and close air support for hundreds of boardings during interdiction work. During Praying Mantis, SAGs Bravo and Charlie were tasked with attacking oil platforms, while SAG Delta attacked and destroyed the Iranian frigate *Sabalan*. Praying Mantis was the largest US military engagement since the Vietnam War, and the largest sea-air battle since World War II.

Prominent among US intervention at world trouble spots to which SH-2Fs deployed was Operation Desert Shield and Desert Storm in 1990 and 1991, respectively. Six SH-2F-equipped frontline HSLs served in these operations, providing two-plane detachments aboard guided-missile cruisers and destroyers. One dozen SH-2Fs

THE PERSIAN GULF

Few Seasprites are known to have been painted white to reflect assignment aboard special-project ships. The HH-2D BuNo 149750 is seen here in June 1972 at NAS Lakehurst, freshly painted White over Gull Gray in preparation for duty with Sixth Fleet Task Force 60 in the Mediterranean during the Yom Kippur War. *Courtesy of Stephen Miller*

In 1974, no. 750's exterior shows the effects of two years of service with HSL-30, Det. 40, aboard USS *La Salle* in the Middle East. Painted white for its diplomatic role and stationed at Bahrain, *La Salle* was the flagship for the commander of Middle East Force. The ship's name is worn above the national insignia. *Author's collection*

participated in the Iraq conflict, with sorties averaging ninety per aircraft, while maintaining the highest availability rates among participating aircraft. The SH-2Fs' MEF modifications proved a highly efficient force multiplier. Commanders were highly supportive of LAMPS MK I, relying on them for essential tactical information.

MAGIC LANTERN

In response to the mine hazard in the Persian Gulf, a highly classified mine detection system made its first appearance in early 1991 during the Gulf War, mounted to an SH-2F that operated from the frigate USS *Vreeland* (FF-1086). Developed by Kaman, the unit was the "Magic Lantern" ML-30 laser subsurface mine detector. Using a sophisticated array of components, Magic Lantern could detect mines at depths greater than the deepest draft (keel level below the surface) of all US Navy ships. It used laser pulses and six cameras that took photos simultaneously at six different depths, and a mine could be detected if the laser light was reflected or if shadows were seen at lower depths. Identification of the object was done by a computer that filtered out all contacts not having mine characteristics. The system, which weighed approximately 1,000 pounds,

On a stormy day in the North Arabian Sea, "Seasnake 2-0" returns to the destroyer escort USS *Kirk* (FF-1087) after the successful rescue of an A-7 pilot from USS *Midway* who went down on July 13, 1985. *Courtesy of US Navy*

After the frigate USS *Stark* was attacked in May 1987 in the Persian Gulf, HSL-32, Det. 3, went aboard guided-missile frigate USS *Stephen W. Groves* (FFG-29) for the remainder of its deployment. "Invaders" Seasprites, such as BuNo 151330 (*pictured here*), accordingly were fitted with missile-warning equipment and chaff and flare dispensers mounted forward of the cargo door. *Courtesy of US Navy*

consisted of an externally mounted laser housing, an operator's display, equipment racks, and a ground support station for reviewing and analyzing recorded mission data. The large laser pod replaced the MAD on the starboard side of the Seasprite—turned mine hunter. All ASW equipment was removed.

During more than eighty missions in the northern Persian Gulf, the Magic Lantern detected large minefields in areas previously thought to be clear of mines. After ML-30's initial test phase in the gulf, HSL-34 Det. 5, aboard the destroyer USS *Kidd* (DD-661), was directed to take custody of the Magic Lantern–equipped SH-2F at Manama, Bahrain. Arriving at Manama on April 6, 1991, Det. 5 personnel found that the aircraft had received such minimal maintenance that they deemed the helicopter unsafe. After a monthlong rebuild of the SH-2F, *Kidd* returned for the aircraft, and in mid-May HSL-34 began mine-hunting operations in the North Arabian Gulf. Magic Lantern's complex technology greatly reduced the likelihood of a mine-hunting ship striking a mine. Success with the initial version of the ML-30 led to an advanced development model, called ML (ADM), which was earmarked for installation in the follow-on model of the SH-2F, the SH-2G. In November 1997, HSL-94 flew the ML (ADM) system at the Coastal Systems Station at Panama City, Florida, as part of the Navy's ongoing evaluation of laser mine detection systems.

On December 12, 1987, "Seasnake 2-1" of HSL-33, Det. 6, aboard guided-missile destroyer USS *Chandler* (DDG-996) rescued crew members of the burning Cypriot supertanker *PIVOT*, the victim of an Iranian attack 10 miles off Dubai in the Strait of Hormuz. *Courtesy of US Navy*

In 1989, the SH-2F BuNo 161914 of HSL-33 was equipped with a Hughes AN/AAQ-16 night vision system in a turret below the pilot's station. The device detected tiny differences in heat to produce a TV-like picture on a cockpit display. The system had been in production since 1985 for the US Army and the Navy's F/A-18 Hornet aircraft. *Courtesy of Hughes Aircraft Company*

Flying without doors, the SH-2F BuNo 161914 in the fully updated MEF conversion in May 2009. The MAD launcher had been removed, and an improved ALQ-16 night vision system, also called forward-looking infrared radar (FLIR), was installed, along with ECM equipment consisting of two flare launchers and two ALQ-144 "disco ball" missile jammers on the upper tail boom, plus an M60 machine gun in the rescue doorway. Sixteen MEF conversion SH-2Fs were deployed to the Persian Gulf. *Courtesy of US Navy*

A Seasprite AW manning a 7.62 mm M60D machine gun during Operation Praying Mantis in April 1988. Seasprites hunted Iranian bog hammers (Iranian high-speed patrol boats) and small craft staging from oil platforms to attack tankers. *Courtesy of US Navy*

With its Texas Instruments ARR-75 sonobuoy receiver antenna deployed, BuNo 162577 of HSL-32 "Tridents" goes on the hunt. In addition to highly effective AN/ALQ-144 IR guided-missile jammers, AN/ALE flare dispensers were included in the MEF configuration to jam first-generation IR-guided missiles. *Courtesy of US Navy*

Although a lesser-quality photo, this illustrates the variety of weapons systems for which the Seasprite qualified. The torpedo is an odd mix with a Maverick missile and nineteen-tube, 2.75-inch FFAR launcher, both of which are surface weapons. *Courtesy of US Navy*

The initial success of the early version of Magic Lantern spurred Navy interest in airborne laser mine detection systems, resulting in the development of several systems. This appears to be a fit check for one of those systems on an SH-2F during the mid-1990s. The US Postal Service emblem was commonly spotted on Seasprites as a humorous touch, in reference to the UH-2's duty of mail delivery at sea. *Courtesy of US Navy*

BuNo 162577 with a better view of the ALQ-144 IR jammers, or "disco balls," atop the tail boom. The jammers were always on. A pedestal-mounted M60 machine gun is barely visible in the rescue doorway. Purple jerseys of the deck crew identified fuel handlers, while red signified ordnancemen. Here, no. 577 hot-refuels aboard guided-missile cruiser USS *Wainwright* (CG-28) in May 1988. *Courtesy of US Navy*

During 1993 and 1994, VX-1 evaluated the Magic Lantern Mine Warfare System at NAS Patuxent River and Panama City, Florida. Here, BuNo 161641, the first new production SH-2F, mounts an initial Magic Lantern unit at the NAWC. The aircraft was later bailed to Kaman for further testing. *Courtesy of US Navy*

An SH-2F of HSL-94 prepares a Magic Lantern–equipped SH-2G for flight from amphibious assault ship USS *Inchon* (LPH-12) for Joint Task Force Exercise 1997 (JTFX-97) off North Carolina. Green jerseys identified equipment and maintenance personnel, while purple identified fuel handlers. *Courtesy of Matt Russ*

Pilot and copilot of HSL-34 preflight their MEF-configured SH-2F at NAS Norfolk in 1993. *Courtesy of US Navy*

Bailed to Kaman, Magic Lantern–equipped BuNo 163214, which first flew as an SH-2G in July 1994, is put through its paces at Panama City, Florida. This Seasprite became the first operational Magic Lantern Seasprite. *Courtesy of Kaman Aerospace Corp.*

Somewhere in the Mediterranean, aboard an MEF-modified SH-2F (BuNo 161657) of HSL-35, Det. 6—pilot to copilot: "If you're looking for our AW, he stepped out to get some air." *Author's collection*

CHAPTER 11
THE SUPER SEASPRITE

After production of the SH-2F reopened in 1982, the realization came that improvement of the LAMPS platform was best achieved not by costly development of a new aircraft, but by upgrading the highly successful SH-2F. Giving rise to the plan was Kaman's Engineering Change Proposal 469, submitted to NAVAIR, which would upgrade the new model with GE-T700-401 engines. Confirmation of the plan came in 1985, when the decision was made during new SH-2F production to build the last six of the sixty-unit contract as advanced models designated SH-2Gs, or "Super Seasprites," Kaman model K-894. After SH-2F production ended, SH-2G production began in 1990. The new model began with SH-2F BuNo 161653 serving as a test bed for the 1,723 shp General Electric YT700-GE-401/C turboshaft. To support the heavier, more powerful engine, the structure atop the SH-2F was rebuilt with titanium. Already adopted by the Navy for Sikorsky's SH-60B Seahawk and Bell's AH-1W Supercobra for the Marines, the new engine produced 10 percent more power and 20 percent lower fuel consumption than the T58; range extended to 390 miles, its service ceiling extended to 10,000 feet at maximum gross weight, and top speed then reached 172 mph. Although the new engine pushed maximum takeoff weight to 13,800 pounds during flight tests, the 13,500-pound limit was retained. The power increase enabled the Super Seasprite to carry two Mk. 46 torpedoes at the second convergence zone for 1.5 hours of on-station time. Equally beneficial were lower maintenance manhours per flight hours required—eight for the SH-2G compared to twenty-two for the UH-2A—and commonality with SH-60 and AH-1W engines. For safety, the T700 delivers 30 percent more single-engine power. A T-62 gas-turbine APU (auxiliary power unit) enables the aircraft to self-start, eliminating the need for ground support equipment. As Kaman's YSH-2G prototype, BuNo 161653 had flown for the first time on April 2, 1985. The first flight with the full, new avionics package was made on December 28, 1989.

In 1987, when funding appropriations were to have ended new SH-2F production, the Navy was faced with the option of upgrading sixty-one SH-2Fs with the new engines, while ordering 103 new-build SH-2Gs. Cessation of the Cold War in 1989, however, had the Navy ending its requirement for more smaller ships and helicopters. During more than three years of engineering, in addition to production time, the Navy elected to phase out and decommission the largest number of ships upon which the Seasprite operated—the FF-1052 frigate. As a result, HSLs were decommissioned and the aircraft were placed in Arizona desert storage. In 1994, only twenty-four SH-2Gs had been completed, which were dispersed among three newly formed reserve squadrons. All the SH-2Gs featured state-of-the-art mission electronics, making the Super Seasprite a self-contained anti-submarine-warfare and anti-surface-warfare (ASuW) platform. Largely responsible for this dual function is the Canadian-built AN/UYS-503 acoustic processor, which processes gathered information on board, permitting operations independent of the parent ship. Sonobuoys, which use a ninety-nine-channel receiver, are either SSQ-41 or AN/SSQ 53F

HSL-94 took delivery of the first two SH-2Gs so equipped on December 7, 1996. The Magic Lantern airborne laser mine detection system added 900 pounds to the aircraft. *Courtesy of Don Brabec collection*

directional-frequency analysis and recording (DIFAR passive), or SSQ-62 or AN/SSQ 62E directional-command active sonobuoy system (DICASS active). The SH-2G's multimission modular design is built around a digital data bus and multifunction display, which ties together all its mission equipment, navigation, and tactical-information systems. This enables the aircraft to be flown by a crew of two, or with a standard crew composed of pilot, copilot / tactics officer, and enlisted crewman operating ASW or Magic Lantern equipment. Typically, the latter crewman, called an aviation warfare systems operator (AWSO), had attended aircrew school, rescue swimmer school, and ASW school, all at NAS Pensacola.

The first operational SH-2G began service with Reserve HSL-84 "Thunderbolts" at NAS North Island, San Diego, on February 25, 1993. The squadron was allocated eight Super Seasprites, while Reserve HSL-94 "Titans," at NAS Willow Grove, Pennsylvania, received the first of eight machines in March 1994. Of the remaining eight SH-2Gs, one was a nonflying parts aircraft, while another was assigned to the Strike Test facility at NAS Patuxent River. Although Sikorsky SH-60B Seahawks had assumed a large portion of the LAMPS III role since the establishment of HSL-41 in January 1983, SH-2Fs and SH-2Gs continued ASW duty. In 1994, SH-2Fs were retired from active service with the US Navy, concurrent with proposed retirement of the last of the Vietnam-era Knox-class frigates, which were unable to accommodate the new and larger Sikorsky SH-60 Seahawks that replaced the aging Seasprites. In 1997, the Navy chose to protect its twelve carrier battle groups from defense cuts by disposing of the majority of its Seasprite-capable Knox-class 1052s and FFG-7 Oliver Hazard Perry–class frigates to foreign customers and the Naval Reserve Force—1052s went to Egypt, Taiwan, Thailand, Turkey, Mexico, and Greece, while FFG-7s went to Poland, Pakistan, Spain, Taiwan, Bahrain, Egypt, Turkey, and Australia. Of the forty-six Knox-class frigates built, twenty-seven were sold abroad and fifteen were scrapped or sunk. As of 2000, SH-2Gs operated only from Naval Reserve short-hull FFG-7 frigates, which could not accommodate the larger 22,000-pound SH-60B Seahawk. Remaining FFG-7s were earmarked for foreign sales by 2001. As of March 2021, fifteen Oliver Hazard Perry–class frigates were moored at Naval Inactive Ship Maintenance Facility at Philadelphia, Pennsylvania. Kaman would benefit from the overall arrangement, since countries that purchased the still very capable frigates required ASW helicopters to keep the ships combat capable.

The first flight of the SH-2G demonstrator, BuNo 161653, which occurred on December 28, 1989, at Kaman's facility in Bloomfield, Connecticut. The YSH-2G prototype was first flown four years earlier. *Courtesy of Kaman Aerospace Corp.*

The SH-2G during sea trials. Installation of T700-GE-401 engines resulted in a drastic change in engine nacelles. Noteworthy is the odd shape of the upper transmission housing, which incorporated a screened air inlet and flared rotor head fairing. *Courtesy of US Navy*

In 1985 the SH-2F BuNo 149023 of HSL-33 is prepared for transport to Kaman to be reborn as a "Gray Ghost," slang for SH-2Gs, which emerged from production painted in gray tactical schemes. *Courtesy of Gordon Permann*

The SH-2G was equipped with the AN/ASQ-81(v)2 MAD, which could be towed by its 180-foot-long cable at speeds between 12 and 161 mph. Evident in BuNo 163543's profile is the redesign of the upper structure, which reduced the size of the engine nacelle tail fairing familiar to earlier twin-engine models. *Courtesy of Fred Freeman*

A Super Seasprite fires decoy flares, which were elements of its survivability package. *Courtesy of US Navy*

With retired SH-2Fs available for conversion to SH-2Gs, along with SH-2Gs available for remanufacture and tailored to user requirements, Kaman pursued an international market, investing heavily in the research and development of varied systems. Among them were composite main rotor blades, labeled second-generation composite main rotor blades (CMRB2), which had been successfully flight-tested on an SH-2G in August 1996. The CMRB2 blades have an expected service life of 15,000 hours, compared to the 3,700 hours of the "101" metal blades used on SH-2Fs and early SH-2Gs. Composite rotor blades are more durable, extend the lives of control system bearings, improve hover performance, and allow an additional 500 pounds in payload. Although haul-down systems were not deemed a priority for US Navy operations, the SH-2G was used to test the Indal Recovery Assist, Secure and Traverse (RAST) system, which was compatible with Harpoon and other deck-landing systems. Other updates then under review included the addition of forward-looking infrared radar, dipping sonar, chaff/flare dispensers, and Mk. 50 torpedoes, among an array of weaponry that included antishipping missiles with compatible search radar. The Mk. 50 torpedo, which had been authorized for fleet use in October 1992, was designed to counter the fast, deep-diving, double-hull nuclear submarine. The 800-pound torpedo featured increased range, and greater lethality, speed, and depth.

After successful helicopter air-to-surface missile firings during the Falklands War in 1982, the US Navy reexamined the need for LAMPS helicopters to have an offensive capability. Studies led to the development during the late 1980s of the Norwegian-made IR-imaging AGM-119B Penguin Mod. 7 air-to-surface fire-and-forget antishipping missile. The SH-2G also qualified with the Hughes television-guided AGM-65 Maverick, British Aerospace Dynamics' radar-guided Sea Skua, and the laser-guided Hellfire missile. The Super Seasprite can also carry a pair of Mk. 11 depth charges, two Mk. 46 torpedoes, and crew-served 7.62 mm M60 or 12.7 mm machine guns. Lessons learned from helicopters being targeted while operating in the Persian Gulf led to outfitting SH-2Gs with an aircraft survivability equipment package that included Lockheed-Sanders ALQ-144R infrared jammers and Tracor ALE-39 chaff/flare dispensers.

The SH-2G BuNo 161647 of HSL-94 "Titans." What follows are detailed walk-around views of this Seasprite. *Courtesy of John Hairell*

Hinged front cowling, under which was located the rescue hoist / winch drive motor and transmission oil tank. Installation of the T700 engine extended the center of gravity by relocating the combining gearbox from behind the engines to the front, allowing placement of dipping sonar in the aft cabin. This eliminated a nose-up attitude during the dipping hover. *Courtesy of Milosz Rusiecki*

Maintenance walkways covered the engine nacelle tail fairing. Oil cooler vents are at the rear of the rotor head fairing. *Courtesy of John Hairell*

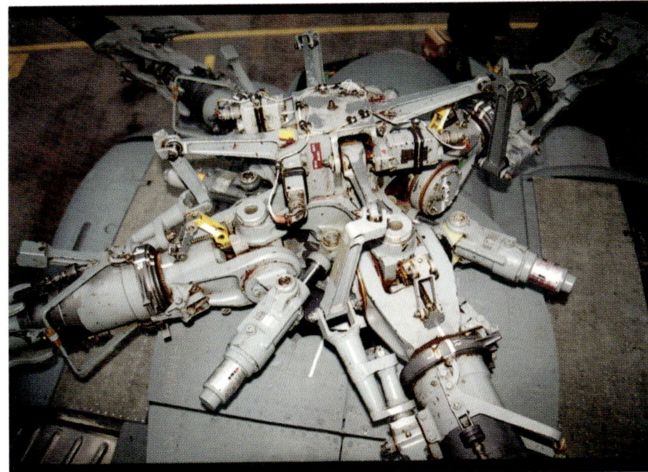

The SH-2G rotor head. *Courtesy of Milosz Rusiecki*

Copilot's instrument panel of the SH-2G. *Courtesy of John Hairell*

Pilots' seats formed a partial bulkhead between the cockpit and cabin. Fold-down steps in the bulkhead frame replaced retractable steps of earlier models. Rearview mirrors first appeared on the UH-2C. *Courtesy of John Hairell*

Attached to the trailing edge of the tail rotor pylon is an AN/ALR-66 ESM antenna. The tailplane is braced. The ventral blade antenna corresponds to UHF radio equipment. *Courtesy of John Hairell*

Pilot's instrument panel of the SH-2G. *Courtesy of John Hairell*

Located midbelly is the ARR-75 folding sonobuoy receiver antenna, which allowed transmitting sonobuoy data to the ship. *Courtesy of John Hairell*

Shown to good advantage is the SH-2G's tail rotor linkage, along with AN/ALR-66 radar-warning receivers on both sides of the tail rotor pylon. *Courtesy of John Hairell*

The SH-2G's rescue hoist was a folding affair that retracted downward inside the aircraft to allow closing of the rescue/pilot's door. *Courtesy of John Hairell*

Left: The SH-2G's tail fin supported a tail rotor that was 8 feet, 1 inch in diameter, along with a 90-degree gearbox and navigation light. "NW" was the tail code for all three SH-2G reserve squadrons. *Courtesy of John Hairell*

Right: To manage landings on ship decks, the SH-2G's main landing gear used forward-retracting legs with liquid spring shock absorbers. Titanium wheels with eight-ply tires incorporate rings for securing chain. *Courtesy of John Hairell*

The SH-2G's nonretractable tailwheel with oleo-pneumatic shock absorber is fully castoring but locked fore and aft for takeoff and landing. Aft of the tailwheel are dual AN/APN-171 radar altimeter antennas and a UHF blade aerial. *Courtesy of John Hairell*

Barely noticeable is the transition of aircraft color to darker gray forward of the cockpit and on the upper fairing. *Courtesy of US Navy*

SH-2G BuNo 163541 presents a fine study of the Super Seasprite's redesigned domed superstructure and the tactical color scheme. *Courtesy of US Navy*

Guided by a yellow-shirted landing signalman, enlisted (LSE), an SH-2G completes its landing cycle aboard the guided-missile frigate USS *Fahrion* (FFG-22). *Courtesy of US Navy*

The Super Seasprite armed with a pair of AGM-114 Hellfire missiles. *Courtesy of US Navy*

Despite an uncertain future—and the Navy on the verge of relegating its frigates to history—Super Seasprite crews of HSL-84 and HSL-94 routinely trained in alternate missions, including over-the-horizon targeting of vessels for antisurface warfare, search and rescue, medical evacuation, utility work, vertical replenishment, and drug enforcement with the US Coast Guard. Success with the Magic Lantern airborne laser mine detection system led to a contract for Kaman to modify five additional SH-2Gs for fleet deployment. Plans called for HSL-94 to deploy seventeen-member detachments aboard active-duty US Navy destroyers. The handwriting was on the wall, however, since various phases of LAMPS development ended up on the budgetary chopping block, and funding remained only for LAMPS Mk. III, the "ultimate LAMPS." As the LAMPS mission range requirement grew, so, consequently, did the weight, with the Super Seasprite yielding to the Seahawk and larger ship decks. The last official US Navy flight of the SH-2G was made in June 2001 in conjunction with disestablishment of HSL-84. So extensive was the Seasprite's growth history and its multimission capabilities that it had captured the interest of naval leaders on a global scale. At the SH-2G's retirement, Kaman already had invested four years in a vigorous program for export sales. Kaman's selling points were based on the SH-2G's proven performance and versatility, the application of continual technology, and growth potential. The airframe had proven its robustness in US Navy service, and the aircraft proved adept in a wide range of roles. Kaman officials were keenly aware that international customers demanded multimission capability in their maritime helicopters—Kaman vowed not to disappoint.

Finally, after the Seasprite left the US Navy inventory, they were scattered to the four winds; foreign service, museum displays, relegated to storage. This example was turned into a monument at NAS Barbers Point, Hawaii, to honor RAdm. Alvin Holsey, past commander of HSL-37 at the base. The display was established in early 1992, when the squadron transitioned from the SH-2F to the SH-60B, the first unit to do so. HSL-37 "Easy Riders" had been established on July 3, 1975, with the SH-2F. *Author's collection*

A number of Seasprites became gate guards and museum displays. This Super Seasprite is displayed at the Patuxent River Naval Air Museum, Maryland. BuNo 161642 went from SH-2F production in 1983 to the NATC Rotary Wing Aircraft Test Directorate for a few months and was then assigned to HSL-37 until October 1991. After conversion to SH-2G, it went back to the test directorate in 1993 and ended up at the museum in 1998. *Courtesy of Pam Bone, Patuxent River Naval Air Museum*

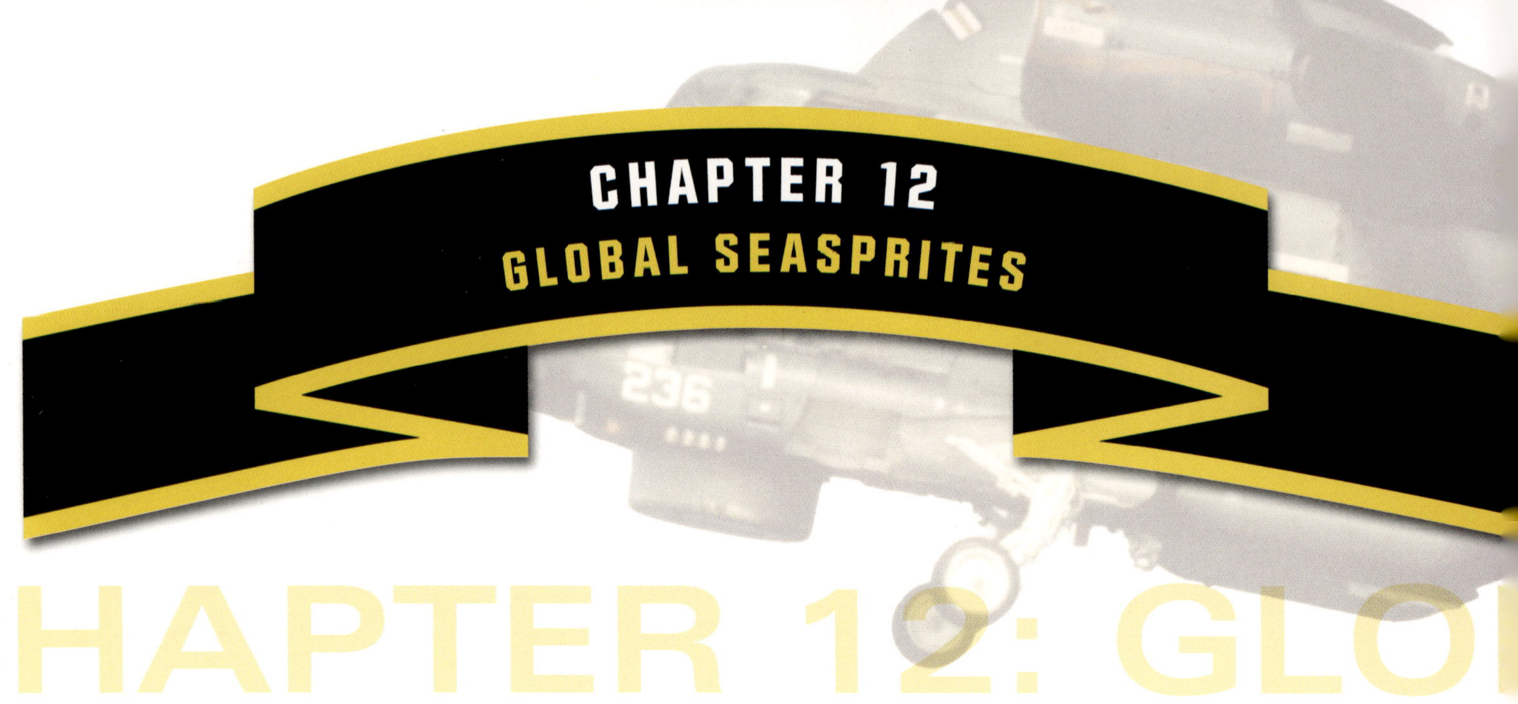

CHAPTER 12
GLOBAL SEASPRITES

CHAPTER 12: GLO

Despite the end of the Cold War and subsequent downsizing and reorganization of the US military, new missions and threats demanded new priorities on a global scale. New technology, then, had to compensate for less military hardware. The result was a leaner yet more capable combat force.

Early retirement of the US Navy's low-hours SH-2Gs appealed to international customers as relatively new aircraft that had been built with 10,000-hour airframe life. Kaman also offered airframes that were upgraded SH-2Gs, or SH-2Fs remanufactured to SH-2G standard, all with 10,000-hour airframe life and with a wide array of systems to meet customer demands. The installation of GE-T700-401 engines greatly increased their capability, ease of maintenance, commonality with other helicopters in their inventory, and, subsequently, their combat readiness. Myriad electronic systems give the Super Seasprite superior adaptability in the changing world while complying with reduced defense budgets. Regardless the SH-2G's capabilities, competition in the maritime helicopter market remained keen among Kaman, Sikorsky, Eurocopter, and Westland. It was not lost on competing firms that small- and intermediate-sized multimission helicopters prove vital to nations that are hard-pressed to deploy battle groups with ships dedicated to countering surface and subsurface threats.

Upgrades for foreign sales followed the pattern that Kaman used for SH-2Fs brought up to SH-2G standard. Airframes pulled from AMARC storage went first to Kaman's facility in Moosup, Connecticut, where they were stripped and blasted. The shells then went to the Bloomfield factory, where the aircraft were remanufactured, including the installation of components specified by the customer. Among the many variations of electronic packages specified by foreign customers, MAD units were seldom seen on Super Seasprites. The effectiveness of MAD units diminished with the increased capability of dipping sonar and aircraft-launched sonobuoys. However, MAD systems remained effective in the final phases of fixing and killing submarines. Advanced Soviet submarines with titanium hulls, since they are all but invisible to MAD units, possess a significant measure of stealth.

After the last official US Navy flight of the SH-2G in 2001, Kaman began in earnest its global marketing strategy, to the extent of relabeling the Super Seasprite the SH-2G International, or SH-2G(I). Outfitted with the latest in electronics and a variety of weapons, the SH-2G(I) was hailed as an advanced maritime weapon system and proven day/night/all-weather multimission helicopter. Boasting the highest power-to-weight ratio of any maritime helicopter, the International fulfilled numerous roles. International prospects began during the late 1990s with offers of surplus SH-2Fs as foreign aid to Greece (six aircraft) and Turkey (fourteen); however, they rejected the offer in light of tension between the two nations. Egypt initially acquired four SH-2Fs under the aid program. Taiwan was to have obtained twelve SH-2Fs in 1993; however, lack of funding shelved the deal. In 1996, Kaman made a bid to Malaysia, which sought a replacement for its Westland Wasps. Further prospects were the Philippines,

AL SEASPRITES

Torpedo away from an SH-2G. *Courtesy of US Navy*

Indonesia, Mexico, Bangladesh, Morocco, South Africa, Pakistan, and Thailand. In most cases, Kaman played a support role to foreign military sales (FMS) managers at NAVAIR. International purchases were handled as foreign military sales, which included overhaul both of ships and aircraft, plus a complete logistics package of two years of spares, support equipment, test equipment, and training. This FMS template was used to support all foreign sales. A landmark event in Kaman's marketing program occurred in September 2008, when the company brought an SH-2G(I) to the Black Sea Defense Aerospace & Security Exhibition at Bucharest, Romania. Kaman's public-relations endeavors met with success on April 14, 2014, when the first New Zealand SH-2G(I) began production flight testing at the Bloomfield facility.

This SH-2F BuNo 162582, like its host ship, the guided-missile frigate USS *Horne* (DLG-30), was mothballed in 1994. The Seasprite got a new lease on life with the Egyptian navy; however, in 2008 USS *Horne* became a target ship, now resting on the bottom off Kauai, Hawaii. By mid-1996, more than sixty SH-2Fs had joined no. 582 at the AMARC storage facility at Tucson, with six stored at Fort Rucker, Alabama, and one at NAS Pensacola. *Author's collection*

EGYPT

Egypt was the first export customer for the Seasprite through a 1995 foreign military sale agreement for ten aircraft, plus spares and training. Although Westland's Lynx, followed by Sikorsky's S-70B, dominated the international market, the sale of Seasprites to Egypt gave notice that the type retained ample potential and cost less than its rivals. Egypt's ten aircraft are former SH-2F airframes that were in various

The SH-2G BuNo 163214, seen here during qualification with the Penguin AGM-119/Mk. 2 missile, was the last-built SH-2F. *Courtesy of Fred Freeman*

Egypt was Kaman's first overseas customer for the SH-2G, acquiring ten examples remanufactured from SH-2Fs. Under the terms of a March 1995 FMS agreement, the aircraft were embarked aboard four FFG-7 frigates and two Knox-class vessels transferred from the US Navy. Egypt's SH-2Gs were the first variants equipped with AQS-18A dipping sonar and a digital hover coupler. The first SH-2G(E) was delivered on October 21, 1997. The sonar detects underwater contacts by using echo ranging to determine the bearing, range, and closing speed of the target relative to the Seasprite's position. *Courtesy of US Navy*

US Navy lieutenant commander Andrew Howerton, the air boss of Helicopter Maritime Strike Squadron (HSM) 48 "Vipers," greets an Egyptian air force SH-2G pilot aboard guided-missile destroyer USS *Jason Dunham* (DDG-109) on July 31, 2018, during "Eagle Salute 18," an exercise with Egyptian naval forces in the Fifth Fleet area of operations. *Courtesy of US Navy*

stages of construction during the mid-1990s Their BuNos are 163212, 163213, 162577, 162581, 161652, 161906, 162587, 162582, 161909, and 161645. The first SH-2G(E) configured for Egypt, BuNo 162580, was retained by Kaman to test the dipping-sonar system at NAS Patuxent River in early 1997. The dipping sonar is a primary feature of the SH-2G(E) since it is more effective in noisy environments, and the Egyptians intended to work in the busy sea lanes of the Mediterranean. Built by Allied Signal, the digital AQS-18A's transducer unit, which is lowered into deep or shallow water, weighs 200 pounds, with a cable that can reach a depth of 1,444 feet. The unit is used in conjunction with a hover coupler that enables the pilot to precision-hover in low visibility and at night at a programmed altitude. On the pilot's command, the helicopter automatically departs from the hover. Although the SH-2G(E) has no sonobuoy launcher, the AQS-18A processor can manage passive buoy signals. Since US Navy Seasprites dropped torpedoes in forward flight, tests flown at NAS Pax River cleared the SH-2G(E) to drop torpedoes while in a sonar-dipping hover. The senso in the Egyptian crew of three could adjust the weapon's cable offset to allow safe separation of the falling torpedo. As with US Navy SH-2Gs then in service, Egypt's SH-2Gs were equipped with the Litton LN-66HP multimode chin-mounted radar, which was capable of detecting both submarine periscopes and aircrew down at sea.

Egypt's SH-2G(E)s were to be partnered with two former US Navy Knox-class frigates and three Oliver Hazard Perry–class frigates. In August 1997 the first SH-2G(E) began flight testing, with rollout on October 21. After the presentation to Egyptian general Hazim Awad, Charles Kaman said, "This is a milestone event for the SH-2G Super Seasprite as it marks the beginning of its new mission in international military service." Monthly deliveries to Egypt's Borg al-Arab Air Base followed, with deliveries completed in 1998. Egypt also took advantage of a US foreign-aid program that offered surplus SH-2Fs by acquiring four airframes to be used as spares in support of their forthcoming SH-2G(E)s. Initially, twenty Egyptian air force pilots attended flight training at NAS Pensacola, where they accomplished more than two thousand day and night landings on the base's Helicopter Landing Trainer. Ten sonar operators and thirty maintenance technicians also underwent training. For logistics training, Kaman had teamed with Logistics Services International of Jacksonville, Florida, while the Navy provided hangar and training facilities at Pensacola.

In 2005, the Egyptian air force awarded Kaman a contract to modernize two SH-2G(E)s with digital automatic flight control, FLIR, health and usage monitoring systems, and ALE-47 countermeasures. The pair of modernized SH-2(E)s was delivered in February 2009. In 2006, an Egyptian SH-2G(E) had crashed into the sea and was lost.

THE AUSTRALIAN EXPERIENCE

Australian and New Zealand orders for SH-2Gs were linked through a collaborative ANZAC-class frigate program between the two nations. The frigates were to be joined by offshore patrol vessels (OPVs) built as a collaborative effort with Malaysia. It was hoped that both countries then would procure the same helicopter, increasing the potential for Australia to enlarge its Seasprite force to twenty aircraft. Early in the program, the Australian government suggested that if New Zealand selected the Super Seasprite, it could be advantageous to both nations due to common acquisitions and support infrastructure. Although often viewed as identical aircraft, Seasprites for Australia and New Zealand navies are SH-2Gs, but they are as different as the kiwi and the kangaroo emblazoned on their aircraft's national insignia. A main requirement of the Royal Australian Navy (RAN) was that the helicopter operate at high ambient temperatures and perform a multitude of maritime helicopter functions with a two-person crew (pilot and copilot), plus the capability of flying the aircraft hands off. Included was Australia's option for Kaman to establish a helicopter support center adjacent to its naval air station at Nowra. The Royal New Zealand Navy (RNZN) stressed performance in rough seas with SH-2Gs that were similar to those of the US Navy, with a few changes.

Richard Collier, whose thirty-year career with Kaman included direct involvement with H-2 procurements for Australia and New Zealand, reflects:

> Australia and New Zealand posted teams of RAN, RNZAF, and RNZN personnel at Kaman during the lives of these programs to oversee engineering, production, and logistics. These teams worked and interfaced with Kaman personnel and its vendors for the duration of this effort. The New Zealand program, which was lower risk due to the proven technology of various systems, proceeded as scheduled with SH-2G deliveries. The Australian program software requirements were much more complicated due to greater system integration that was required for a two-man crew and hands-free flight.

Prior to export to the Royal Australian Navy, this Penguin-armed Seasprite was the SH-2G prototype. Here in September 1999, it is registered N351KA for rebuild to RAN specifications. Eventually it would be back at Kaman, registered N167KM, for rebuild for the Royal New Zealand Navy. *Courtesy of Kaman Aerospace Corp.*

This SH-2G(A) of the Royal Australian Navy wore its former US Navy BuNo, 152205, beneath its RAN no., 846. Australia's troubled Super Seasprite program was canceled in early 2008 after it fell seven years behind schedule and suffered 40 percent budget overruns and ongoing technical issues. *Courtesy of US Navy*

Wearing US registration as required for testing at Kaman following its return from Australia in 2006, former US Navy BuNo 149773 carries flight test telemetry equipment during upgrade to SH-2G(I) for New Zealand. *Courtesy of Johan Ragay*

Remanufacture of SH-2Fs to SH-2G(A)s included a cockpit featuring four active-matrix liquid-crystal color multifunction displays, below which were two data entry and display units. This arrangement was designed for operation by a crew of two, comprising pilot and tactical coordinator / sensor operator (TACCO). The highly automated system displayed both flight and tactical data. The Super Seasprite wears US registration N318KA while at Kaman between transfer from Australia to New Zealand. *Courtesy of Johan Ragay*

The mission profile for Australia's intermediate-size naval helicopter stated surface surveillance, ASW, boarding search and seizure, naval gunfire support, and SAR, with tactical navigation capability. In particular, Australia set its sights on the Super Seasprite to satisfy its requirement for Project SEA 1411, which called for a weapon system that was compatible with its new fleet of eight ANZAC-class frigates, the first of which began service in April 1996. Request for tender for fourteen helicopters was issued in October 1995, and by March 1996, Kaman's SH-2G Super Seasprite and Westland's Super Lynx were in contention. Kaman was selected in January 1997; however, budget woes had Australia's SH-2G order reduced to eleven aircraft under a contract signed on June 26, with deliveries slated to begin in early 2001. Since the aircraft was to play a major ASW role, missiles were a main area of interest in providing long-range protection of its parent ship. Weapon systems entered into the competition consisted of the Norwegian Penguin, Hughes Maverick, British Aerospace, Sea Skua, and Italian Sea Killer / Marte. It came down to the Sea Skua and Penguin, with the latter becoming the prime contender. The sea-skimming Penguin, with armor-piercing warhead, had a range of 25 nautical miles. Specifically, the RAN specified that its Seasprites be equipped to carry the IR-guided Kongsberg Mk. 2 mod 7 Penguin antiship missile, which was designated the AGM-119 in the US Navy. The SH-2G had been cleared for Mk. 44, Mk. 46, and Mk. 50 torpedoes. Included in the contract was Kaman's responsibility for training all personnel involved, and operation of a mission flight simulator at Australia's NAS Nowra.

Since Kaman was determined to dispel the notion that its Seasprite was an ASW aircraft only, after contract signing the company suggested to the Australian Defense Force (ADF) an offer of a Seasprite gunship, given that the type had successfully tested in that role years earlier. Kaman also briefed the ADF on the possibility of modifying Seasprites for troop transport.

All SH-2G(A) airframes were former US Navy SH-2Fs recovered from AMARC storage for remanufacture at Kaman's Bloomfield facility. Safe Air Ltd. was responsible for reassembly after shipment to Australia.

Included in the SH-2G(A)'s massive array of state-of-the-art electronics was development of an Integrated Tactical Avionics System (ITAS) for operation by a crew of two consisting of pilot and tactical coordinator / sensor operator (TACCO). High-end communication, navigation, and avionics systems were managed by using twin displays in the center console of the SH-2G(A)'s automated glass cockpit. Integrated into the ITAS suite were

The SH-2G BuNo 163214, seen here during qualification with the Penguin AGM-119/Mk. 2 missile, was the last-built SH-2F. *Courtesy of Fred Freeman*

Another view of the Kongsberg AGM-119 antiship missile. The Norwegian passive IR seeker Penguin was introduced to the US Navy in 1993. *Courtesy of US Navy*

synthetic-aperture radar, Raytheon AAQ-27 FLIR, laser-warning system, missile approach warning system, and ALE-47 or ALE-39 flare/chaff countermeasures. As a component of the then most sophisticated Seasprite model, the system was operated by the TACCO in the left-hand seat. Multistores pylons on both sides of the aircraft could accommodate Mk. 46, Mod 5 torpedoes (which was replaced by the MU 90), Penguin antiship missiles, Mk. 11 depth charges, or 100-gallon auxiliary fuel tanks. The 300-pound Mk. 11 depth charge was effective for submarines on the surface or at periscope depth. A crew-served MAG 58 7.62 mm machine gun could be mounted in the cabin doorway. The SH-2G(A) was equipped with the Indal RAST system for shipboard recovery. The RAST already was in use by the RAN for recovery and deck handling of Sikorsky S-70B Seahawks. Completing the Australian Super Seasprite were composite rotor blades and a crashworthy fuel system.

Many felt that acquisition of the Super Seasprite by the Australian government was flawed from the outset. The ITAS was a highly ambitious technical goal for its time. It replaced a proven tactical navigation computer, and a newly developed digital Automated Flight Control System (AFCS) replaced the Seasprite's reliable automatic stabilization equipment, which had been proven during more than one million hours in US Navy service. By late

2000 the ITAS system, which Kaman heralded as being tailor-fit for two-crew operation of Australia's Super Seasprites, fell seriously behind in its developmental track. The relationship between contractor Litton Guidance & Control Systems and Kaman soured, Litton withdrew from the project, and Kaman received rights to build the system. Adding to the upheaval following a costly three-year delay was the Royal Australian Navy chief's refusal to accept the first SH-2G(A) when it arrived in September 2001, maintaining that the aircraft was not fit for its original purpose; the hands-free capability had still not been resolved to Australia's satisfaction. The minister of defense overturned the action, clearing the way for the delivery of eight aircraft in provisional training configuration. Problems persisted with regard to cost, scheduling, and technical risks, not to mention wrangling between Kaman and the Australian defense department. It became obvious that exorbitant monetary loss could not be recovered, and the Australian government would have to "bite the bullet" and wait grimly for the helicopter that Kaman had promised. Kaman's recovery included redevelopment of the ITAS system with the aid of US and Australian companies.

The Commonwealth provisionally accepted the first SH-2G(A) as an interim trainer on October 18, 2003, for the RAN to begin testing and training in advance of delivery of the full weapon system. Ten SH-2G(A)s were delivered to NAS Nowra, with the last aircraft of the order remaining with Kaman for testing until late 2004. The incremental acceptance process had maintenance personnel of No. 805 Squadron—which had been recommissioned for the SH-2G(A)—attending a four-month training program, followed by aircrew training.

The SH-2G(A) made its first shipboard landing on November 5, 2003, aboard the ANZAC frigate HMAS *Warramunga*, remaining embarked to evaluate shipboard handling. Land and shipboard trials continued through 2004, with Kaman's goal being delivery of a fully functional and Penguin missile-armed SH-2G(A) by year's end. All eleven SH-2G(A)s could then be operational aboard ANZAC frigates by late 2005.

In May 2006, the Seasprite's Australian Military Type certificate that had been issued in 2004 was withdrawn due to concerns with the automatic flight control system, and all Seasprites were grounded. On May 25, 2007, the government announced continuation of the program, but it would be short lived. On March 5, 2008, a newly installed government, after reviewing the troubled history of its Seasprites, canceled the SH-2G(A) project. In June, No. 805 Squadron was summarily decommissioned, and the eleven Australian SH-2G(A)s, plus spares and support, were purchased back by Kaman. Eventually, they were reconfigured for sale to the Royal New Zealand Navy.

MEANWHILE, ACROSS THE TASMAN SEA

Royal New Zealand Navy ships and embarked helicopters are tasked with patrolling the nation's territorial sea and 200 nautical miles beyond, which form the fourth-largest Economic Exclusion Zone. For nearly thirty years, four Westland Wasp helicopters that were embarked aboard Leander-class frigates were vital elements in maintaining the goals of New Zealand's defense policies. Efforts by the Royal New Zealand Navy (RNZN) to procure a successor to the venerable Wasp actually had begun as far back as 1988 under a study named "Project Amokura." This was replaced by a more resolute acquisition program named simply "Replacement Naval Helicopter" (RNH). Despite their independent procurement policy and affinity toward British influence, RNZN officials, while closely watching Australia's Seasprite experience, were attracted to the Super Seasprite since its sensor package and avionics paralleled that of the US Navy's SH-60 Seahawk. To satisfy the RNH requirement, on March 10, 1997, two months after Australia's minister of defense announced that the RAN would acquire eleven SH-2G(A) Super Seasprites, the RNZN also selected the SH-2G. The contract was signed in June for four new-construction SH-2G(NZ)s, with the option to procure a fifth aircraft two years later. The order coincided with the acquisition of two ANZAC frigates and a smaller Leander-class frigate. Unlike Australia, New Zealand opted for new-build SH-2Gs to avoid fatigue problems sometimes associated with remanufactured airframes, although Kaman guaranteed a 10,000-hour life with both types; the RNZN also specified long-life, all-composite rotor blades. To enable the RNZN's thirty-two-year-old Westland Wasp to be phased into retirement, a contract provision included the delivery of four SH-2Fs for use as interim aircraft to continue naval operations. Their US Navy BuNos were 150154, 150171, 161641, and 162585, which the RNZN registered NZ3441–NZ3444.

Taken from AMARC storage, the first SH-2F arrived in New Zealand by sea in August 1997, followed in December by the next three, plus a fifth airframe for spare parts. Budget and manpower issues permitted the restoration of only three aircraft to flight status, relegating the fourth airframe to a parts source. The first refurbished SH-2F was rolled out at Auckland on February 27, 1998. Like the Wasps they replaced, the SH-2Fs were assigned to Naval Support Flight of 3 Squadron of the Royal New Zealand Air Force. The SH-2F received high praise from aircrew during its performance as a training platform to enable the transition from Wasp to Super Seasprite. A unique arrangement had the helicopters flown by naval crews but maintained by air force personnel. They were under naval control when embarked. An embarked flight consisted of pilot, observer, aircrewman, and seven maintainers. An added dividend was the rebirth of the RNZN's observer branch. Observers were selected among naval officers who had obtained their bridge-watching certificate and had served at sea. Their extensive

Former US Navy SH-2F BuNo 150171 was one of four SH-2Fs that Kaman supplied to the RNZN in mid-1997 to replace its Westland Wasps, pending the arrival of SH-2Gs. Here, in 1998, NZ3443 was assigned to No. 3 Squadron Naval Support Flight. *Author's collection*

March 6, 2015, marked the arrival of three SH-2G(I)s of an order of ten to replace earlier SH-2G(NZ)s. Prior to assignment to RNZAF No. 6 Squadron at Base Auckland, an acceptance ceremony was held that included Maori warriors, whose ancient warrior tradition won them a reputation as some of the fiercest warriors of the South Sea. *Courtesy of A/Sgt. Judith Boulton*

Putting aside its alliance with British industry in selecting Kaman's Super Seasprite over Westland's Lynx, the RNZN changed direction from its Australian counterpart, trading a lesser capability for a new airframe to reduce cost and ensure longevity. Evidence of the change lies in the favor shown the SH-2G(NZ), such as NZ3603 (shown here in 2012) and the later SH-2G(I). *Courtesy of Erik Roelofs*

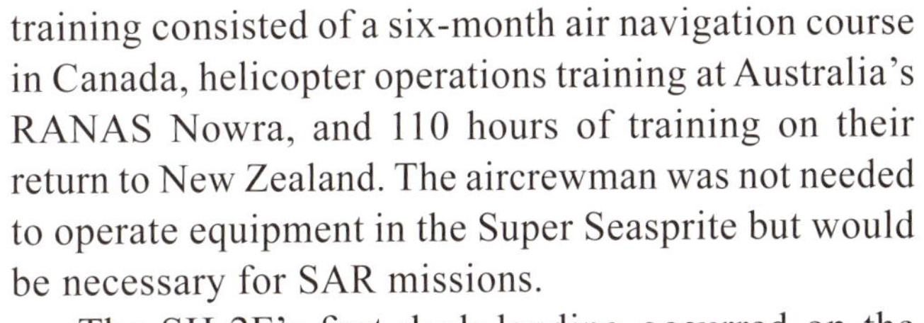

training consisted of a six-month air navigation course in Canada, helicopter operations training at Australia's RANAS Nowra, and 110 hours of training on their return to New Zealand. The aircrewman was not needed to operate equipment in the Super Seasprite but would be necessary for SAR missions.

The SH-2F's first deck landing occurred on the Leander-class frigate HMNZS *Canterbury* on September 18, 1998. Operations from ANZAC-class frigates included trials from ANZAC frigates HMNZS *Te Kaha* and *Te Mana*, and deployments to East Timor and the Persian Gulf, the latter in support of United Nations operations.

Lt. Cmdr. John Toon, a Royal New Zealand Navy pilot, said of the SH-2F, "The F is a very impressive performer and extremely compatible in the small-ship environment. It has exceeded early expectations, is providing invaluable as a training platform, and will enable us to hit the deck running when the G arrives."

The arrival of the first two SH-2G(NZ) Super Seasprites brought to a close the short but productive career of the RNZN SH-2Fs. The trio of operational SH-2Fs was withdrawn from service in June 2001, with one returned to the US and the remaining two used as spare parts; SH-2F and SH-2G components had 75 percent commonality. The first two SH-2G(NZ)s were formally presented at a rollout ceremony at RNZAF Base Whenuapai on August 18, 2001, with the third and fourth examples delivered later that year. The fifth and final SH-2G(NZ) arrived in February 2003. During 2002 and 2003, RNZN Super Seasprites were embarked aboard *Te Kaha* and *Te Mana* in the Persian Gulf in support of Operation Enduring Freedom.

On October 31, 2005, the Royal New Zealand Navy's No. 6 Squadron was reestablished to assume No. 3 Squadron's duty of operating the navy's air element. Based at Whenuapai under the Air Component commander, Headquarters Joint Forces New Zealand, No. 6 Squadron deployed helicopters aboard navy frigates

Located in the nose section of New Zealand's SH-2G(I) are radar-based missile-warning systems, Raytheon AN/AAQ-16 FLIR, and search and landing lights. The tublike radome houses either LN-66HP or APS-143 search radar with AN/AAQ-22 thermal imager. *Author's collection*

Te Kaha and *Te Mana*, the multimission *Canterbury*, and offshore patrol vessels *Otago* and *Wellington*. This action separated the Naval Support Flight from No. 3 Squadron RNZAF, although the SH-2Gs were still maintained by the air force personnel, who at times were assigned to the Seasprite unit, including aboard ship. The aircrewman's position was changed to navy helicopter loadmaster, who, after training by the RNZAF, performed such tasks as hoist operation, aerial photography, and cargo handling.

Unlike its counterpart in the US Navy, New Zealand's Seasprites were optimized for antiship rather than antisubmarine operations. Functioning, therefore, primarily as surveillance platforms, the Kiwi Seasprites could also fill ASW, troop transport, and SAR roles. The SH-2G(NZ)'s range of equipment included APS-143(V)3 advanced search radar, AAQ-22 thermal imager, and an analog cockpit based on Litton's ASN-150 tactical navigation system. The firm Telephonics claimed that its AN/APS-143 had a range of 200 nautical miles and could detect a 1-meter target in sea state 3 at 20 nautical miles. The ability to carry two Raytheon TV or IR-guided AGM-65 Maverick missiles made New Zealand's Super Seasprite the only helicopter in the Southwest Pacific able to engage surface targets. Three test firings had been conducted by BuNo 163214 in mid-February 1996. Other armament included two Mk. 46 torpedoes, and provisions for pintle-mounted 7.62 mm M60D machine guns for embargo and counter-drug operations. Early in 2008, Fabrique Nationale MAG-58M 7.62 mm machine guns replaced the M60Ds. Eight Mk. 25 marine markers in two launchers were also carried. A 3,000 psi hydraulic Harpoon deck lock was used to recover the SH-2G(NZ) in high sea states, with a three-wire traversing system for moving the aircraft into the ship's hangar. This combination system was considered less complex and less costly than the RAST system used on Australia's ANZAC ships.

The third batch of Seasprites acquired by the New Zealand Defense Force consisted of six various former US Navy models taken from AMARC storage for use as ground instructional airframes. These were US Navy BuNos 150146, 150152, 150173, 151323, 151333, and 152199, which in 2009 were shipped to the Royal New Zealand Air Force ground-training wing at Woodburne.

Since the five SH-2G(NZ)s were due for midlife upgrades or were experiencing corrosion issues, the RNZN instead decided in 2012 to purchase ten of the eleven SH-2G(A)s rejected by the Royal Australian Navy. Kaman modernized the ex-Australian Super Seasprites, which the company redesignated its "International" model SH-2G(I). Noteworthy among the upgrades in the International model

The Royal New Zealand Navy's SH-2G(NZ) NZ3605 in 2006 preparing to land aboard the carrier USS *Abraham Lincoln* (CVN-72). Located at midfuselage is the launcher for four Mk. 25 smoke markers. Support braces were necessary for the stores station. *Courtesy of US Navy*

The crew-served Belgian 7.62 mm FN MAG 58 machine gun for New Zealand's SH-2Gs. *Author's collection*

The downward-folding rescue hoist of the SH-2G, with the time-honored horse collar. Below the hoist hinge are folding steps. *Courtesy of Milosz Rusiecki*

Royal New Zealand Navy SH-2G(I) NZ3612 in 2012. Among numerous features introduced in the SH-2G(I) were crashworthy self-sealing fuel tanks, a deck-landing system, provisions for six crashworthy passenger seats, and NVG-compatible internal lighting. *Courtesy of Erik Roelofs*

The orange radome of NZ3618 houses a transmitter beacon that jettisons in a crash. Midfuselage is the smoke float launcher, and a SATCOM antenna tops the tail boom. *Courtesy of Royal New Zealand Navy*

With US registration N352KA censored from the photo, the SH-2G test-fires a Raytheon AGM-65D TV-guided maverick missile. Intended for arming RNZN SH-2Gs, the missile was tested at the US Army's Yuma Proving Ground during February 1996 and during December 2000. *Courtesy of US Navy*

was the switch from the Maverick missile to the more lethal Penguin antishipping missile. The I model's first flight occurred in April 2014, with the first aircraft accepted by the New Zealand Defense Force in December. Deliveries were completed in early 2016. April 21 of that year saw the last flight of the SH-2G(NZ), when they returned from cyclone disaster relief duty in Fiji. Eight of the SH-2G(I) s were made operational, with the remaining two used as spares. In Kiwi service, all SH-2G(I)s were registered NZ3611 through NZ3620; their former US. Navy BuNos were 163210, 150156, 161913, 161656, 152205, 151329, 161914, 150160, 151310, and 149773, respectively. While at Kaman during transitional periods between different nations, US N-number registrations for testing were worn on the aircraft. New Zealand's original five Super Seasprites were sold to Peru in October 2014.

POLISH DRAGONS

The first ship-deck landing of a Polish helicopter occurred in November 1978, when an Mi-2RM sea-rescue variant of the "Hoplite" landed on the helipad of the large landing ship 773KL/3. The landing was for demonstration only, since the vessel was built in Poland for Libya. A decade later, when the PZL W-3t "Sokol" (Falcon) helicopter was introduced to the Polish navy, deliveries of eight SAR versions, the W-3RM "Anakonda," followed. Tests of ship-helicopter operations in the Baltic Sea remained low priority since shore-based helicopters proved up to the task. Further limiting helicopter ship operations was the existence of only one helicopter-capable ship, the ORP *Warszawa*, which had a permanent helipad but no hangar.

The standard weapons load for New Zealand's SH-2G Super Seasprites was the Mk. 46 torpedo and the AGM-65D Maverick missile, or two Mavericks. The Maverick was a logical choice since it was included in the arsenal of RNZAF A-4 Skyhawks. Live Maverick firings took place in September 2008 as part of a joint exercise, using floating shipping containers off Great Barrier Island. *Courtesy of Royal New Zealand Navy*

During the 1990s the Polish navy became involved with NATO activities, with membership secured at the end of the decade. Since NATO members were obligated to participate in the Atlantic naval force team, the US government provided two Oliver Hazard Perry–class frigates commissioned as ORP *Gen. Kazimierz Pulaski* (formerly USN Clark) and ORP *Gen. Tadeusz Kosciuszko* (formerly USN *Wadsworth*). Delivered in 2002 and 2003, respectively, they would host the Polish navy's first permanently embarked helicopter units. Since the frigates were short-hull versions, the choice of helicopter type was limited, prompting the US Navy to suggest the proven Seasprite. In April 2000, the commander of the Polish navy sent a letter of request to the US for the transfer of four SH-2Gs for assignment to the two frigates. After financial haggling, a contract was signed in August 2002.

The four SH-2Gs, which were the last four delivered to the US Navy, were recovered from AMARC storage. The first two refurbished Super Seasprites (BuNos 163544 and 163546) were flown by Kaman pilots to the former USS *Wadsworth* for the ship's delivery voyage to Poland, arriving at the end of September 2002. The four, having construction nos. 247–250, retained their US Navy BuNos in Polish service; 163543–163546. The aircraft were not armed for delivery, which limited the crew of three to search, track, and identify targets, the results of which were transferred to the ship for possible attack. American instructors arrived with the pair of SH-2Gs. During a ceremonial baptism of the two aircraft on October 25, 2002, the Super Seasprites flew demonstration flights with mixed Polish-American crews. Four Polish pilots and two navigators soon arrived at Kaman's training center at Bloomfield, where, despite their helicopter experience, they had to learn new techniques familiar to Western helicopters. The main rotor rotation is opposite that of Polish and Soviet helicopters, and transition to the imperial measurement system was required. Poland's two SH-2Gs remaining in the US that were used for training were shipped to Germany for collection by Polish crews and US instructors for destination Gdynia.

On August 25, 2003, all four Super Seasprites formed the 28th Naval Air Squadron "Dragonflies." Training in shipboard operations was followed by landings on a simulated flight deck at Babie Doly Air Base. Each crew accomplished a hundred landings, half at night, aboard the ORP *Kosciuszko*. Training ended by October, when the Dragonflies became operational as the only NATO unit flying the SH-2G. In October 2003, the Dragonflies were deemed fully operational. During ongoing training, SH-2G aircrews learned the lessons of gradual acceptance by ship crews and the importance of cooperation. Training activities grew, along with participation in international exercises. The farthest northern cruises brought the Dragonflies to the coast of Norway, including crossing the polar circle in 2014 and 2017. From the outset, the SH-2Gs were based at Gdynia, which is Poland's largest and most vital naval air base, which borders a major naval shipyard.

In 2007, Poland's Super Seasprites underwent upgrades to carry MU-90 "Impact" torpedoes, along with updated electronics. The weapon, however, was not launched until October 30, 2013. Further improvements, based on service in the Mediterranean and Black Seas, saw the installation of a 7.62 mm PK/PKM machine gun in the cabin doorway.

A Polish navy Seasprite was aboard frigate *Gen. T. Kosciuszko*, berthed at Cruise Line Terminal of England's Liverpool Pierhead in late May 2013 in celebration of the seventieth anniversary of the Battle of the Atlantic. More than twenty-five warships from six nations participated. *Author's collection*

Polish navy SH-2Gs retained their US Navy bureau numbers. In 2013, no. 163546 was given a dramatic paint scheme adopted for the tenth anniversary of the 28th Naval Air Squadron "Dragonflies." Inspired by the squadron's name, Polish army helicopter pilot Mariola Andrasik creatively turned the dragonfly into a sea dragon for the special marking. Called the "Jubilee Dragon," the artwork, which was on the port side only, was printed on special foil, which survived for three years before it was removed. *Courtesy of Milosz Rusiecki*

A Polish navy crewman loads AN/SSQ 53F passive sonobuoys into the SH-2G 163546.
Courtesy of Milosz Rusiecki

The sensor operator's station in the Polish navy's modernized SH-2G(I) in 2008. *Courtesy of Miroslav Gyurosi*

The SH-2G was also used as a platform for a special-forces sniper, especially for antipiracy operations.

By 2018, the Polish navy's Seasprites were nearing half of their factory-guaranteed airframe life. With significant upgrades and technical support from Kaman, they could provide many good years of service. In May 2018, Poland's Ministry of National Defense announced an impending withdrawal of SH-2Gs from service, citing mainly the cessation of support from Kaman. By 2020, Poland, in the midst of revamping its Soviet-legacy helicopter fleet, prepared to replace the Super Seasprites with four to eight Leonardo AW159 or PZL W-3 Sokol ASW variants. The program to acquire a multipurpose shipborne helicopter was code-named "Kondor."

As of this writing, the Kondor program has slowed down, due mainly to the priority given other defense projects such as multirole helicopters and attack helicopters. The decision on these has not been forthcoming. Also slowing the retirement process of the Polish SH-2G is the replacement of aging mother ships with new Swordfish-class frigates.

THE PERUVIAN NAVY SH-2G(P) SUPER SEASPRITE

In a move to bolster its antisubmarine and antisurface warfare capabilities, the government of Peru and General Dynamics Canada in October 2014 agreed to acquire and modernize four SH-2Gs scheduled for retirement from the Royal New Zealand Navy. The following month, a contract was let by Kaman and General Dynamics to proceed with the upgrade, with support of a fifth airframe provided by Kaman. The five aircraft composed the first batch of Super Seasprites acquired by New Zealand; their RNZN serial nos. were NZ3601, NZ3602, NZ 3603, NZ3604, and NZ3455. On September 4, 2008, NZ3602 had been the first Super Seasprite to fire the Maverick missile against a floating target.

The "front office" of the Polish navy SH-2G. *Courtesy of Milosz Rusiecki*

Although the Polish navy completed SH-2G modifications to use the MU90 torpedo in 2007, the first MU90 launch took place in October 2013. *Courtesy of Grzegorz Waletko*

The protective shrouds that protect avionics from water are unfastened while nose doors are open on this Polish SH-2G at Gdynia-Babie Doly Air Base in October 2022. *Courtesy of Milosz Rusiecki*

A Polish SH-2G keeps company with an Mi-14PL ASW "Haze" helicopter in 2008. Derived from the earlier Mi-8, Mi-14 is the Soviet shore-based ASW helicopter, six of which were partnered with Poland's SH-2G ASW force. *Courtesy of Milosz Rusiecki*

French and Italian collaborative design in the 1980s led to development of the MU90 torpedo, which featured a shape charge warhead that can penetrate any known submarine hull, especially the Soviet double hull. The torpedo is 9 feet in length, weighs 670 pounds, and can be launched from aircraft or ship. *Courtesy of Marian Kluczynski*

After operations in the Mediterranean and Black Seas in 2008, the Polish navy equipped its SH-2Gs with 7.62 mm PK/PKM machine guns in the rescue/pilot's doorway. Foldable mounts allowed cabin doors to be closed. The Soviet weapon also armed Mi-2, Mi-8/17, and Mi-24 helicopters. *Courtesy of Milosz Rusiecki*

Polish Super Seasprites were overall Light Ghost Gray (FS36375) with Dark Ghost Gray (FS36320) upper surfaces. The separation of the two colors is barely visible on no. 163544's nose and top structure. *Courtesy of Milosz Rusiecki*

Polish special-operations troops fast-rope from an SH-2G to board the frigate *Gen. T. Kosciuszko*. The ship, one of two Oliver Hazard Perry–class guided-missile frigates donated to Poland in 2002, is the former US Navy USS *Wadsworth* (FFG-9). In 2000, the US government donated USS *Clark* (FFG-11) to Poland, which became the ORP *Gen. Kazimierz Pulaski*. *Courtesy of Milosz Rusiecki*

The arrival of Peru's first remanufactured SH-2G at Lima in January 2021. Peruvian Super Seasprites initially were assigned to Escuadrón Aeronaval de Ataque No. 22, eventually joining Naval Air Squadron 21. *Courtesy of Santiago Rivas, Pucara Defensa*

Central to the SH-2G(P)'s integrated mission systems were General Dynamic's sonobuoy and stores management system. Like with all US Navy and international SH-2Gs, search-and-rescue, surveillance, and utility capabilities were retained.

Since Peru's fifth airframe was not remanufactured, it was first to arrive in January 2016 but was damaged during unloading at El Callao Harbor. After extensive repair, it was fit for duty in May 2018. The first two completed rebuilt SH-2G(P)s were tested by the Peruvian navy at Kaman's Bloomfield facility in March 2019. The final contract for all mission integration systems was signed in mid-2020. In 2021, all four aircraft joined Agusta-Bell 212 and Bell 206B helicopters of Naval Air Squadron 21 for service aboard four Italian Lupo-class frigates.

Above: The Peruvian SH-2G(P), four of which were remanufactured following service with New Zealand. *Courtesy of Kaman Aerospace Corp.*

Left: The SH-2G's T700-GE-401 turbojet engine. *Courtesy of Miroslav Gyurosi*

Despite modernization, the SH-2G(I) Super Seasprite retained the familiar profile of earlier models. Here, Kaman's demonstrator SH-2G (international) was featured at the Black Sea Defense Aerospace & Security Exhibition at Bucharest, Romania, in September 2008. *Courtesy of Miroslav Gyurosi*

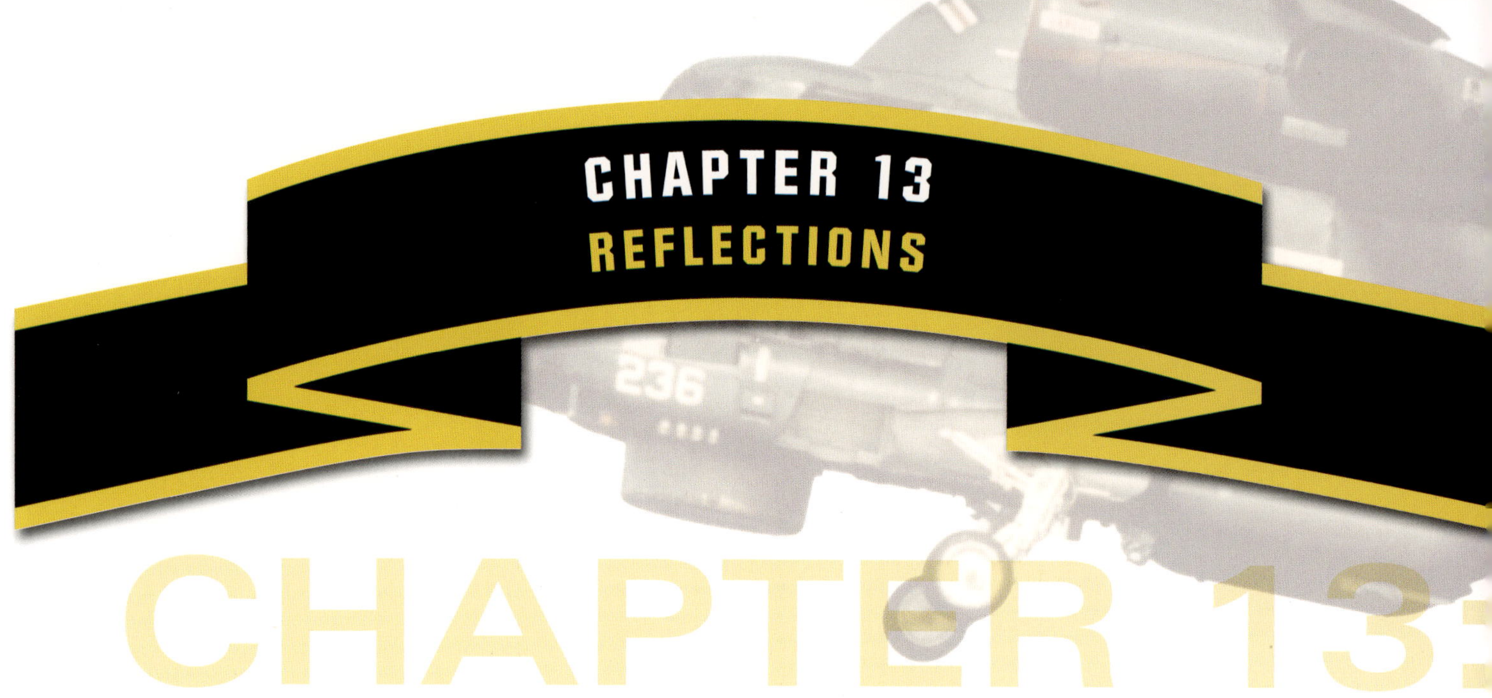

CHAPTER 13
REFLECTIONS

Stories of people and aircraft that rose to prominence throughout the Seasprite's long history could fill another volume. Countless individuals gave rise to the Seasprite's legacy, often when many felt that the helicopter was nearing its twilight. But dedicated engineers, leaders, and tacticians continually breathed new life into the machine that proved a most vital cog in the US Navy's top warfare priority: antisubmarine warfare, the systems of which must operate in a complex and variable ocean environment.

The US Navy's original intent was to create the most versatile helicopter possible, designed specifically for shipboard multipurpose missions. The Navy got more than it bargained for when one looks at the Seasprite's long history of adaptation to configurations and missions. To satisfy changing requirements, the H-2 leapfrogged from the single-engine UH-2A/B to the twin-engine UH-2C, to the armed and armored HH-2C, to the uprated HH-2D, to the SH-2D LAMPS, to the SH-2F, to the modernized SH-2G, and test variants and international designations in between. Having won favor over the famed Bell HueyCobra gunship, it was ordered in large numbers by the US Army until politics came into play. As was often the case, changes occurred with a particular aircraft that was singled out to prove the type's versatility, thereby extending the life cycle of the breed. Like the Douglas DC-3, which grudgingly passed into history, the Seasprite, although serving in the shadow of more-popular helicopters, dutifully soldiered on for more than half a century. During metamorphosis, the Seasprite's basic fuselage dimensions remained unchanged but carried increases in gross weights totaling more than 3,000 pounds.

Considering all that was asked of the Seasprite, having endured its share of growing pains and periods of dubious reputation, it provided long-term usefulness at minimal expense. Often, one of the run is singled out to serve as a test platform, which, typically, is given a nickname. Probably the most notable of Seasprite helicopters, however, was known simply as "number 981." Having begun life as an HU2K-1 (construction no. 14) assigned US Navy BuNo 147981, this Seasprite best illustrates the entire evolution of the series. Frequently bailed to Kaman since it was accepted by the Navy on December 28, 1960, no. 981 was the most prolifically tested H-2 airframe, resulting in multiple, successive designations.

No. 981 began its testing career in 1961 as one of five HU2K-1s selected for the Navy's Board of Inspection and Survey (BIS) trials after the type was approved for production. From June until August it was tested at the Langley AFB wind tunnel and later participated in the BIS flying-qualities demonstration at the NATC, Pax River. From September 1962 until February 1963, no. 981 underwent environmental testing at Eglin AFB, Florida, where it was subjected to temperature extremes of −65 degrees to 130 degrees Fahrenheit in a climatic chamber. Climatic testing included airborne icing tests at Ottawa, Canada. When bailed to Kaman during 1963 and 1964, it flight-tested various rotor blade designs and associated vibration analyses. In June 1964 the fish-pole rescue boom was installed for testing, often in conjunction with a collapsible "ladle" rescue net.

In 1961, BuNo 147981 was one of five airframes that underwent Bureau of Inspection and Survey (BIS) trials when the HU2K-1 was approved for production. From June to August 1961, no. 981 was the subject of wind tunnel tests at Langley AFB, Virginia, followed by flying-quality demonstrations at NAS Patuxent River. An explanation based on firsthand experience of 981's vastly altered fuselage is elusive; however, it is likely that various airframe designs were considered. *Courtesy of US Navy*

The HU2K-1 BuNo 147981 was subjected to icing trials at Ottawa, Canada, then went to Eglin AFB, Florida, for climatic hangar cold testing. The aircraft was sprayed with –4-degree Fahrenheit fog and was started without preheating after being "cold-soaked" at –65 degrees Fahrenheit for three days. *Courtesy of US Navy*

Undoubtedly the most significant change in 981's life occurred in October 1964, when it was selected as the prototype for the twin-engine installation, becoming the first UH-2C, then designated NUH-2C. No. 981 continued flight and static testing with the twin power plant into early 1967, when all UH-2A/Bs had been earmarked for the major modification. During this period, 981 served as the test platform for payload evaluation, Kaman-developed bearings, and experimentation of antiresonant vibration isolators. Other test programs related to the twin-engine installation included evaluation of a new fire-extinguishing system and a 200-foot rescue hoist cable, both of which became standard on H-2s. To better manage the UH-2C's increased gross weight for the vertical-replenishment mission, no. 981 performed initial trials with a four-blade tail rotor.

In August 1968, 981 was fit with stub wings for mounting a variety of stores, including ordnance and auxiliary fuel tanks; these wings also were "wet," having internal tanks.

No. 981 served first as the mockup and later the prototype twin-engine UH-2C. It is seen here on March 22, 1966, fitted with nose-mounted instrumentation. The tailplane and braces were painted red and yellow-striped. The aircraft designation on the tail rotor pylon was "UH-2-C." *Courtesy of US Navy*

Seasprite pilot Scott Milner, who was extensively involved with development of the H-2, offered his recollection of a segment of 981's testing career:

> In 1969, the Navy believed that the H-2 needed enhanced vision at night for surveillance of foreign shipping. Night vision goggles either were not yet developed or were in their infancy; low-light-level television (LLLTV), however, did exist. A system was mounted into 981, with the monitor being placed on the console between the pilots. We flew three or four flights over the countryside in Pennsylvania and Connecticut. Unfortunately, the ambient lighting wasn't ideal, as there were always some lights from houses nearby. It was apparent that placement of the monitor in the cockpit could lead both

The fish pole and hoist rescue system was first tested on no. 981 in June 1964. Here, the fish pole at maximum extension is used in conjunction with the rescue net. *Courtesy of US Navy*

Wearing the stylized "W" of the Weapons Test Directorate, NUH-2C no. 981 during tests with the AIM-7 Sparrow missile at the Pacific Missile Range, Point Mugu, California, in July 1972. The tests successfully demonstrated that a Sparrow missile could be launched from a helicopter against a moving target. *Courtesy of US Navy*

Since the Navy had been mounting equipment on test bed helicopters to augment the weapons and radar systems of ships since the 1960s, unsurprisingly, on March 29, 1971, AIM-9G missiles were test-fired from NUH-2C no. 981, assigned to NADC. The AIM-9G, which had an improved seeker over its predecessor, the AIM-9D, had been adopted by the Navy in 1970. A camera was mounted over the NADC title on the tail boom. *Courtesy of US Navy*

pilots to focus on it and not flying the aircraft. That was not a good idea, and downright dangerous. We recommended that further evaluation be conducted, so the system was removed from 981 and was sent to HC-5 at NAAS Imperial Beach, where it was installed in a UH-2C. Just to try a dumb idea twice, again the monitor was installed in the cockpit. Lt. Dennis Christian and crew flew at Ft. Huachuca, Arizona, a very, very dark environment. There, the miles of desert floor gave them the opportunity to thoroughly test the concept. After several late-night flights with no moon, again it was concluded that the monitor should never be in the cockpit, as it was too distracting. When they returned to Imperial Beach, the configuration was removed and never again tested in an H-2. Bureau Number 147981 was an interesting old airframe; a unique aircraft.

Earlier tests with external stores led to more-advanced weapons evaluations beginning in early 1971 with the AIM-9G Sidewinder missile. Developed for the US Navy and based on the AIM-9D, the AIM-9G was a short-range air-to-air missile with an improved seeker head. In early 1972, the NUH-2C BuNo 147981 flew to Raytheon's facility at Hanscom Field, Bedford, Massachusetts, where an AIM-7 Sparrow III medium-range air-to-air missile was mounted, with corresponding fire direction control radar housed in a nose section from an F-4E Phantom. No. 981 was then airlifted by C-5A from Kaman's Bradley Field to the Navy's Pacific Missile Range, Point Mugu, California. In July 1972, four Sparrows and several Sidewinders were successfully air-launched at moving surface targets. No. 981 was then returned to Kaman for conversion to an HH-2D and labeled NHH-2D. External LAMPS equipment was mounted, along with the 101 rotor system, uprated engines, and new landing gear, all of which were earmarked for the SH-2D, and later SH-2F. As the SH-2D prototype, no. 981 was also experimentally fit with the AN-ASQ-81 MAD unit and an early version of an associated data link.

No. 981's time on the research trail seemed endless. In 1973 it was on to Lakehurst, where the NAEC used 981 to experiment with both "Beartrap" and "Harpoon" haul-down, rapid-capture securing systems. In spring 1974, 981 came under a new master to perform simulated shipboard landing operations on a mock Knox-class flight deck, in preparation for enlargement of the frigates' hangars and flight decks to accommodate the LAMPS Mk. 1. The test also served as validation of new flight deck markings and other visual aids.

Showing no signs of fatigue, no. 981 in fall 1979 was modified to be Kaman's demonstrator of the XH-2/CCR circulation control rotor, with the first flight made on September 18. The XH-2/CCR program, under a Naval Air Systems Command contract, examined replacing conventional cyclic pitch with direct cyclic control of blade life, using compressed airflow ejected from full-span slots of the rotor blades' trailing edge.

No. 981 eventually ended its career as an SH-2F. In the words of test pilot Scott Milner, "Good ol' 981. It was a real trooper." The final entry on 981's individual record card is dated November 1981.

Edward W. Barewich, one of the USMC UH-2B pilots, wrote of the Seasprite:

> The UH-2B Seasprite's short tenure with the Marine Corps demonstrated what has been a hallmark of the Marine Corps, using what you have and exploiting it to its maximum advantage. Thanks to the Seasprite's design features and unique capabilities, together with its dedicated and motivated crew, it performed its mission in a near-flawless manner and even in unexpected ways, such as the light-water experiment. And then consider those individuals, who in their respective extreme moments of need, saw the Seasprite as their savior. With confidence I believe I speak for all those pilots and fellow crew chiefs who flew the Seasprite, or who helped to maintain her, the feelings of pride and accomplishment that come with successfully completing your mission and all the while proudly representing our Corps. The UH-2B Seasprite served us well.

Designated an NHH-2D, BuNo 147981 at NADC, NAS Lakehurst, on March 19, 1973. *Courtesy of Stephen Miller*

Wearing the emblem of the Naval Air Test Facility on its cargo door, as an SH-2F, no. 981 performs simulated shipboard operations on a mock Knox-class flight deck at NATF NAS Lakehurst in April 1974. During the 1970s, Knox-class frigates had a flight deck and hangar for DASH helicopters, which were enlarged to accommodate LAMPS Seasprites. *Courtesy of US Navy via Brian Miller collection*

Among the ranks of naval aviators are individuals whose names ring synonymous with the H-2 helicopter. Rod Stoker provides this insight explaining why his father, LaRon Stoker, easily stands out as one of those responsible for the Seasprite's success:

> Everyone I have spoken with says he was a hell of a good pilot. I think it helped knowing how much he absolutely loved it. The Navy and flying were his life. He was scheduled to join the Air Force when he was in college, but he was rejected as a result of injuries sustained in a car crash. When he fully recovered, the Navy was making its rounds through campus and signed him into the Naval Cadet program. He never looked back. LaRon Stoker began his helicopter career in 1957, going from flight school to HS-1 at Key West, to VX-6 in Antarctica, to becoming a flight instructor at Pensacola. The remainder was mostly at San Diego from squadron to squadron as he moved up the ranks. He was there from the start to full development of the LAMPS program. The H-2 was his mistress! He loved that bird! I've been told many times that there were few that knew it as well as he did, and not many could fly it the way he did. He knew her limits and loved pushing it to the edge to get the most out of it. He was a bit of a "seat of your pants" pilot. I guess the crop-dusting days when he first learned to fly never wore off.
>
> The H-2 was not a high-profile aircraft, but those who flew them seem to hold them in high esteem. His flight logs show his first flight in an A model in December 1965. The last log I have ends in April 1977, when he had 5,447 total flight hours, more than 2,000 of which were in H-2s. He was still flying them through 1980, when we left Japan, so that number grew. Anytime he could get time on the stick, he did. I am quite proud of

Although we might question the authenticity of this photo, it is safe to say that aircraft evaluated by other services sometimes wore the markings of that service. As the UH-2C prototype, BuNo 147981 underwent cold-weather testing at an Air Force facility. Nor was it unusual for manufacturers to feature their products in various schemes and markings to elicit sales to that service. *Courtesy of US Navy*

my dad and the men like Scott Milner, who flew with him.

Scott Milner received his wings in 1966 and was assigned to HC-1 CVA detachment flying the UH-2A/B. In 1969 he was assigned to HC-5 as a UH-2C instructor. As the first OIC of LAMPS at NADC, he was involved with configuring the aircraft, learning systems, writing procedures, and flying with unusual equipment attached to HH-2Ds that were dedicated to the project. Milner delivered the first SH-2D to HC-5 in early 1971. The following year, he sailed with the first West Coast deployment aboard USS *Sterett* (DLG-31), and the first East Coast deployment aboard USS *Belknap* (DLG-26). Milner says about LaRon Stoker:

Ron was our mentor and leader during the R&D phases of LAMPS. He was a special guy to all of us who were fortunate to have been a part of that growing program. Ron was involved in many special projects that led to phenomenal innovations. He was the first to actually accomplish HIFR with 30-gallon barrels in the cargo compartment of the H-2. Not pretty, but it worked and later became standard procedure for all naval helicopters.

To gain all-around perspective of the H-2's history, Richard "Dick" Collier provides insight to the manufacturer's role in the life of the Seasprite, beginning in 1970:

I spent thirty years working for Kaman Aerospace. During my early years I was logistics support representative working at NAS North Island, Barbers Point, Cubi Point, and Atsugi, supporting the various LAMPS squadrons. I was also involved with the SH-2D BIS at Pax River in the early 1970s. In the 1980s, I was Kaman's integrated logistics support (ILS) manager, working with NAVAIR on procurement of the SH-2F and SH-2G. In the 1990s, I was heavily involved with H-2 procurement for Egypt, Australia, and New Zealand. I retired from Kaman in 2000 as the director of customer service.

From the very introduction of the H-2 to the US Navy, Kaman's primary point of contact with the Navy users was its service department. This department was established years earlier in support of the H-43 series of rescue helicopters utilized by the US Air Force. The service department consisted of an administrative section, service publications, service engineering, and the field service group. Field service reps assigned to various bases from which H-2s operated worked with the squadrons to provide on-site assistance and technical support, as well as a direct line back to the factory. Field reps provided Kaman with daily and weekly reports on aircraft status and issues that arose during fleet operations. Service engineers analyzed field problems, consulted with design and structural engineers, and provided recommendations to improve aircraft maintainability. Kaman logistics personnel were required to sign off on engineering drawings to ensure that reliability and maintainability issues had been addressed. Service engineering sponsored publication of the bimonthly magazine *Rotor Tips*, which reported squadron activities, maintainability improvements, and articles of interest within the H-2 and H-43 communities. Besides ensuring that issues of *Rotor Tips* reached units and field service offices, Kaman awarded pins to pilots and crewmen involved with rescues, and plaques to pilots when they achieved one thousand through four thousand flight hours in the aircraft.

In the early 1980s, the service department experienced significant growth as a result of the expanded ILS requirements that came with the purchase of new aircraft. Thanks to input from field service reps, logistics personnel could identify potential fleet problems to NAVAIR so that fixes could begin; similar practice existed in the production program, with problems identified at monthly program reviews. Kaman developed a component-forecasting program to assist the government in the purchase of long-lead-time finite-life components. Flight hours on these components were tracked at the squadron level for feeding into the forecasting system. Often-needed components could be diverted from production assets to satisfy fleet operational requirements.

Kaman, as a company, was totally committed to supporting the needs of the operators. Never were considerations such as cost or manpower given priority over the needs of the users. This approach and commitment to customer service carried forward to all Kaman customers, both foreign and domestic.

As the Seasprite went through a series of upgrades during the 1960s, mostly related to reliability improvements, Kaman was developing engineering change proposals to offer the Navy various upgrades to improve components' reliability and maintainability. Kaman, under contract with the Naval Air Engineering Service Unit (NAESU), deployed airframe, avionics, and logistics representatives to major H-2 installations, including Lakehurst, Norfolk, Imperial Beach, and North Island. These reps provided daily assistance and interface between squadrons and engineering, customer service, and supply support departments at Kaman. When the Navy elected to add an additional engine to the H-2, Kaman developed a modification program whereby fleet aircraft entered a production line for modification to the twin-engine model, and standard depot-level maintenance (SDLM).

With the transition of the H-2 mission from detachments of three to four aircraft aboard aircraft carriers to single aircraft operating alone at sea, the logistics of supporting this concept became more important than ever. With the deployment of multiple aircraft and the large storage capacity of a carrier, more spares could be carried. Intermediate-level maintenance capabilities aboard the carrier could handle shipboard repairs, and, in the worst cases, parts could be removed from one aircraft to keep another mission ready. Due to the limited storage aboard LAMPS ships, a shipboard "pack-up" of spares was developed to provide the aircraft ninety days of support while deployed. These pack-ups, which consisted of about 600 pounds of spares, to include everything from nuts and bolts to main rotor blades, batteries, and tires, were refined over the years to support aircraft configuration changes. "Out of Area" supplemental pack-ups were made available for ships that deployed to the Indian Ocean and Australia.

NAS Cubi Point was the primary support hub for LAMPS units in the WestPac area. Helicopter detachments flew off the ship upon entry to Subic Bay to perform needed maintenance. The air station originally was manned by Kaman field service reps until mid-1972, when HSL-31 assigned a liaison officer to Cubi Point to assist detachments. Ultimately, HSL-31's assignment became permanent. To support LAMPS in both the Pacific and Atlantic, pack-ups were rotated between LAMPS ships as they deployed. Upon cruise completion, pack-ups were offloaded, inventoried, and restocked ready for the next deployment. NAS Sigonella performed the same function for East Coast units.

With thc reopening of H-2 production in the 1980s, NAVAIR initiated a major logistics program by contracting with Kaman to perform a logistics support analysis to bring the aircraft support concept in line with organizational maintenance aboard small ships. This resulted in the development of new support equipment tailored to the shipboard environment, and establishment of the position of integrated logistics support manager.

I appreciate the opportunity to shed light on the significant impact that Kaman and its people had on the success of H-2 programs. There is not a day that goes by that I don't miss the rush of those days and the great people that I've had the pleasure of meeting and working with.

Testimony to the resiliency of the Seasprite lies in its continuation of service more than six decades after its first flight in 1959. The H-2 was a most vital element in the challenging world of antisubmarine warfare. With the collapse of the Soviet Union and end of the Cold War, the submarine threat dwindled and ASW proficiency suffered as defense priorities changed; ASW came to mean antisurface warfare . . . but we can no longer be fooled into thinking that the submarines of Russia, China, North Korea, and Iran lack the capability for supremacy.

The legacy of the Seasprite lies in the thousands of lives saved and the crewmen lost during the performance of their duties.

APPENDIX A

ACRONYMS, INITIALISMS, AND ABBREVIATIONS

AAA	antiaircraft artillery
ADF	automatic direction finding
Adm.	admiral
AGC	general communications vessel
ARG	amphibious ready group
AMARC	Aerospace Maintenance and Regeneration Center, Davis Monthan AFB, Arizona; prior to 1984 was MASDC (Military Aircraft Storage and Disposition Center)
ASE	automatic stabilization equipment
ASMD	antiship missile defense
ASROC	antisubmarine rocket
AUTEC	Atlantic Undersea Test and Evaluation Center

ANZAC	historical term for linked forces of Australia and New Zealand Army Corps
AW	naval aircrewman
BIS	Bureau of Inspection and Survey
BUWEPS	Bureau of Naval Weapons
Cmdr.	commander
CLG	light guided-missile cruiser
CNO	chief of naval operations
COD	carrier onboard delivery
CSAR	combat search and rescue
CV	fleet aircraft carrier
CVA	attack aircraft carrier
CVS	antisubmarine carrier
CVT	training aircraft carrier

DASH	drone antisubmarine helicopter
DCASO	Defense Contract Administration Services Office
DD	destroyer
DDE	destroyer escort
Det.	detachment
DLG	guided-missile frigate
ECM	electronic countermeasures
ESM	electronic support measures
FFAR	folding-fin aerial rocket
FFG	guided-missile frigate
FIP	fleet introduction program
FLIR	forward-looking infrared radar
FMS	Foreign Military Sales
FRAM	Fleet Rehabilitation and Maintenance Program
HC	helicopter combat support squadron
HCT	helicopter combat support training squadron
helo	Navyspeak for helicopter
HIFR	helicopter in-flight refueling; also referred to as hover in-flight refueling
HS	helicopter antisubmarine squadron
HSL	helicopter antisubmarine light
HU	helicopter utility

IFR	Instrument Flight Rules
JRB	joint reserve base
LAMPS	Light Airborne Multi-Purpose System
Lt. Cmdr.	lieutenant commander
LOH	light observation helicopter (US Army)
LSE	landing signalman, enlisted
Lt. (j.g.)	lieutenant junior grade
MAD	magnetic-anomaly detector
MCAS	Marine Corps air station
MEF	Middle Eastern Force
NAAS	naval auxiliary air station
NADEC	Naval Air Development Center, Johnsville, Pennsylvania
NAEC	Naval Air Engineering Center
NARF	Naval Air Rework Facility
NAS	naval air station
NASA	National Aeronautics and Space Administration
NASC	Naval Air Systems Command
NATC	Naval Air Training Center
NATO	North Atlantic Treaty Organization
NATF	Naval Air Test facility (NAS Lakehurst, 1958–77)
NATOPS	Naval Air Training and Operating Procedures Standardization

NAVAIR	Naval Air Systems Command, successor to BUWEPS in 1966, headquartered at Patuxent River, Maryland
NAWC	Naval Air Weapons Center
NFO	naval flight officer
NMNA	National Museum of Naval Aviation
NS	naval station
OIC	officer in charge
ONR	Office of Naval Research
ORP	Traditional prefix of Polish navy ships: stands for Okret Rzeczypospolite Polskies, which translates to Warship of Polish Republic
PAR	Point and Return, modification facility at Dothan, Alabama
PIRAZ	Positive Identification Radar Advisory Zone
R&D	research and development
RAdm.	rear admiral
RAN	Royal Australian Navy
RAST	Recovery Assist, Secure and Traverse system
RDT&E	research, development, test, and evaluation
RIO	radar intercept officer
RNZAF	Royal New Zealand Air Force
RNZN	Royal New Zealand Navy
RWTD	Rotary Wing Test Directorate
SAM	surface-to-air missile
SAR	search and rescue

SARDIP	selective aircraft reclamation and disposal in place
SDLM	Standard Depot Level of Maintenance; in 1995 transferred to civilian contract depot support at Pemco World Air Services, Dothan, Alabama
shp	shaft horsepower
senso	sensor operator
SO&ES	station operations and engineering squadron (USMC)
SONAR/sonar	sound navigation and ranging
TACAN	Tactical Air Navigation System
TACCO	tactical coordinator and sensor operator
T-AGS	Navy oceanographic survey ship
TF	task force
UHF	ultrahigh frequency
USAAVNTBD	US Army Aviation Test Board
USNS	United States Naval Ship
VAdm.	vice admiral
VERTREP	vertical replenishment
VFR	Visual Flight Rules
VU	utility squadron
VX	air development squadron
WestPac	western Pacific

APPENDIX B

US NAVY H-2 SEASPRITE BUREAU NUMBERS / KAMAN CONSTRUCTOR NUMBERS

[LISTED BY MODEL DESIGNATION AT TIME OF ENTRY INTO SERVICE]

This listing is by no means complete but is representative of facts obtained from various sources, including official documents, photographs, visual aids, and data such as records and logbooks provided by those who flew, maintained, and supported the H-2 Seasprite helicopter.

Among the information on Individual Aircraft Record Cards of some Seasprites are abbreviations that denote the presence of representatives at various US Navy concerns. Typically, on-site managers represented Naval Air Systems Command (NAVAIRSYSCOM), more commonly called "NAVAIR," and Bureau of Aeronautics (BUAER). Assigned to production and modification facilities, personnel of these offices represented NAVAIR interests in accepting new aircraft and ensuring compliance. Kaman H-2s underwent modifications at a small firm located at Dothan (Alabama) Airport. US Navy representative offices were Naval Plant Representative Office (NPRO), Defense Contract Administration Services Office (DCASO), Bureau of Aeronautics Representative (BAR), and Bureau of Naval Weapons Representative (BWR). BAR/BARR frequently was broken down as Maintenance & Support (M&S) and Research & Development (R&D).

Common throughout this list is the term "written off," which often is termed "struck off charge." However, there is interpretive distinction between the two: "written off" refers to an aircraft lost or damaged by accident or combat, to the extent it is uneconomical or militarily impractical to restore it to service. Aircraft that were struck off charge might have become obsolete, were in storage, or were struck off charge while undergoing rework. An administrative strike refers to aircraft removed from the frontline Navy inventory for transfer to other agencies or foreign air arms, ground training, testing, museum display, or technical purposes. A strike date often is not necessarily the date an accident occurred, or an aircraft might be stricken later than the date it was placed in storage. As of mid-June 1996, Kaman recorded a total of 145 Seasprites officially stricken, of a total of 250 produced; seventy were in storage, sixty-three at AMARC, six at the Dothan facility, and one in a museum.

Kaman constructor numbers follow the bureau numbers.

YHU2K-1 (REDESIGNATED YUH-2A IN 1962)

147202/1	accepted by USN on April 29, 1959; retained by Kaman for M&S/R&D; BARR/BAR with zero flight hours flown, was an administrative strike at Kaman on November 24, 1959
147203/2	first flight on July 2, 1959; administrative strike at Kaman on December 10, 1961; to UH-2B March 1965; withdrawn from use on June 9, 1965
147204/3	to UH-2B in March 1965; to NUH-2B in May 1968; administrative strike at Kaman on March 13, 1970
147205/4	accepted by USN on December 31, 1959; retained by Kaman for RDT&E/BWRR/BWR; administrative strike at Kaman on July 17, 1964, for use as airframe at structural test facility; mockup of ASW configuration for proposed Republic of China Navy in 1983

HU2K-1 (REDESIGNATED UH-2A IN 1962)

147972/5	administrative strike at Kaman on October 21, 1961
147973/6	to UH-2B in March 1965; administrative strike at Kaman October 18, 1967
147974/7	accepted by USN on June 29, 1960; retained by Kaman Bloomfield facility/BWR/BWRR; written off following accident during RDT&E on July 26, 1963, with 897 hours; salvaged for parts
147975/8	accepted by USN on July 28, 1960; retained by Kaman Bloomfield facility for testing/BWRR/BWR, destroyed during RDT&E on April 19, 1962, with 192 hours, possibly at NAS Patuxent River
147976/9	BUWEPS HU-1; ditched at sea at night, capsized, remained afloat, and recovered September 12, 1963, by USS *Bon Homme Richard,* written off October 30

147977/10	accepted by USN on September 29, 1960; retained by Kaman Bloomfield facility/BWR for testing; to NATC in April 1961 for RDT&E, with only 15 hours flown, was written off on April 17, 1961, possibly at Eglin AFB, Florida, following accident while assigned to RDT&E at NAS Pax River; salvaged for parts
147978/11	R&D; under bailment contract from factory for high-speed research, Army jet test; redesignated NUH-2B in May 1968; administrative strike at Kaman on March 17, 1969
147979/12	used in early 1965 for evaluation of static electricity discharge system; HC-4 Det. 36 "Scooter 5-4" "Gray Ghost" aboard amphibious force flagship USS *Estes* (AGC-12); crashed into sea off Vung Tau, South Vietnam, on April 8, 1968
147980/13	HC-1 Det. E 1965; HC-4 Det. 47 Kaman test aircraft aboard USS *Little Rock* (CLG-4) in 1969; HC-1 Det. 61, 14, 31; to HH-2D 1971; HSL-30 Support Det. aboard USS *Shreveport* (LPD-12); HSL-32 Det. 4 aboard USS *Capodanno* (FF-1093) in 1976; assigned to every East Coast LAMPS squadron as SH-2F; HSL-34 Det. 4, 2 aboard USS *Conolly* (DD-979), Det. 1 aboard USS *Moineste* (FF-1079), Det. 8 aboard USS *J. Hewes;* HC-4 Dets. 83, 49 aboard USS *Austin* (LPD-4); Dothan, Alabama, facility in 1981; HSL-84 1985–88; HSL-74; AMARC in December 1993
147981/14	UH-2C mockup / first UH-2C; most tested H-2 airframe with multiple designations, mainly NHH-2D
147982/15	HU-2 Det. 62 aboard USS *Independence,* crashed in Caribbean and sank on May 16, 1965, two crewmen missing
147983/16	NAWC/NATC; NAS Jacksonville; HC-2 Det. 16 aboard USS *Saratoga,* Det. 11 aboard USS *Intrepid,* crashed into sea due to engine failure on June 14, 1967
149013/17	HC-2; HSL-33; HH-2D 1970; SH-2D 1973; HSL-36 Det. 7; HSL-94; HSL-74; AMARC in December 1992
149014/18	HC-2 aboard USS *America,* lost on maintenance flight in bay at Istanbul, recovered, inspected, and sunk at sea, written off on April 9, 1966
149015/19	HC-2 Det. 60 aboard USS *Saratoga;* HH-2D 1970; SH-2D 1973; SH-2F 1973; HSL-33 crashed/ destroyed during night approach to NAS Lemoore on January 22, 1977

149016/20	first UH-2A to begin fleet duty, HU-1; HH-2D in 1970; loss at NAS Oceana on August 14, 1973
149017/21	HC-2 Det. 66; HC-4 Det. 47, 44; HH-2D in 1970; SH-2D in 1972; SH-2F in 1973; HSL-30; HSL-33; HSL-84; HSL-74; AMARC in January 1994
149018/22	HU-2 Det. 1; HU-1 Det. 1 Unit Q aboard USS *Bennington,* operational loss on July 1, 1964
149019/23	HU-2 recovered following crash into sea on December 11, 1963; written off on January 14, 1964
149020/24	HU-2 written off on August 13, 1963, at NAS Lakehurst
149021/25	HC-1 Det. A, USS *Midway* (CVA-41) (overall orange); NAS Adak HC-5; HH-2D in 1971; SH-2F Rotary Wing Test Directorate, 1982–86; storage at NAS Pensacola as N8059T; to USS *Hornet* Museum, Alameda, California, in 2006
149022/26	HU-1; HC-1 Det. A aboard USS *Midway in* 1965; SH-2F; HSL-33; HSL-35; static display at NAS North Island in 1992
149023/27	HU-2/HC-2; HC-4; HSL-34; HSL-35; HSL-33; AMARC in March 1993; to Kaman in 2009
149024/28	HC-2; HC-1 Det. E. Det. 5 (camo) aboard USS *King;* HC-7 as UH-2A; HH-2D; SH-2F HSL-32 "Dirty Sally"; HSL-34; HSL-94; AMARC in August 1993; to Kaman; to Royal Australian Navy
149025/29	HU-1 Det. 1; HC-5 (overall orange); UH-2A of HSL-30 based at NAS Atsugi; crashed into Houdai Mountain near Yokohama on October 6, 1964, six killed

149026/30	HC-5 (overall orange); HSL-30 written off at NAS Norfolk on June 25, 1986, after ditching in Atlantic from power loss on takeoff from USS *Compte de Grasse*; display at Norfolk
149027/31	HU-2 Det. 65 aboard USS *Enterprise,* written off on August 20, 1964
149028/32	HC-7; to HH-2D; HSL-31 Det. Alpha aboard USNS *Chauvenet;* HSL-30 Det. Alpha, crashed during instrument training flight at Londonderry, New Hampshire, on May 20, 1979, all five aboard killed
149029/33	HU-1; HU-2 damaged on July 23, 1964, at Key West; written off on August 31
149030/34	HU-1; HC-1 Det. 43 aboard USS *Coral Sea;* HC-7 no. 33; HH-2D HSL-31 Marine Coast & Geodetic Det. A Korea, in 1972–73; HSL-32 Det. 4; AMARC in July 1993; to New Zealand as SH-2G NZ3441
149031/35	one of two HH-2Ds not converted to LAMPS; HU-2 Det. 38; HC-1; HC-2 Dets. 42, 38; HC-4 Det. 3; HSL-30 Dets. A, 32, 35, 36; HSL-31 Det. B "SHAKA 1-4," USNS *Chauvenet* / USNS *Harkness;* BUWEP; Kaman, updated with SH-2F 101 rotor and -8F engine but retained aft tailwheel; last HH-2D in inventory; Pensacola museum, loaned to American Helicopter Museum
149032/36	HU-2 Det. 60 aboard USS *Saratoga;* HC-7; HSL-31 Det. 32 HH-2D COMSEVENTHFLT USS *Oklahoma City;* HSL-32 Det. 4 aboard USS *Donald B. Beary,* lost at sea off Martha's Vineyard on March 25, 1982
149033/37	HU-2 aboard USS *Independence;* HH-2D NADC in early 1970s to test LAMPS MK III; HC-7; BQM drone controller, NAF China Lake, in 1971; tests with HSL-31 aboard USS *Fox in* 1972; to YSH-2E, to SH-2F in 1976; HSL-36 Det. 3 aboard USS *Vreeland*, written off on May 28, 1980
149034/38	HU-2 Det. 62 aboard USS *Independence,* written off on July 17, 1963
149035/39	HU-2; HC-2 aboard USS *Shangri-La;* HSL-35 Det. 9, crashed at sea off USS *Davidson* due to tail rotor failure on October 27, 1982

149036/40	HC-1; HC-4; HC-7 no. 8; HSL-31 in film *Airport 77*; HSL-30; AMARC in June 1992
149739/41	HU-1 Det. R; HC-1 Det. E aboard USS *Ticonderoga,* impacted water due to power loss off San Diego on May 10, 1967; written off on September 5, 1967
149740/42	HC-2 aboard USS *Roosevelt,* written off on August 16, 1965
149741/43	HU-2; along with BuNo 150139, were first operational UH-2Cs to HC-1 on August 11, 1967; HC-1 Det. 61 aboard USS *Ranger;* blade flap failure and control loss aboard USS *Bon Homme Richard* on December 4, 1967; written off next day
149742/44	HC-1 Det. C aboard USS *Kitty Hawk;* HC-2 Det. 42; HSL-31; HH-2D; written off at NAS Imperial Beach on May 11, 1972
149743/45	HC-1 Det. 43 aboard USS *Coral Sea;* HC-7 no. 6, crashed/destroyed while heavily loaded with ammo at Cubi Point on May 14, 1968, three killed
149744/46	HC-1 Det. 3, 34; HU-1 Det. L; HC-7 no. 7; HSL-33; HSL-32 Det. 14 aboard USS *Voge*; crashed at sea due to engine failure off NAS Jacksonville, on August 17, 1984, one killed
149745/47	HU-1; HC-1 Det. 34, Det. F ship's flight aboard USS *Ticonderoga;* HSL-34 Det. 3 aboard USS *Aylwin;* crashed at sea off Newport, Rhode Island, on June 17, 1975, two killed
149746/48	HU-2 Det. 60 aboard USS *Saratoga;* written off on October 19, 1964
149747/ 49	HU-1 Det. A; HC-1; HSL-35; HSL-94; AMARC in April 1993

149748/50	HC-1; HC-2 Det. 7; HC-7 no. 3; HSL-30; HSL-34; HSL-74; AMARC in January 1994
149749/51	HU-2 Det. 65 aboard USS *Enterprise;* written off on April 14, 1964
149750/52	HU-2; HC-1 Det. M aboard USS *Enterprise;* HC-2 Det. 60 aboard USS *Saratoga;* Det. 66 aboard USS *America;* to UH-2C 1969; first HH-2D; HC-4 Support Det. Middle East in 1972; HC-4 redesignated HSL-30 Det. 40 aboard USS *La Salle* (AFG-3); based at Bahrain until 1973, painted White and Gull Gray; to SH-2F in 1974; NATC RWTD 1978 to 1981; VX-1 1988; storage at Dothan, Alabama, as N8061P
149751/53	HC-1 Det. L aboard USS *Hancock;* crashed at sea due to engine failure on January 10, 1966
149752/54	HU-1 Det. F, Point MUGU, USS *Ranger;* written off on May 17, 1965
149753/55	HC-1; HC-2 Det. 62; HSL-30; AMARC in March 1993
149754/56	HU-2 Det. 62 aboard USS *Independence;* written off on February 16, 1964
149755/57	HU-2; HC-1; HSL-32 LAMPS Det. 6; crashed off Florida coast on June 10, 1979
149756/58	HC-4; HC-5; to HH-2D; MAD-equipped for "Iron Barnacle" in Southeast Asia; MAD evaluation aboard USS *Truxtun* in Pacific in 1970, then to HH-2C; NAF China Lake RDT&E in April 1970; HSL-31 MC&G; written off on July 4, 1973
149757/59	HU-2 Det. 42 aboard USS *Roosevelt;* HC-2 Det. 11 aboard USS *Intrepid;* HC-1 aboard USS *Bon Homme Richard;* crashed into Gulf of Tonkin on night launch on August 10, 1969, three killed

149758/60	HC-2 Det. 42; HC-1 Det. 7; HC-7; HSL-35; HSL-84; HSL-74; AMARC in December 1993
149759/61	HU-1/HC-1 Det. B; damaged at NAS Jacksonville on March 3, 1969; written off on April 16, 1969
149760/62	HU-2; written off on April 7, 1964, following crash into wooded area on March 20
149761/63	HU-1/HC-1 Det. 3 aboard USS *Coontz* (DLG-9); HC-7 no. 15 (camo), "OMYASSIS DRAGON" extensive battle damage January 6, 1967, attempted rescue of Lt. Cmdr. Richard Mullen, one crewman KIA; HSL-33 Det. 3; AMARC in August 1992
149762/64	HC-1 Dets. 3, 11 aboard USS *Gridley;* crashed into sea due to power loss on March 18, 1967
149763/65	HU-2 Det. 59 aboard USS *Forrestal;* crashed into Tyrrhenian Sea on December 14, 1964, one killed
149764/66	HU-1 aboard USS *Ranger;* HC-1; HC-7 Det. 104 no. 14; Lassen Medal of Honor; USS *Dale,* ditched off North Vietnam due to fuel starvation on January 7, 1969
149765/67	HC-1; HU-1 Det. M, crashed into sea (West Pac) off USS *George K. MacKenzie* (DD-836) on January 23 1965, but was recovered on January 28 by *MacKenzie* or USS *Rupertus* (DD-851); HC-7 no. 2, NAS Atsugi base flight / Det. 101 VIP; VX-1 as SH-2F no. 31; crashed inverted on final approach to NAS Patuxent River when engine access door opened and flew into main rotor on June 24, 1977, three killed
149766/68	HU-2; to HH-2D, MAD-equipped for "Iron Barnacle" in Southeast Asia; MAD evaluation aboard USS *Truxtun* in Pacific in 1970; HSL-33; HSL-37, administrative strike on December 31, 1993, at NAS North Island
149767/69	HC-1 Det. 1 aboard USS *Bon Homme Richard;* off USS *Sterett* on August 10, 1969; crashed into Gulf of Tonkin due to rotor blade failure

149768/70	HC-2 aboard USS *Shangri-La*; HC-1; HSL-32; HSL-34; HSL-30; AMARC in May 1993
149769/71	HC-2 Det. 60; HC-1 Dets. M, F, modified with AN/AQS-10 dipping sonar for evaluation at NAS Key West in 1965; HSL-34; HSL-36, as SH-2F on August 10, 1984; crashed on landing at NAS Oceana due to power loss; written off at NARF Pensacola on February 19, 1985
149770/72	HC-2 Det. 66: modified with AN/AQS-10 dipping sonar for evaluation at NAS Key West 1965; HSL-34; HSL-36; HSL-30; HSL-32; AMARC in May 1993
149771/73	HC-2 Det. 66, modified with AN/AQS-10 dipping sonar for evaluation at NAS Key West in 1965; HSL-36 Det. 3; as SH-2F on May 1, 1983; crashed into Red Sea landing aboard USS *Trippe* when starboard landing gear collapsed, pilot killed
149772/74	HU-2/HC-2 Det. 62; HC-1 (roof modification); HC-2 Dets. 59, 67, 66; HSL-74; AMARC in June 1992
149773/75	HU-2; HC-2; as HH-2C with HC-7 no. 20; HSL-34; HSL-30; AMARC in April 1993; to Royal Australian Navy; returned to Kaman as N318KA, to Royal New Zealand Navy
149774/76	HC/HU-1 Det. 1, Unit G; destroyed in fire aboard USS *Oriskany* on October 26, 1966
149775/77	HU-2 Det. 38; HC-7; HC-1 Det. 2; HCT-16 aboard USS *Lexington*; as UH-2C on December 13, 1975, crashed off Texas coast
149776/78	HU-1 aboard USS *Midway;* on September 17, 1963, crashed into sea due to power failure, one flotation bag failed, and aircraft rolled over and sank
149777/79	HU-1; on January 28, 1963, went down overwater off Ream Field, pilot killed

149778/80	HU-2; HC-5; HC-1 Det. 64; on June 13, 1969, crashed into sea 7 miles off Point Loma, California, flying casevac from USS *Constellation* to Balboa Island, California, five killed
149779/ 81	HU-1; HC-7 nos. 1, 2, 5; HSL-31; HSL-37; HSL-33 administrative strike on May 8, 1992
149780/82	HC-2 Det. 11; HC-1 Det. 31; HC-7; HC-5 Det. COMSEVENTHFLT; HCT-16; HSL-37; HSL-35; HSL-84; HSL-94; AMARC in February 1994
149781/83	HC-2 Det. 59 aboard USS *Forrestal;* on July 29, 1967, received combat damage; written off at NARF on December 19, 1967
149782/84	HU-1 Dets. R, N aboard USS *Hornet* "Trick or Treat"; operational loss on deck of USS *Kearsarge* on September 17, 1964
149783/85	HU-1 Det. C aboard USS *Kitty Hawk*; HC-1 Det. G aboard USS *Oriskany;* HC-2 Det. 11 aboard USS *Intrepid;* on June 14, 1966, crashed into sea due to engine failure; written off at NARF North Island on October 11, 1966
149784/86	HU-2 damaged on April 18, 1963; written off at NAS Lakehurst on April 30
149785/87	to US Army as proposed UH-2A "Tomahawk" gunship; HC-2 Det. 38 aboard USS *Shangri La;* on January 3, 1967, crashed at Grottaglie Airfield, Italy; written off next day
149786/88	to US Army as test aircraft during which Army flew this aircraft to Pikes Peak on August 8, 1963; HU-1 Det. R aboard USS *Kearsarge;* operational loss in Southeast Asia on August 9, 1964

150139/89	HU-2; to HH-2C; HC-7 no. 22; this aircraft, "the Big E," and BuNo 149741 were first operational UH-2Cs to HC-1; on August 11, 1967, as SH-2F with HSL-36 Det. 2 on September 28, 1967, flew into water; written off at Mayport, Florida, on December 7, 1982
150140/90	NAS Atsugi station SAR; HC-2 Det. 11; HC-1; HSL-35; AMARC in October 1992
150141/91	HU-1 drone recovery; HC-2; HSL-37 Det. 3; HSL-33; HSL-74; AMARC in August 1992
150142/92	HC-5; HC-1 Det. 63; to HH-2C; HC-7 no. 23; HSL-33 LAMPS Det. aboard USS *Sterett;* on March 11, 1977, as "Sea Snake 1-4," crashed into Pacific on night approach to USS *Worden*, one killed
150143/93	HSL-37 AUTEC; HSL-74; AMARC in November 1992
150144/94	HC-2 Det. 60; HC-1 Det. 43 aboard USS *Coral Sea;* on February 21, 1969, crashed due to power loss of both engines; written off next day
150145/95	11th Naval District Point Mugu, California; damaged on September 2, 1964; written off on September 30
150146/96	HC-5 (overall orange); HC-1 Det. 1; Unit L aboard USS *Hancock;* HSL-30; AMARC in May 1993; to RNZAF ground-training wing in 2009
150147/97	HU-1 aboard USS *Bennington;* written off on October 29, 1963
150148/98	HU-4; HC-1 Dets. 61, 43; HCT-16; HSL-30, written off following crash aboard USNS *Harkness* off Somalia on April 24, 1986; cockpit preserved at Ferguson Airport, Pensacola

150149/99	HC-2; HC-4; written off on March 11, 1966
150150/100	NAS Lemoore; HC-2 Det. 38; HSL-37 Det. 10, USS *Hepburn* (FE-1055); HSL-94 on May 14, 1990; crashed off coast of Ponte Vedra Beach, Florida, four killed
150151/101	NAS Lemoore, written off on July 3, 1965
150152/102	USMC; HU-4; HC-1 Det. 61, 3; HC-7 no. 55; to SH-2D; HSL-35 aboard USS *Knox*, "the Mighty Mosquito"; HSL-84; HSL-74; AMARC in January 1994; to RNZAF ground-training wing in 2009
150153/103	NAS Atsugi station SAR in 1964; HC-1; HC-7 Det. 108 aboard USS *Coontz;* on October 4, 1967, shot down during rescue attempt, ditched off North Vietnam
150154/104	HC-1 Dets. 7, 9, 40, 19; HC-7 no. 26; NAS Atsugi base flight; HSL-31; HSL-36; HSL-32; AMARC in August 1993; to RNZAF as SH-2F NZ3444, nonflyable-parts source, December 1997, later fire trainer
150155/105	HSL-31; HSL-33; HSL-37; HC-5; AMARC in April 1978; storage at Pensacola as N8062J, loaned to Pima Museum
150156/106	HC-1 Det. 64; HSL-34 Det. 3; HSL-94; AMARC in February 1994; to Kaman as N319KA; to Royal Australian Navy; to Kaman as N201KM; to Royal New Zealand Navy as NZ3612
150157/107	HU-4; HU-2 aboard USS *America*; NATC Weapons Test, Pax River; NAS Pax River station SAR; HC-2 aboard USS Independence, later *America;* HC-4; to SH-2D; HSL-30; storage at Dothan, Alabama, 1974–75; HSL-35 aboard USS *Kinkaid*; HSL-31; HSL-33; HSL-37 Dets. 10, 1, 5; administrative strike for storage at NAS North Island on April 1,1994; USS *Midway* Museum
150158/108	HC-1; HSL-37; administrative strike, NAS Barbers Point Museum in January 2014
150159/109	HC-4; SH-2D; SH-2F prototype and first SH-2F; written off at Kaman in June 1994

150160/110	HC-1 Det. 7; HSL-36; HSL-84; HSL-74; HSL-33; AMARC in February 1994; to Royal Australian Navy; returned to Kaman in 2008 as N654KM; to Royal New Zealand Navy as NZ3618
150161/111	HC-1 Det. 65, 6: HSL-35 LAMPS Det, en route to USS *Fox*; written off on December 7, 1977
150162/112	HC-1 Det. C aboard USS *Kitty Hawk;* on April 15, 1966, crashed due to tail rotor failure, pilot killed
150163/113	HC-1; HSL-32 Det. 1; HSL-94; AMARC in August 1993
150164/114	USMC; HC-1; to HH-2C; HC-7 no. 21; HSL-33; HSL-31; on November 19, 1985, crashed at NAS North Island
150165/115	HC-1; NAS Oceana SAR; HSL-30; AMARC in August 1992
150166/116	USMC in 1964; HC-2 Det. 38 aboard USS *Shangri-La*; USMC in 1965–67; HSL-33; HSL-31; AMARC in 1978; HSL-32 Det. 7 aboard USS *Truett;* on April 11, 1984, ditched following engine failure
150167/117	USMC; returned to service as first SH-2D LAMPS test platform; HSL-31; AMARC; HSL-34 aboard USS *Fahrion;* on March 10, 1986, crashed into Indian Ocean
150168/118	on June 8, 1965, written off at Adak, Alaska
150169/119	HC-1; to SH-2D for DV-98; HC-5; HH-2D prototype; to YSH-2E in 1970 / LAMPS II DV-98 Phase II; tested aboard USS *Fox* in 1971–72; HSL-31; HSL-37; AMARC in October 1993
150170/120	HU-1; HC-1 USS *Standley;* HC-2 Det. 66; SH-2D; HSL-30 LAMPS Det; written off on June 21, 1972

150171/121	HU-1; HC-2 aboard USS *Shangri-La;* as SH-2D served as test platform for LAMPS avionics at NADC in 1972–73*;* NAS Atsugi base flight; HSL-33; HSL-84; HSL-94; HSL-74; AMARC in January 1994; to RNZAF naval support flight in December 1997 as SH-2F NZ3443; in 2001, returned to Kaman to support SH-2G contract
150172/122	HC-2 Det. 60; airborne firefighting tests at NAS Miramar in 1965; HC-4 aboard USS *Bowen;* SH-2D; HSL-30 LAMPS Det.; on August 28, written off at NAS Lakehurst
150173/123	HC-1 Det. L; HC-2 SH-2D LAMPS evaluation aboard USS *Sims* (DE-1059) in 1971; HSL-36; HSL-32; HSL-30; AMARC in March 1993; to RNZAF ground-training wing
150174/124	HC-2; HC-5; HSL-31; HSL-33; HSL-35; AMARC in July 1992
150175/125	HC-2; HSL-31; HSL-35; HSL-33; HSL-84; HSL-74; AMARC in January 1994; display aboard USS *New Jersey,* Camden, New Jersey, in 2008, marked as BuNo 150141
150176/126	HC-4; HC-1 Det. 31 aboard USS *Bon Homme Richard*; as UH-2C (UP-81) on July 10, 1968, crashed due to mechanical failure near Clark AB, Philippine Islands, five USN personnel and one Filipino steward killed
150177/127	HC-2 no. 32, named "Maverick" for *Project Maverick* missile tests; HC-1 Det. 65 aboard USS *Enterprise;* written off on November 16, 1968
150178/128	HSL-30; HSL-94; AMARC in December 1993
150179/129	USMC; HC-2 Det. 11; HH-2C prototype; HC-7 no. 24; HSL-84; HSL-33 Det. 10; AMARC in December 1992
150180/130	USMC; damaged at MCAS Cherry Point on August 15, 1964; written off August 31
150181/131	USMC; HC-2; HC-5; HC-4; NADCYSH-2E LAMPS Mk. III prototype, remodified to SH-2F; HSL-31; HSL-37; storage at Pensacola as N8064F; loan to Mobile, Alabama, museum in 2005

150182/132	HC-1; HC-2 Det. 67 aboard USS *John F. Kennedy;* as HH-2D, crashed into Mediterranean Sea due to tail rotor failure on June 11, 1972
150183/133	HC-1 Det. 1, Unit G; destroyed in fire aboard USS *Oriskany* on October 26, 1966
150184/134	HC-4 Det. 36; VIP "Gray Ghost" (overall gray) aboard USS *Mount McKinley* (LCC-7), flagship of commander, Seventh Fleet Amphibious Force, anchored at Da Nang, South Vietnam; written off at NAS Patuxent River on August 5, 1965
150185/135	HC-1 Det. 36, Da Nang AB, South Vietnam; HSL-31; HSL-33; HSL-31 featured in film *Airport '77;* written off on October 6, 1993, at Wasilla, Alaska; display at Museum of Alaska Transportation and Industry
150186/136	HC-1 Det. M; HC-4/HSL-30; served aboard oceanographic survey ships; HC-2 as HH-2D conducted deck-strength tests aboard USS *W. S. Sims in* November 1970, as SH-2F HSL-34; written off at NAS Norfolk on June 14, 1982
151300/137	HC-1 Det. 5; HSL-31 Det. Bravo aboard USNS *Chauvenet;* HSL-30 as HH-2D painted all-white (named "White Whale" with "Our Baby" painted on fuel tanks) until 1983, then repainted standard USN, Det. Alpha, aboard USNS *Harkness;* crashed on July 30, 1984; written off next day
151301/138	Damaged at NS Sigonella, Italy, in December 1964; written off December 16
151302/139	HC-4 VIP aboard USS *Oklahoma City;* HC-7 nos. 1, 5; as HH-2D at NARF, NAS Lakehurst; AMARC in April 1993
151303/140	HC-1 Det. 6; HSL-34 Det. 5, 8; HSL-32; NAS Jacksonville station aircraft; HSL-30; AMARC in April 1993
151304/141	USS *Lexington* COD flight; HSL-35 CVT SAR in 1973; HSL-30; AMARC in November 1991

151305/142	HC-1; as UH-2B written off at NAS Imperial Beach on December 22, 1968; AMARC in April 1993
151306/143	USMC; HC/HU-1 Det. A aboard USS *Midway*; HC-7 no. 13; HSL-31; HSL-30; HSL-33 Det. 7; damaged when collective control rod broke and aircraft made uncommanded takeoff to 20 feet, pilots chopped throttles and aircraft fell back to ground; written off at NAS North Island on January 6, 1983
151307/144	HC-1 Det. 6, damaged aboard USS *Oriskany* on January 27, 1970; written off on February 18, 1970
151308/145	USMC; NAS Patuxent River station aircraft; HC-7 no. 1; HC-4/HSL-30, first SH-2D for Atlantic Fleet in February 1970 aboard USS *Belknap;* HSL-35; HSL-33; AMARC in January 1992
151309/146	HC-1 Det. E; HC-7 no. 4; HC-4/HSL-30 Support Det. 31, Sixth Fleet Med; HSL-32 VIP; AMARC in June 1992
151310/147	HC-1; NAS Jacksonville station aircraft; HSL-30 Det. Alpha aboard USNS *Chauvenet;* AMARC in June 1993; to Royal Australian Navy; returned to Kaman 2008 as N705KM; to Royal New Zealand Navy as NZ3619
151311/148	HC-1; first UH-2C to HC-2 on September 23, 1968; HSL-37; HSL-74; AMARC in November 1992
151312/149	HC-2 Det. 38, 66; HSL-31; HSL-34; storage at Pensacola as N8064H; display at NAS Pensacola
151313/150	HC-1; HU/HC-4 Det. 40; HC-5; HSL-30 administrative strike on November 21, 1989, following engine failure, ditched in James River, Virginia
151314/151	HU/HC-4 Det. Galveston; HC-7 no. 22; NAS Naples as UH-2C; HSL-37 Det. 8, 4, 7; HSL-31; AMARC in October 1991

151315/152	HU/HC-1; HC-7 Det. 104 aboard USS *Dewey;* M60 accident on January 23, 1968, when crewman's machine gun round struck main rotor blade, crashed into sea
151316/153	HC-2; HC-4 aboard USS *Wright* command ship; HSL-32; AMARC in June 1993; to Royal Australian Navy for spares and ground instruction
151317/154	HC-1 Det. Unit L aboard USS *Bon Homme Richard;* on February 27, 1967, crashed into water on takeoff; written off next day
151318/ 155	HC-1; HC-2 Det. 59 aboard USS *Forrestal;* combat damage on July 29, 1967; written off on December 19, 1967
151319/ 156	USMC airborne firefighting tests in 1967; first SH-2D, which made first flight on March 16, 1971; HC-4; HSL-37 Det. 2 aboard USS *Badger;* as SH-2F, crashed into sea off Japan on September 17, 1983
151320/157	Destroyed in accident on transport mission 40 miles west of NAS Chase Field, Texas, on September 5, 1969
151321/158	HC-5; AMARC in May 1978; HSL-30; HSL-32 "Zulu Invader"; HSL-30; NMNA storage at Dothan, Alabama; to Evergreen Museum, McMinnville, Oregon, in 2006
151322/159	HC-4, commander, Amphibious Squadron (COMPHIBRON) 11; HSL-33; HSL-30; HSL-36 Det. 5; as SH-2F aboard USS *O'Brien*, written off on March 7, 1980
151323/160	HC-2; HSL-36; HSL-32 Det. 7; AMARC in May 1993; to RNZAF ground-training wing in 2009
151324/161	As HH-2D, was one of two testing ASMD system with HC-5 1970-71 DV-98 Phase II aboard USS *Fox*; HSL-35 Det. 3; written off aboard USS *Barbey* on June 27, 1983

151325/162	HC-2 Det. 62; HSL-31; written off at NAS Imperial Beach on November 25, 1985
151326/163	HC-1 Det. 10, 64: HC-2; HSL-33 Det. 9; as SH-2F aboard USS *Reasoner*, crashed into San Diego Bay on July 15, 1976
151327/164	HH-2D; HC-4 aboard USNS *Chauvenet;* HSL-33 Det. 5; crashed into Indian Ocean on takeoff from USS *Leftwich* on August 18, 1984, two killed
151328/165	HSL-30 Det. 2 aboard USS *Standley;* HSL-34; HSL-36 Det. 7 aboard USS *Estocin;* written off on September 7, 1982, aboard USS *Paul*
151329/166	HSL-30; AMARC in May 1993; to Royal Australian Navy; returned to Kaman as N424KM; to Royal New Zealand Navy as NZ3616
151330/167	HC-1; HC-5; HC-2 Det. 60; HSL-30; HSL-32 Det. 3; USS *Lexington* COD flight; AMARC in August 1993; to Royal Australian Navy as spares and ground instruction
151331/168	HC-1 Det. 19; HC-7 no. 25; SH-2F HSL-32 Det. 2, 5, aboard USS *Moinester*, USS *Donald B. Beary in* 1978; wore markings of USS *Julius Furer* and USS *Thomas C. Hart*; crashed at NAS Cubi Point, PI aboard *Beary;* written off on December 15, 1981
151332/169	JUH-2C; HSL-34; as HH-2D, tested Sparrow missile and 101 rotor system; HSL-94; AMARC in September 1993
151333/170	HC-1 Det. 61; HC-7 no. 6; rebuilt to HH-2C following crash on January 23, 1968; HC-5, first SH-2D for Pacific Fleet in December 1971 aboard USS *Sterett;* HSL-31; HSL-36 AUTEC; HSL-34; AMARC in July 1993; to RNZAF ground-training wing in 2009
151334/171	HU-1; HC-2 aboard USS *John F. Kennedy;* HH-2D; HC-1; HSL-30; AMARC in May 1992

151335/172	HU-2; HC-1 Det. 61; HC-7 no. 25; HSL-33; HSL-74; AMARC in August 1992
152189/173	USMC; HSL-31; HSL-33 written off at Bakersfield, California, on April 23, 1993
152190/174	HC-1 Det. 5; HC-4, horizontally installed 12-tube sonobuoy launcher; HSL-32; HSL-30; HSL-74; HSL-94; in film *Ice Station Zebra*; DV-98 aircraft aboard USS *Belknap* with HC-4, followed by WestPac combat cruise in 1972 aboard USS *Biddle;* AMARC
152191/175	NAS Whidbey Island; HC-7; HC-2; HC-5 Det. 101, VIP flagship helo for commander, Amphibious Forces Seventh Fleet, "Miss Bessy"; as HH-2D, inflatable radar modification in 1972; HSL-30; HSL-33; HSL-34; HSL-36; VX-1 test bed for LAMPS III; AMARC in June 1993; to RNZAF as SH-2G
152192/176	HC-1, first HH-2D to HC-4; HSL-31; HSL-37; written off at Kauai, Hawaii, on April 4, 1990
152193/177	HSL-32 aboard USS *Guam;* crashed on pier at NAS Norfolk; written off on November 1, 1973
152194/178	*HC-2 Det. 60 aboard USS Saratoga;* ditched during VERTREP in Mediterranean Sea on September 3, 1966
152195/179	HC-2 Det. 60; HC-1 Det. 63 aboard USS *Kitty Hawk;* crashed into Gulf of Tonkin due to power loss on April 30, 1968
152196/180	HC-1 Det. 1, Unit G, aboard USS *Oriskany;* on September 16, 1966, engine flamed out when hit by wave while picking up survivors
152197/181	HC-1 Det. 14 aboard USS *Ticonderoga;* on February 15, 1968, crashed into sea due to power loss

152198/182	HC-1; HSL-31 Det. 1; as SH-2D, crashed into sea after losing power in one engine after takeoff from USS *Sterett* between Guam and Philippines on March 25, 1973
152199/183	HC-2 Det. 61; HC-1 Det. 2 aboard USS *Kitty Hawk*; HC-4; HSL-36; HSL-31; HSL-33; HSL-34; AMARC in June 1993; to Kaman as SH-2G training aircraft
152200/184	HC-4; NAS Lemoore base flight; HSL-36 Det. 4; HSL-30; stricken on September 1, 1991, following crash from engine failure into James River on training flight May 31, near NAS Norfolk; to Kaman as SH-2G training aircraft
152201/185	HC-4 Det. 82 aboard icebreaker USCGC *Westwind* (WAGB-281) in 1966; first UH-2 to cross Arctic Circle en route to Thule Air Base, Greenland; Operation SUNEC (Support of Northeast Command); HC-1; HC-7; HC-5; VX-1 in 1979–88; VIP commander, Seventh Fleet, at NAS Atsugi; HSL-30; display at Louisiana Military Museum
152202/186	JUH-2B; HC-1 Det. 64, WESTPAC aboard USS *Kinkaid;* USS *Coral Sea;* USS *Constellation;* HC-4; HSL-35 Det. 2; as SH-2D, stricken aboard USS *Leftwich* on December 11, 1982; to Royal Australian Navy as SH-2G
152203/187	HC-2 aboard USS *Franklin D. Roosevelt;* HSL-30 Det. 4 aboard USS *Biddle;* HSL-32 Det. 7; HSL-94; HSL-74; AMARC in February 1994
152204/188	HC-4 Det. 45; HC-2 Det. 17; HSL-37; HSL-35 Det. 10; AMARC in August 1992; to Royal Australian Navy as spares and ground instruction
152205/189	HC-2; HSL-36 Det. 8 aboard USS *Paul;* HSL-35; HSL-34; AMARC in April 1993; to Royal Australian Navy; to Kaman as N332KM; to Royal New Zealand Navy as SH-2G(I) NZ3646 spare aircraft
152206/190	HC-2; HSL-34 Det. 2 aboard USS *Paul;* HSL-30; AMARC in June 1993; to Royal Australian Navy as spares and ground instruction

161641/191	NAWC; first new production SH-2F LAMPS Mk. I in 1983; "Magic Lantern" test aircraft at Kaman in late 1990s; to RNZAF naval support flight in November 1997 as NZ3441; to Kaman in 2001 to support SH-2G contract
161642/192	NATC RWATD in 1983–84; HSL-32 until October 1991; to Kaman for conversion to SH-2G; test aircraft at NAS Patuxent River in 1993–97; on December 20, 1988, with HSL-32 at NAS Norfolk, first H-2 to surpass one million flight hours; display at NAS Patuxent River in 1998
161643/193	HSL-35 Det. 6; HSL-37; upgraded to SH-2G; HSL-84; HSL-94; AMARC in June 2001
161644/194	HSL-36; HSL-84; HSL-94; AMARC in April 2001
161645/195	HSL-33; AMARC in December 1993; to Egypt as SH-2G(E)
161646/196	HSL-34 aboard USS *McCandless;* written off on March 30, 1988
161647/197	HSL-35 Det. 3; HSL-94; AMARC in December 2000
161648/198	HSL-34; written off at NAS Norfolk on March 3, 1989, following crash due to engine failure near Smithfield, Virginia
161649/199	HSL-34; HSL-33 SH-2F aboard USS *Reid;* on January 21, 1985, crashed into Pacific 325 miles southwest of San Diego
161650/200	HSL-32; SH-2G selective aircraft reclamation and disposal in place (SARDIP); removed from flight status in June 2005 and used for parts at Kaman
161651/201	HSL-33 "Seasnake 1-7"; crashed into Persian Gulf on approach to frigate USS *Barbey* on November 11, 1988, three killed

161652/202	HSL-36 Det. 9; HSL-32; AMARC in September 1993; to Egypt as SH-2G(E)
161653/203	YSH-2G prototype in 1985, with first flight on April 2, 1985; stricken at Kaman for parts on September 1, 1994
161654/204	HSL-32 aboard USS *Yorktown;* HSL-37 Det. 7; written off on January 11, 1987, following crash into Gulf of Mexico from electrical malfunction
161655/205	HSL-37; HSL-35 aboard USS *Reid;* written off on August 10, 1988
161656/206	HSL-34; HSL-94; AMARC in February 1994; to Kaman as N356KA; to Royal Australian Navy in 2001; to Kaman as N314KM; to Royal New Zealand Navy as NZ3614
161657/207	HSL-37 Det. 6; HSL-33; HSL-35; AMARC in April 1994; to RNZAF as SH-2G
161658/208	HSL-36; HSL-94 (Magic Lantern); AMARC in November 2000
161898/209	HSL-35; HSL-37 aboard USS *Oldendorf;* written off on November 28, 1989
161899/210	HSL-35; HSL-36; HSL-32; HSL-33; AMARC in April 1994; to New Zealand as SH-2G
161900/211	in June 1993, first SH-2F to SH-2G conversion; HSL-33; HSL-84
161901/212	HSL-30; HSL-32, sank next to ship; written off on April 14, 1993

161902/213	HSL-37 aboard USS *Oldendorf;* ditched in western Pacific on September 21, 1988
161903/214	HSL-36 aboard USS *Vreeland;* written off on May 8, 1988
161904/215	HSL-35; SARDIP cocooned at Kaman in June 2005
161905/216	HSL-32 "Magic Lantern" test aircraft at Kaman in late 1990s; New England Air Museum in December 2011
161906/217	HSL-37; HSL-94; HSL-33; AMARC in March 1994; to Egypt as SH-2G(E)
161907/218	Beginning with this BuNo, gross weight increased to 13,500 lbs. and external fuel tank capacity increased from 60 gal. to 100 gal.; HSL-34 Det. 2; HSL-33; HSL-94; AMARC in June 2010
161908/219	HSL-37; upgraded to SH-2G; HSL-94; AMARC in May 1997
161909/220	HSL-36; HSL-34; AMARC in July 1993; to Egypt as SH-2G(E)
161910/221	HSL-35 Det. 7 aboard USS *Bagley;* written off on March 5, 1988
161911/222	HSL-32; crashed/destroyed at NAS Norfolk on November 20, 1990
161912/223	HSL-33; HSL-94; AMARC in April 2001

161913/224	HSL-34; AMARC in September 1993; to Kaman as N351KA; to Royal Australian Navy; to Kaman as N244KM; to Royal New Zealand Navy
161914/225	HSL-33; AMARC; to Royal Australian Navy; to Kaman as N523KM; to Royal New Zealand Navy as NZ3617
161915/226	HSL-35; HSL-36 aboard USS *Rodger;* written off on October 2, 1986
162576/227	HSL-35; HSL-94; display at JRB Willow Grove, Pennsylvania
162577/228	HSL-32; HSL-94; AMARC in January 1994; to Egypt as SH-2G(E); VX-1 GPS fit for Magic Lantern systems training
162578/229	HSL-33; HSL-94; AMARC in November 2000
162579/230	HSL-34; lost North Atlantic; written off on September 16, 1987
162580/231	HSL-35; dipping-sonar tests at NAS Pax in 1997; AMARC in July 2001; first SH-2G configured for Egypt but retained at Kaman
162581/232	HSL-36; HSL-32; HSL-94; AMARC in April 1994; to Egypt as SH-2G(E)
162582/233	HSL-33; HSL-37; AMARC in October 1993; to Egypt as SH-2G(E)
162583/234	HSL-32; HSL-36; display at Alabama Space Museum

162584/235	HSL-34; AMARC in September 1993
162585/236	HSL-33 supertanker *Pivot* rescue in Persian Gulf in December 1987; AMARC in March 1994; to RNZAF naval support flight in 1997 as SH-2F NZ3442; to Air Force Museum of New Zealand
162586/237	HSL-34; HSL-36; crashed/destroyed at Mayport, Florida, on March 14, 1989
162587/238	HSL-33; AMARC; to Egypt as SH-2G(E)
162650/239	
162651/240	
162652/241	
162653/242	
162654/243	Egypt
162655/244	

163209/245	conversion from SH-2F; HSL-36; SARDIP at Kaman in June 2005
163210/246	to Kaman as N351KA; to Royal Australian Navy as SH-2G(A); to Kaman as N167KM; to Royal New Zealand Navy as NZ3611
163211/247	HSL-37 aboard USS *Leftwich;* crashed in Straits of Hormuz due to gearbox failure on March 15, 1993, three killed
163212/248	HSL-34; AMARC in September 1993; to Egypt as SH-2G(E)
163213/249	HSL-33; AMARC in December 1993; to Egypt as SH-2G(E)
163214/250	HSL-34; HSL-94 (first operational Magic Lantern aircraft); Kaman test aircraft for AGM-65 Maverick missile firing and qualification at Yuma Proving Ground on February 14–15, 1996; also tested Kongsberg Mk. 2 Mod. 7 Penguin missile; AMARC in December 2000
163541/251	HSL-84; AMARC
163542/252	HSL-84; AMARC in July 1996
163543/253	HSL-84; AMARC in January 2001; to Polish navy in August 2003
163544/254	HSL-84; AMARC in October 2000; to Polish navy in 2002
163545/255	HSL-84; AMARC in June 2001; to Polish navy in 2002
163546/256	HSL-84; AMARC in October 2000; to Polish navy in 2002
163547-552	order for six SH-2G canceled

APPENDIX C
COLORS AND MARKINGS

The UH-2B BuNo 150171 at NAS Lakehurst, in October 1968, displays the standard markings for UH-2A/Bs. All numbers, lettering, and window trim are white, which contrasted well with the aircraft color Engine Gray. Seasprites of HC-2 assigned to USS *Shangri-La* provided SAR support for East Coast carriers. BuNo 150166 (*in the background*) in 1970 completed a world cruise aboard *Shangri La*, including Vietnam. *Courtesy of Roger Besecker*

Dark Sea Gray Seasprites with International Orange markings became a familiar sight on US Navy aircraft carriers, and as station SAR aircraft. Seen here with HU-4 at NAS Lakehurst in 1963, BuNo 150157 served numerous assignments before ending its career as a display aboard the Midway Museum. *Author's collection*

Although the Navy specified Engine Gray for helicopters prior to Seasprite production, a few examples were finished in glossy Sea Blue. The UH-2A BuNo 147983, the sixteenth machine to roll off the production line, is seen here in the rare blue livery at NAS Pax River in August 1962. It wears the stylized "W" of the Weapons Test Directorate, NATC. *Courtesy of Stephen Miller*

Early in their careers, Seasprites wore their squadron letter codes on the upper fuselage and tail rotor pylon. The fish pole boom of BuNo 149023 was painted barber-pole high visibility. The aircraft is well secured to the deck of USS *Guadalcanal* (LPH-7) at Portsmouth Dockyard, UK, in 1970. *Guadalcanal* was an Iwo Jima–class amphibious assault ship (helicopter). *Courtesy of R. A. Scholefield*

Seasprites serving in Vietnam were a mix of camouflage patterns and markings, often dependent on unit preference. The UH-2A BuNo 149761 served both HC-1 and HC-7 in the war zone. *Courtesy of US Navy*

A torpedo is loaded on QH-50D DASH s/n 05-1526 aboard USS *Alan Sumner* in 1969. For visual identification of the ungainly aircraft, portside components were painted orange, while starboard components were painted green. *Courtesy of US Navy*

Markings on the rescue/pilot's door of an SH-2G. "CHWR" stands for Command Helicopter Wing Reserve, the "S" is the Wing Safety Award, and the wrench is the Wing Maintenance Award. Dots represent consecutive awards, each given annually. *Courtesy of John Hairell*

Wearing an "A" for excellence, BuNo 150156 shows the marking change of the SH-2F's tail rotor warning band from an angled position on the lower tail rotor pylon to a vertical band. *Courtesy of US Navy*

Unit pride was abundantly reflected in the appearance of some Seasprites. Among the array of markings of the SH-2F BuNo 151331 of HSL-32 are the "E" Efficiency Award, with hash mark for consecutive award, and the Safety "S" Award on the rescue/pilot's door. Other special markings include the squadron emblem on the forward landing-gear fairing, white trim around the nose antiglare panel, engine-warning markings, and antiskid areas of the auxiliary fuel tank, and the host ship's name on the tail boom; the ship was guided-missile frigate USS *Julius A. Furer* (FFG-6), called "the Jolly JAF." Noted aviation photographer Stephen Miller captured this image at Andrews AFB on May 20, 1978.

Barely visible immediately forward of the Excellence and Safety Awards of this SH-2F of HSL-37, Det. 9 "Terminators," is a red "A" signifying the annual award of the Arnold J. Isbell Trophy for ASW Excellence. BuNo 161906 was photographed aboard USS *America* (CV-66) at Perth Australia in June 1989. The "E" was also termed the Battle Efficiency Award, or "Battle E." *Courtesy of Wally Civitico*

The nose antiglare panel of SH-2F BuNo 149023 of HDL-33 was outlined in the squadron colors. The star of the national insignia points forward, per US Navy regulation. *Courtesy of Gordon Permann*

Resplendent in its glossy Engine Gray coat, HH-2D BuNo 151326 of HC-2 in 1971 wears its aircraft number in six locations: nose, auxiliary fuel tank, forward landing-gear fairing, upper walkway, transmission fairing, and rotor head tail fairing. No. 326 also wears the early-style tail rotor warning band. "RESCUE" applied to the upper tail boom and "ABANDON CHUTE" applied to the Seasprite's underside were common markings. *Courtesy of Stephen Miller*

Seasprites usually wore the name of their host ship on the upper tail boom. This unique marking was used by HSL-35, Det. 5, aboard USS *John Hancock* (DD-981). *Courtesy of Paul Taylor*

Its flashy painted Mk. 46 torpedo complemented the good looks of this SH-2F of HSL-34 "Green Checkers," whose Seasprites wore a green checkered band on the tail rotor pylon. *Courtesy of Stephan De Bruijn*

During BuNo 149750's busy career, it went through four model designations and as many color schemes. In its final version as an SH-2F, seen here at NAS Patuxent River in 1981, it wore a liberal amount of International Orange. *Courtesy of Stephen Miller*

The color scheme of SH-2D BuNo 151306 was as unusual as its demise. Painted dark gray with black markings, remnants of its Orange-Yellow tail rotor warning band were retained as background to highlight the data block. The Seasprite destroyed itself during an unpiloted takeoff at NAS North Island in November 1982. *Courtesy of US Navy*

The Seasprite was born in the era of glossy paint schemes and colorful markings that was the signature of naval aviation. In 1957, when Kaman and the US Navy signed the contract to begin production of the YHU-2K-1, the Navy specified the color Gloss Engine Gray for helicopters, replacing the standard aircraft color Glossy Sea Blue. The blue, a carryover from World War II, had been reformulated in 1948. Until the present, gray has stood as the predominant color for US Navy equipment. To eliminate the befuddling nature of identifying colors, in 1956 a color code system was devised, titled Federal Standard (FS) 595a, which used five-digit numbers for identification. The first digit of the guide established sheen: 1 for gloss, 2 for semigloss, and 3 for flat (often termed nonspecular). Over the years, numerous shades of gray appeared under the guide, to the extent that correctly identifying a Seasprite color became a lesson in frustration. Adding to the confusion is the number of times that H-2s were routed through rework for modification or model change, which included repainting. Depending on differently mixed color batches, weathering, aging, and the range of tones in photography, the Engine Gray of Seasprites appeared in hues ranging from near black to light gray; in canvassing Seasprite crewmen and maintenance personnel, "green" was the predominant response to their remembrance of the aircraft color. Standard gray played tricks on the eye, but even standards change, dependent on myriad factors such as geographical location, aircraft configuration, mission, unit policies, etc. Under the color standard, the names of some colors changed according to their sheen; the Seasprite's Engine Gray, for example, became Dark Gray and later Gunship Dark Gray with gloss sheen, and Seaplane Gray with semigloss sheen. Color and marking directives kept pace with changes in tactics and technology. Exemptions included overall International Orange for Seasprites assigned aboard US Coast Guard ships, and overall solar-heat-reflecting Insignia White for Middle East–based Seasprites. Seasprite models, up to and including SH-2Fs, especially aircraft assigned SAR and training roles, appeared with upper fuselage structures, empennages, and noses painted International Orange. Some sources cite the use of Fluorescent Red-Orange (FS28913) on those areas. Although fluorescent Paintit saw extensive use on naval aircraft since its introduction in February 1959, the Navy discontinued its use in May 1965 due to its inability to withstand weathering effects.

As war in Southeast Asia intensified, the morale-building flashiness that identified US Navy and Marine units and their aircraft gave way to maximizing survivability; "minimal visual detectability" became the name of the game. Recall Medal of Honor recipient Lassen's comment that camouflage aided him and his crew in accomplishing their lifesaving mission in Vietnam. Of necessity, the "wow factor" of color schemes and markings dwindled, thankfully with no loss of pride and comradeship so prevalent among the ranks. Land schemes and some camouflage paint schemes fell under Navy guidelines, while others were born of necessity at the unit level. Combinations of camouflage appeared, often from whatever paints were available in various shades of tan, brown, green, and gray. Some combat Seasprites wore the tritone camouflage adopted by the US Air Force in 1965. Other schemes were the result of unit policy, or the whim of detachment or squadron commanders, as often was the case when regulations were sidestepped in combat theaters.

Even the drab tactical paint scheme could not dampen the crewmen's enthusiasm for applying traditional artwork to the sonobuoy cover of this SH-2G, BuNo 162576 of HSL-94, in 1997. Embodied in the artwork is the wording "UNITAS XXXVI" and "HSL-94 TITANS." *Courtesy of Geoff Russell*

Variations of the ever-popular shark's mouth appeared on Seasprites during its decades of service. This toothy SH-2G belonged to the HSL-94 Titans, which operated Seasprites from 1985 to 2000. *Courtesy of Eric Scheie*

Sonobuoy cover artwork of HSL-36, Det. M. Art by Phil Friddel. Names surrounding the artwork are Rick Stevenson, Terry Nichols, Greg Neher, Wayne Durant, Fran Congdon, and Joe Cushing. *Courtesy of Rick Morgan Collection*

Prior to a radical change in Navy aircraft color and marking schemes, Seasprites of HSLs were a colorful display of high-visibility markings that contrasted with their Engine Gray livery. Markings included but were not limited to large national insignia, Insignia White NAVY titles, aircraft numbers, the "last four" of bureau numbers, and awards and warnings. Included in the latter were broad vertical, or angled, Orange-Yellow tail rotor warning bands. Horizontal stabilizers, or tailplanes, and their strut braces wore an eye-catching pattern of narrow, alternating Red and Orange-Yellow stripes. Personal markings and artwork were in vogue on Seasprites that crossed oceans on cruises, special projects, and training exercises. Names of ships to which Seasprites were assigned often were proudly worn on external fuel tanks or tail booms.

Sonobuoy cover artwork of HSL-33, Det. 8, aboard frigate USS *Marvin Shields* (FF-1066) during Operation Desert Storm in 1991. Art is by Theodore Hull Miller and Michael Miller. *Courtesy of Gordon Rzewnicki*

Sonobuoy cover art by Ray Trygstad aboard USS *O'Bannon* (DD-987) in 1991. *Courtesy of Ray Trygstad*

Sonobuoy cover art of "Bill the cat" of HSL-33, Det. 4, aboard USS *Kirk* (FF-1087) during its 1992–93 deployment. Art is by Theodore Hull Miller and Michael Miller. *Courtesy of Gordon Rzewnicki*

Sonobuoy cover artwork of HSL-35, Det. 2 "the Deuces." Art is by Lt. T. Culora (1984). *Author's collection*

Sonobuoy cover artwork of HSL-35, Det. 7, aboard USS *Lockwood* (FF-1064). *Author's collection*

Sonobuoy cover artwork of HSL-37, Det. 7, at NAS Atsugi in 1979, extended to the SH-2F's fuselage, which included crew names, mission tallies, and naval aviators' wings. Within the artwork, the three islands represented frigates on which the detachment was embarked, while lettering included "Nomads of DESRON 15" (Destroyer Squadron), and "HUMPIN THRU WEST-PAC 79–80." *Courtesy of Richard Burgess*

Sonobuoy cover artwork of HSL-35, Det. X, aboard USS *Stein* (FF-1065) in 1987. *Author's collection*

The favored canvas to which Seasprite aircrew applied artwork was the panel that protectively covered the fifteen-tube sonobuoy launcher on the aircraft's port side. Framed in candy-cane-striped warning and fastened with six quick-attach fasteners, sonobuoy launcher covers displayed caricatures, sultry pinups, crew names, and patriotic priding and told the story of missions and adventures that spanned the globe.

An April 18, 1985, Tactical Paint Scheme MIL-STD-2161 (AS) superseded directives that had controlled painting schemes and markings for years. This scheme effectively brought to a close the era of colorful US Navy aircraft. Patterns of the new gray-on-gray scheme were based on optical principles that called for certain nonreflective colors, configurations, and proportions. The new standard essentially used various shades of flat gray, with all markings reduced in size and in a color that contrasted to the background color. For example, if the overall aircraft color was FS36320 Dark Ghost Gray, then markings were to be FS35237 Blue Gray. If background color was FS26375 Light Ghost Gray, then markings were to be FS36320 Dark Ghost Gray. Colors were to blend into each other at demarcation lines. Flat black and even white often were substituted for contrasting gray markings. Nations that acquired Seasprites typically adopted the gray color schemes under the Tactical Paint Scheme worn by those in US Navy service.

The original dark grays familiar to the family of Seasprites were replaced in the 1980s by a light Sea Gray scheme with light-gray undersides and subdued markings. This "Gray Ghost" was the SH-2F BuNo 149761. *Courtesy of US Navy*

Tactical color schemes that combined gray colors beginning in the 1980s presented as varied hues. This SH-2G of HSL-94 in 1997 was painted Dark Ghost Gray with Medium Gray top surfaces and Light Gray undersides. *Courtesy of Robert F. Dorr*

Emblazoned on the white empennage of this UH-2C assigned to Naval Support Activity, Naples, Italy, in 1972 is the emblem of the US Naval Forces Europe-Africa, and the four stars representing Adm. William F. Bungle, commander of US Naval Forces Europe. *Courtesy of Jack Morris*

This SH-2G BuNo 163214 of HSL-94 at NAS Willow Grove, Pennsylvania, in June 1999, wore the squadron's "Titans" emblem on the fuselage. Written below the doorway are the squadron commander's and plane captain's names, and the CO's call sign, "Titan One." *Courtesy of Erik Roelofs*

The SH-2F BuNo 151311 of HSL-74 at Andrews AFB, in May 1992, sports a replacement empennage. Red letters GHWR appear on the rescue/pilot's door. *Courtesy of Bryan Wilburn*

15042	Sea Blue
16081	Engine Gray, Dark Gray, Navy Gray
26081	Seaplane Gray, semigloss version of Engine Gray
36231	Dark Gull Gray
36320	Dark Compass Gray, Dark Ghost Gray
36375	Light Compass Gray, Light Ghost Gray
35237	Medium Gray, Blue Gray (viewed as both blue or gray, depending on opinion)
34097	Dark Green (USAF tritone camouflage)
34102	Light Green (USAF tritone camouflage)
30219	Tan (USAF tritone camouflage)
36622	Light Gray (undersurfaces of USAF tritone camouflage)
12197	International Orange
13538	Orange-Yellow
28913	Fluorescent Red-Orange
11136	Insignia Red
33538	Insignia Yellow
15044	Insignia Blue

APPENDIX D
SEASPRITE EMBLEMS

HSL-33, Det. 9

Bad to the Boneyard

Attack Wolf

HSL-36

USNS CHAUVENET

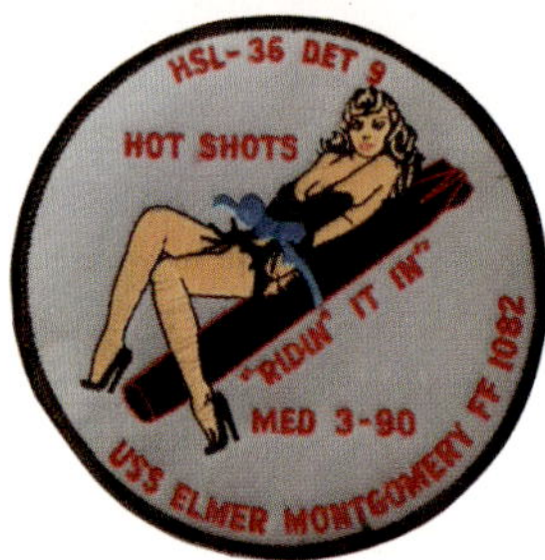

HSL-36, Det. 9

Plane Captain

LAMPS MARK I

Kaman Novelty Company

Helicopter Support Squadron One (HU-1)

HSL-30

HSL-31 Arch Angels

HSL-32

HSL-33

HSL-34

HSL-35

HSL-36

HSL-37

HSL-74

HSL-84

HSL-94

HSL-30, Det. 31

HC-1 LeGare's Bears Det. 5

HSL-33, Det. 8

HSL-35, Det. 10

HSL-33, Det. 9

HC-1/HC-7

Oceanographic Unit Five

HSL-32, Det. 3 Sharks

Helicopter Combat Support Training Squadron 16

USNS Harkness

HSL-35 China Lake Det.

HSL-33, Det. 7

Helicopter Combat Support Squadron Four (HC-4)

LAMPS Maintenance

HSL-32, Det. 5

Helicopter Combat Support Squadron Seven (HC-7)

Tonkin Gulf Yacht Club

Polish Navy SH-2G

Original emblems of Polish Naval Aviation Brigade Shipborne Flight 2003

Polish Shipborne Helicopter Flight 28 Puck (City of Puck Naval Air Squadron) 2011

Polish Navy 43rd Naval Air Base 2021

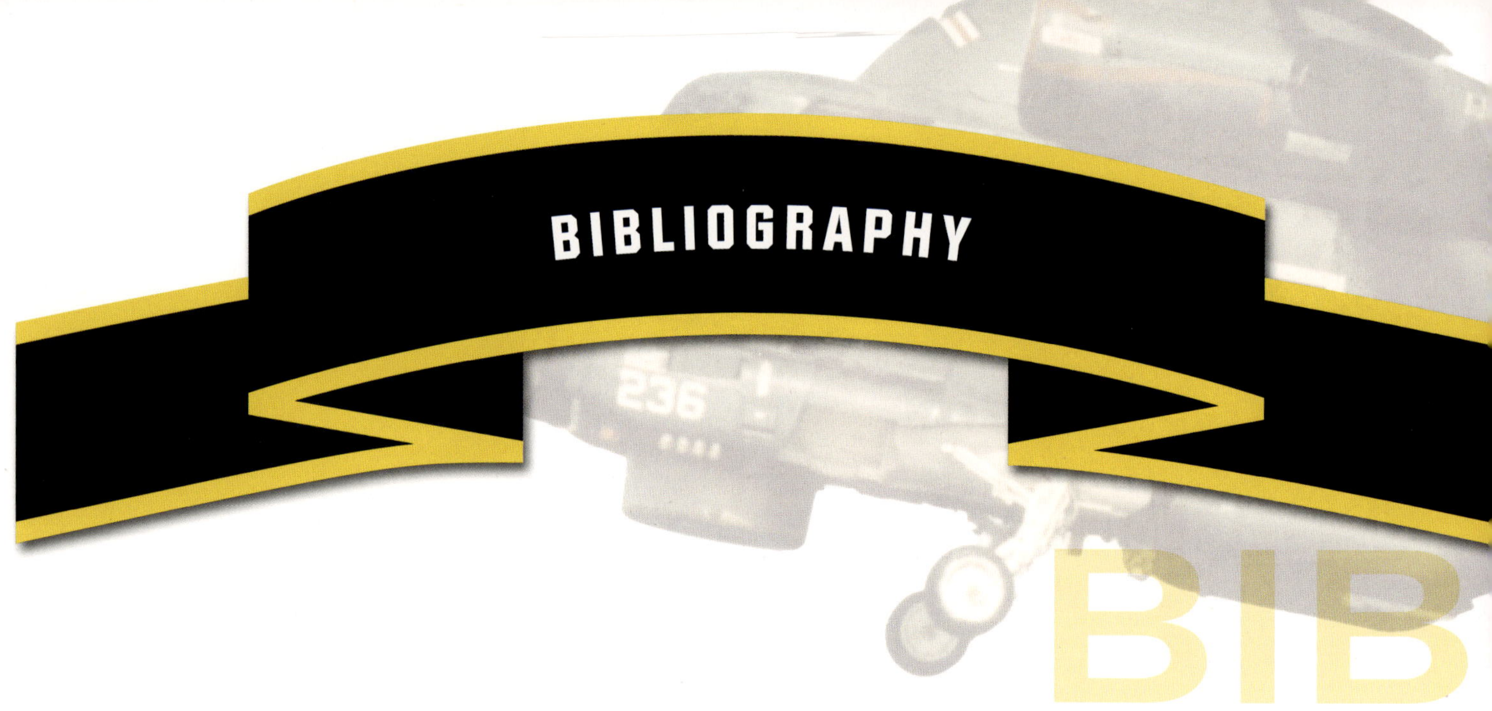

BIBLIOGRAPHY

BOOKS

Elliot, John M., Maj., USMC (Ret.). *The Official Monogram US Navy & Marine Corps Aircraft Color Guide 1960–1993*. Sturbridge, MA: Monogram Aviation Publications. 1993.

Hobson, Chris. *Vietnam Air Losses: United States Air Force Navy and Marine Corps Fixed-Wing Aircraft Losses in Southeast Asia 1961–1973*. Hinckley, UK: Midland, 2001.

Mutza, Wayne. *Helicopter Gunships: Deadly Combat Weapon Systems*. North Branch, MN: Specialty Press, 2010.

Nanson, Sid. *Strikes: US Naval and Marine Corps Aviation Attrition, 1962–1985*. Uxbridge, UK: Mach III Plus, 2003.

NATOPS Flight Manual: Navy Models UH-2A/UH-2B Helicopters. Washington, DC: Office of the Chief of Naval Operations, November 1964.

NATOPS Flight Manual: Navy Models HH-2C/HH-2D Helicopters. NAS Patuxent River, MD: Naval Air Systems Command, September 1970.

Ochadlick, Andrew R. *Iron Barnacle Operation: 1970 Weapons Cache Detection in Cambodia and Republic of Vietnam*. New Hope, PA: Science Dimensions, 2022.

Rusiecki, Milosz. *Kaman SH-2G*. Warsaw, Poland: Edipresse, 2013.

Zumwalt, Elmo R., Jr. *On Watch*. New York: Quadrangle Times Book, 1976.

PERIODICALS

Armstrong, Benjamin "BJ," Commander. "Armaments & Innovations: DASH, Snoopy, and the Night Panther." *Naval Institute*, June 2016.

Armstrong, Benjamin "BJ," Commander. "Unmanned Naval Warfare: Retrospect & Prospect." *Armed Forces Journal*, December 20, 2013.

"Autogiro Lands Four Times on Plane Carrier." *Evening Star* (Washington, DC), September 24, 1931.

Barewich, E. W., USMC. "US Marine Corps UH-2B Seasprite."

Bostock, Ian, Grzegorz Holdanowicz, and Richard Scott. "Second Coming for the Super Seasprite." *Janes Navy International*, May 2004.

Browning, Robert M., Jr. "The Eyes and Ears of the Convoy: Development of the Helicopter as an Anti-submarine Weapon." Coast Guard's Historian's Office, 1993.

Colucci, Frank. "Kaman's Copters." *Air International*, April 1996.

Colucci, Frank. "Kaman's Superior Seasprite." *Vertiflite* 43, no. 3 (May–June 1997).

Dorr, Robert F. "Kaman SH-2G Super Seasprite." *World Airpower Journal* 31 (Winter 1997).

Dorman, Craig E., and Robert S. Winokur. "Anti-submarine Warfare and Naval Oceanography." *Oceanus* 33, no. 4 (Winter 1990–91).

Ehrhard, Thomas P. "Seeds of a Revolution: Maritime UAVs in the 1960s."

Evans, Samuel S. "The Incredible Story of the QH-50 DASH: The First Unmanned Helicopter Turns 50." *Vertiflite* 57, no. 1 (Spring 2011): 36–39.

Fahrenthold, Alex, Lt. Cmdr. "Magic Lantern and the SH-2G." *Rotor Review*, Fall 1997.

Fitzgerald, James R., Vice Admiral, and Richard F. Pittenger, USN (Ret.). "ASW: Will We Ever Learn." *Naval History and Heritage Command*, January 2019.

Goodale, Bruce A., and Robert J. Gilson. "Unique Helicopter Family Proposed for LAMPS." *KamanRotor Tips*, August–October 1969.

"Helo Echo." NAS Imperial Beach, CA: August 10, 1973.

Hobbs, David. "Super Seasprites Fly Down Under." *Air International*, December 2003.

Jones, Robert E., Captain, USN (Ret.) "Squadron History. Kaman Aircraft Receives USA Trecom Contract." *Vertiflite*, June 1964.

"Kaman Emerges in Forefront in Gas Turbine Helicopters." *Hartford Times*, May 3, 1958.

Kaman Rotor Tips. Excerpts from numerous issues.

Liebman, Marc. "Flying the Kaman H-2C/D Sea Sprites." October 27, 2013.

McCracken, David J., Captain, USN (Ret.). "The Adventures and Tribulations of a Helo CSAR Pilots in Vietnam." *Rotor Review* 106 (Summer 2009).

McDonell, Michael G. "LAMPS Is Launched." *Naval Aviation News*, June 1971.

Miller, Stephen H. "Lamps Illuminated." *Air International*, April 1973.

Milner, Scott. "Lamps and the H-2." March 2022.

Morgan, Mark. "Orphans of the 7th Fleet: The Story of HC-7/CSAR."

Mullen, Rick. "Super Seasprite." *Air Force Today*, June 1997.

Murray, William R. "Downed Fliers." *Kaman Rotor Tip*s, January–February 1968.

Nesius, James A., Lt. (j.g.), USNR, and Pehr H. Pehrsson, Capt., CO, LPD-12. "Gator Aviation." *Naval Aviation News*, September 1972.

"New Birds of HC-1 in Double At-Sea Rescue." *Ream Echo*, October 13, 1967.

Rusiecki, Milosz, Dariusz Salata, Krzysztof Salata, and Andrzej Wrona. "Kaman SH-2 Seasprite / SuperSeasprite." *Aeroplan* (special edition), May–June 2013.

Stoker, Ron. "Stories from the Sea."

"Teledyne Ryan Aeronautical Reporter." Fall 1971.

Page references in italics indicate an illustration.

NAVY
9778